African Settings in Contemporary American Novels

African Settings in Contemporary American Novels

DAVE KUHNE

Contributions in Afro-American and African Studies, Number 193

Greenwood Press
Westport, Connecticut • *London*

Library of Congress Cataloging-in-Publication Data

Kuhne, Dave.
    African settings in contemporary American novels / Dave Kuhne.
        p. cm. — (Contributions in Afro-American and African
    studies, 0069-9624 ; no. 193)
    Includes bibliographical references and index.
    ISBN 0-313-31040-8 (alk. paper)
    1. American fiction—20th century—History and criticism.
    2. American fiction—African influences.   3. Africa—In literature.
    4. Setting (Literature)   I. Title.   II. Series.
    PS159.A38K84   1999
    813'.5409326—dc21   98-55344

British Library Cataloguing in Publication Data is available.

Library of Congress Catalog Card Number: 98-55344
ISBN: 0-313-31040-8
ISSN: 0069-9624

First published in 1999

Greenwood Press, 88 Post Road West, Westport, CT 06881
An imprint of Greenwood Publishing Group, Inc.
www.greenwood.com

Printed in the United States of America

The paper used in this book complies with the
Permanent Paper Standard issued by the National
Information Standards Organization (Z39.48–1984).

10   9   8   7   6   5   4   3   2   1

For LR

Contents

Preface

American novelists have placed their stories in a multitude of Africas: the jungle rain forest of the Congo basin, the vast deserts of the Sahara and the Kalahari, the highlands of Kenya, the badlands of southern Ethiopia, and the veldt of South Africa. American authors have not limited their use of African settings to wild or natural Africa; they have placed their novels in African cities from one tip of the continent to the other, from Tangier to Cairo, from Lagos to Nairobi, from Dar es Salaam to Cape Town. As if actual African landscapes, nations, and cities did not provide adequate literary settings, a number of contemporary American novels are set in invented African nations meant to represent the characteristics, values, and conflicts of the entire continent. Americans have written about Africa of the past, Africa of the present, and Africa of the future. African settings have been featured in numerous genres: postmodern fiction, science fiction, historical fiction, and action and adventure fiction.

For many American authors, the appeal of Africa is its "otherness," its difference from the contemporary United States. Africa is a place where Americans go to discover the truth about themselves by comparing their values with African values. Africa is a testing ground that provides numerous challenges; Africa, as Harry Veer—a character in William Harrison's *Africana*—explains, is where you go to "take your gut temperature" (46).

In *Landscapes of Fear*, Yi-Fu Tuan observes that attitudes toward place are not fixed. What one culture fears, another reveres; the rain forest of the Congo, which seems so frightful to European explorers, is a friendly, nurturing, idyllic place to the Mbuti, the Pygmy people who inhabit the forest (37). A similar forest, however, is described by Nigerian novelist Chinua Achebe in *Things Fall Apart* as the home of evil spirits, the place where one disposes of twins and other blasphemies (21).

Furthermore, what is fearsome at one time and place may be comforting at another place and later date. To early Europeans, mountains and dense forests seemed threatening (Tuan, *Landscapes* 7), and colonial Americans viewed the forest "as the enemy . . . the habitat of the godless Indian" (Schama 191). After the Romantic movement in Europe, however, the same mountains and forests became places of beauty that inspired noble, spiritual values. For Westerners living after the Romantic era, the countryside is "inherently wholesome and good" (Tuan, *Landscapes* 131), but most American novels set in Africa equate the open countryside with danger and the struggle to survive. In Africa, as opposed to Europe or America, peace and safety are not to be found in the countryside but in the city, the village compound, or the farm.

A culture's changing attitudes toward place are likely to be reflected in that culture's literature (Lutwack 8); in recent decades, American attitudes toward Africa have begun to change. Novelists such as Alex Haley and Barbara Chase-Riboud have written works in which Africans are portrayed in positive ways that are in contrast to the stereotypical pictures of Africans in earlier fiction. Much of Africa's big game is gone forever, and gone also are safari novels like those by Ernest Hemingway and Robert Ruark; these safari novels have been replaced by ecologically centered thrillers such as William Harrison's *Savannah Blue.*

To some extent what an American author finds in African settings is influenced by the attitude that writer has about African places. Authors expecting to find magic in Africa discover a magical Africa, and those seeking to discover elements of their heritage find their history in African settings. An author's attitude toward Africa often determines the theme of a novel with African settings; therefore, this study is organized by thematic concerns and the various ways in which American authors since World War II have employed African settings in their novels.

Chapter 1, "Africa: What Place Is This?," examines the connotations that Westerners have traditionally associated with Africa and maintains that images of Africa in contemporary American fiction are usually either extensions of or reactions to notions about Africa popularized by earlier European and American authors. Chapter 2, "Antecedents: African Settings in British and American Fiction Before World War II," outlines the use of African settings as they appear in British and American fiction from Aphra Behn to Ernest Hemingway.

Chapter 3, "Filling in the Blank Space: Contemporary American Novels Set in Invented African Nations," deals with novels that are set in invented—as opposed to actual—African nations and regions. These invented Africas incorporate assumptions about Africa into composite pictures that allow American authors to contrast American life and culture with African life and culture. Chapter 4, "Black on Black: African-American Novels with African Settings," examines the ways in which African-American authors have employed African settings in their novels and demonstrates that, for the most part, African-American novels with African settings are didactic works that provide readers with an alternative history of both Africa and of the slave trade to the Americas.

Chapter 5, "Genre Africa," examines the ways in which African settings function in terms of genre and demonstrates that much of the genre fiction featuring African settings rises above genre expectations and deals with themes associated with serious literature. Chapter 6, "Africa: Postmodern, Postcolonial, and 'Other' Wise," considers the role of Westerners and Asians as outsiders in postcolonial Africa and examines the ways in which African settings have been incorporated into postmodern fiction. Chapter 7, "Conclusions: Africa—A Continent of Words," summarizes findings and suggests areas for future exploration.

Each of these chapters deals with the following recurring questions:

First, to what extent are American novels set in Africa didactic? What do these novels teach about the lands and cultures they describe? How do these novels challenge or reinforce stereotypes?

Second, how is the African landscape portrayed in these novels? In what ways do the physical landscapes described become "characters" in the works, and how are the myths, symbols, and characteristics of African settings employed as thematic devices?

Third, how have American writers employed African settings as a way in which to comment on substantial themes such as courage, death, religion, war, and the relationship between an individual and his or her society?

Fourth, how do these novels measure the American character and culture by comparing American characters and cultural traits with African characters and cultural traits? What stereotypes about Africa and America do these novels reinforce or challenge?

For Americans, Africa is becoming less and less a blank space on the map—as it was for Conrad's young Marlow—and more and more a part of daily life. Increased American awareness concerning Africa, Africans, and African affairs since World War II is the result of historical, political, and economic events. The drive for independence that swept Africa after World War II and the civil rights movement in the United States greatly increased public interest in Africa and African cultures. Intercontinental jet travel has also made Africa accessible to American writers—and accessible for characters in American novels as well. In 1949, the Americans in Paul Bowles's *The Sheltering Sky* arrive in Africa after an ocean voyage from New York that takes several weeks; in 1980, the characters in Michael Crichton's *Congo* travel from the United States to Africa in several hours. In the 1990s, as American troops were dispatched to Somalia and as satellite television brings the United States daily images from Rwanda and South Africa, Africa becomes more and more familiar to Americans, and more and more American writers will discover Africa's appeal as a literary setting.

*African Settings in Contemporary
American Novels*

Chapter 1

Africa: What Place Is This?

To understand the role of African settings in contemporary American fiction, it is important to recognize the connotations that Westerners have traditionally associated with Africa. Images of Africa and Africans in contemporary American fiction are usually either extensions of or reactions to notions about Africa popularized by earlier European and American authors. Africa, as it is represented in many British and American novels, is a mysterious and fearsome place. African environments are consistently described as harsh, challenging, frightening, and deadly; Africans are frequently portrayed as primitive, savage, and hostile. In American fiction, African settings are what Leonard Lutwack terms "landscapes of difficulty," places where characters test themselves against challenging conditions (33). For characters in American and British novels, African settings offer the challenges of remoteness, harsh topography, deadly disease, severe climate, dangerous wildlife, and hostile indigenous peoples. Most of all, African settings are landscapes of difficulty because Africa is strikingly different from the United States.

Indeed, Africa is frequently considered to be in binary opposition to the West. Chinua Achebe, for example, maintains that there "is the desire—one might indeed say the need—in Western psychology to set Africa up as a foil to Europe" (*Hopes* 2). Achebe refers to *Heart of Darkness* as a work that "projects the image of Africa as 'the other world,' the antithesis of Europe and therefore civilization," and he maintains that the image of Africa as the "other" is the dominant image of Africa in the West (*Hopes* 3). John Cullen Gruesser echoes Achebe's analysis: the "West is one thing—good, reasonable, bright, and so on—while Africa is its opposite— evil, irrational, dark" (3). Examples of the binary opposition of the West and Africa are numerous. The West is a technologically advanced world; Africa is a world that has not yet experienced technological development. Nature has been tamed in the

West; nature reigns in Africa. The West is a world of science; Africa is a world of magic. Peaceful democracy is the political system of the West; the coup d'etat and rule by violence characterize politics of Africa. The West is a world of wealth and health; Africa is a world of poverty and disease.

In the Western tradition, Africa has always been remote, a place of mystery. For the Greeks and Romans, Africa beyond the Mediterranean rim was a blank space. Herodotus notes that King Necho of Egypt dispatched a fleet manned by Phoenician sailors to circumnavigate the continent from the Red Sea to Gibraltar, but it was not until after the Renaissance, when the Portuguese began to explore Africa, that Europeans obtained approximately correct maps of Africa's outline (Bartholomew xi). Africa south of the Mediterranean rim would remain outside the world as known to Europeans until well into the Middle Ages when Arab knowledge of Africa was spread to Europe through the translation of Joannes Leo Africanus's *A Geographical History of Africa* (Atkinson 16). It would be long after the Age of Discovery, however, before Europeans gained extensive factual knowledge about the interior of the African continent. Indeed, in "On Poetry," Jonathan Swift specifically satirizes European lack of knowledge concerning Africa: "Geographers, in Afric maps,/ With savage pictures fill their gaps, / And o'er inhabitable downs, / Place elephants for want of towns" (177–80). In fact, much of Africa would remain uncharted until the 1930s when the widespread use of aircraft made the more remote regions accessible (Murray 5).

Although the Greeks and Romans knew little about Africa south of the Sahara, they believed that unexplored Africa was the home of strange creatures such as men with no heads and donkeys that never drink (Atkinson 11). As recently as 1798, Africa was believed to be the home of unicorns, and explorer John Barrow spent two years in South Africa searching for this mythical beast (Murray 44). The literary tradition of populating Africa with strange creatures, a tradition that dates at least as far back as the Middle Ages, survives today in such American novels as Michael Crichton's *Congo*.

According to Yi-Fu Tuan, large undefined spaces are causes of fear and anxiety, and boundaries are drawn specifically to protect people from what is outside their circle of control (*Landscapes* 207). For Westerners, African settings are mysterious, challenging, and frightening because they are vast, undefined regions. The deserts of the Sahara and the Kalahari, the "miles and miles of bloody Africa" that make up the veldt, and the seemingly endless rain forests of the Congo basin leave Westerners with the feeling that Africa is beyond human control. Some have seen the open spaces of Africa as symbolic of the Western subconscious mind. For example, in Richard Dooling's *White Man's Grave*, Sisay—an American anthropologist who has gone native and made Sierra Leone his home—explains that he has marked a passage in a book describing the Sierra Leone bush because he believes the passage is the product of a Westerner who attempted to describe African landscape but only succeeded in "describing his own unconscious" (266). The passage Sisay marks describes the Mende-land bush as an "uncanny" place of "low hills" and "swampy valleys" (265).

While the vast, mysterious, and untamed spaces of Africa inspire fear in many American characters, these spaces also offer refuge. In American and British fiction, African settings sometimes become what Lutwack, in *The Role of Place in Literature*, calls "peripheral places," locales where characters can escape to heal wounds and renew heroic dedication (45). In novels such as *The Sheltering Sky* by Paul Bowles, *Henderson the Rain King* by Saul Bellow, and *White Man's Grave* by Richard Dooling, African settings are similar to the territory across the river that appeals to Huck Finn. Because Africa—like Huck's territory—remains wild, open, and uncivilized, it appeals to characters who seek to break away from the dull, regimented, sanitized life of Western culture.

Adding to the mysterious quality of African settings is the timelessness that Westerners tend to associate with Africa. Lutwack cites *Heart of Darkness* and *Henderson the Rain King* to demonstrate that journeys "into the remote interior of Africa are also journeys back in time" (57). Yi-Fu Tuan also comments upon the link between timelessness and remote places. Tuan believes that movement across vast spaces can cause "temporal illusion" and that the narratives of Europeans exploring Africa "give the impression of odysseys into the past" (*Space and Time* 125). Many Africans live lives centered around religion and subsistence farming, a way of living that British and American authors associate with the past, with the way life was lived in England or America before the coming of industrialization. Furthermore, in fiction featuring African settings, it is commonplace for Western characters to discover lost cities that have been frozen in time. The lost-city motif reinforces the notion that Africa is a timeless, unchanging place. Indeed, Westerners have sometimes justified their intervention in African affairs by arguing that Africa is frozen in time and incapable of development without outside assistance (Milbury-Steen 7).

In addition to the remote, mysterious, and timeless qualities frequently associated with African settings, Africa's topography is considered by many in the West to be particularly harsh. Africa is the world's second largest continent—it has a land area of about 11,600,000 square miles—and the dominant feature of the landscape is savanna, or veldt, that resembles the prairie of Texas (Wiedner 6). After the veldt, the next most common topographical feature of Africa is desert; the combined area of the Sahara and the Kalahari deserts is roughly 5,000,000 square miles. The remainder of the African landmass is jungle rain forest and temperate highlands. Africa has fewer mountainous regions than any other continent except Australia, and both Asia and South America have more square miles of jungle rain forest than Africa (Wiedner 6).

From the very beginnings of English fiction, Africa has been pictured as a harsh land where people must struggle with the environment to survive. In some instances, the African topography is so severe that it causes illness and disorientation, and novels set in Africa frequently comment upon the harshness of African topography and link the severity of African topography to psychological changes in characters. The linkage of topography to character change occurs in African as well as British and American fiction. In *Burning Grass*, for instance, Nigerian novelist Cyprian

Ekwensi describes a character's struggle with *sokugo*, the "wandering sickness" that sometimes afflicts Fulani herdsmen. *Sokugo* is caused by the vastness of the plains on which the Fulani live. Another example of the African topography's ability to cause disorientation and illness occurs in *Beau Geste*; the desert causes a number of characters to fall victim to a sort of insanity called the *cafard*. In American fiction, the brutal African topography affects the mental and physical states of characters in such novels as *The Sheltering Sky* by Paul Bowles and *The Coup* by John Updike.

Disease has been repeatedly employed in American and British fiction to demonstrate the severity of African settings, and disease is also an important component in African novels. Achebe's *Things Fall Apart* refers specifically to a disease that causes the swelling of the stomach. The Ibo consider this disease "an abomination to the earth goddess. When a man was afflicted with swelling in the stomach and the limbs he was . . . carried to the Evil Forest and left there to die" (21). Sometimes disease is employed as a plot device as is the case in *Burning Grass*; Mai Sunsaye, stricken with *sokugo*, wanders across the traditional grazing lands of the Fulani and comments upon the tremendous changes that European culture has brought to the Fulani way of life.

Recent years have done little to diminish the terror of disease in Africa. As Eddy L. Harris notes in his 1992 account of his travels across the continent, "Africa is flies and illness everywhere, AIDS and malaria and green monkey disease" (312). Other diseases found in Africa include yellow fever, dengue fever, blackwater fever, Malta fever, bilharzia, onchoceroiasis (river blindness), cholera, bubonic plague, and leprosy. Some authorities maintain that in the early decades of European conquest as many as seventy-five percent of all Europeans in West Africa died of some disease during their first year on the continent (Murray 5).

From the *cafard* that afflicts the characters of Wren's *Beau Gest* to leprosy in Greene's *A Burnt-Out Case*, disease plays an important role in British novels set in Africa. In American fiction, examples of the dangers of African diseases include Harry's death from infection in Hemingway's "The Snows of Kilimanjaro" and Port's death from typhoid in *The Sheltering Sky*. In more recent American fiction, Alice Walker and Richard Dooling include disease as one of the continent's distinguishing characteristics. Boone Westfall, a young American character in Dooling's *White Man's Grave*, learns that according to popular legend, the mosquito was the only weapon needed to defeat the British in Sierra Leone's war for independence (49).

In Alice Walker's *The Color Purple*, an unnamed African character explains why he is reluctant to take up the type of life suggested by the missionaries: "If you do not die, you are weakened by illness. Oh yes. We have seen it all before. You Christians come here, try hard to change us, get sick and go back to England, or wherever you come from" (137). Ironically, the African character himself dies of fever during the next rainy season.

Moreover, Walker specifically comments upon the link between disease and the popular conception of Africa. Walker, however, differs from other American authors by implying that the prevalence of disease in Africa is not an entirely naturally occurring phenomenon. In *The Temple of My Familiar*, she links the Western conception of Africa as a disease-ridden locale with colonialism. For example, Mary Jane Briden, a wealthy white radical who will change her name and flee to Africa, is surprised by what she sees in some early photographs of Africans: "In these photographs she saw Africans whose eyes, skin, clothes, *shone*. With richness and intelligence and *health*. Finally, it was the shine of health that captivated Mary Jane, for she realized that so degraded had Africa become in the mind of the world that a healthy African, like the ones she saw in the photographs, was practically unimaginable" (217). And in *Possessing the Secret of Joy*, Walker implies that some of the disease in Africa has been caused by imperialistic science; an AIDS-stricken character named Hartford speculates that AIDS was created by white scientists conducting vaccine research with monkey cultures (260–62).

The presence of disease in Africa forces Westerners into an awareness of nature that they may escape in the urbanized, sanitized worlds of Europe and the United States. For Westerners, this increased awareness of nature often leads to the realization that nature is indifferent, if not hostile, to humankind. As Tuan observes in *Landscapes of Fear*, "illness directs attention to the world's hostility" (87).

Weather is yet another factor that makes African settings landscapes of difficulty, and, considering the extremes of climate found in Africa, this effect should not be surprising. The world's highest recorded temperature—136 degrees Fahrenheit—occurred in the Sahara desert on September 13, 1922. Africa's lowest recorded temperature—a reading of -11 degrees Fahrenheit—was observed in Morocco, and freezing cold is common in the mountainous regions of Africa. Mount Cameroon receives 400 inches of rainfall annually; the Sahara and Kalahari deserts rarely receive rainfall.

Nigerian novelist Chinua Achebe begins *Things Fall Apart* with a description of the weather, specifically the harmattan—a hot, dry wind, accompanied by clouds of dust, which blows at intervals from the interior of Africa toward the west coast. A severe harmattan sets Achebe's characters on edge in much the same way that Season Affective Disorder (SAD) affects people living in countries that have long, dark winters. In *The Power of Place*, Winifred Gallagher argues that people in native cultures are more in touch with climate and the elements than are people from industrial cultures (42). The rigors of African climate, should, therefore, affect Americans more than native Africans.

African climates, however, are sometimes so severe that even indigenous people have difficulty adjusting to the weather. The natural elements of the African landscape, especially the weather, present Africans with a constant challenge that makes life a struggle. For example, rainfall in Africa is usually restricted to one season of the year, and sometimes there is insufficient rain to support crops (Wiedner 6). The following description of the weather's effect on the people of an Ibo village is from Achebe's *Things Fall Apart*: "It seemed as if the world had gone mad. The first rains were late, and, when they came, lasted only a brief moment. The blazing sun returned, more fierce than it had ever been known, and scorched all the green that had appeared with the rains" (25). The results of such an unexpected break in the reliability of the rainy seasons are tragic for the people of Umuofia: "That year the harvest was sad, like a funeral, and many farmers wept as they dug up the miserable and rotting yams. One man tied his cloth to a tree branch and hanged himself" (27).

Problems with weather and crops also figure into the story of the people of Juffure in Alex Haley's *Roots*. Old Nyo Boto, a respected woman in Juffure, remembers the time the rains failed, causing the death of the weak and sick and driving others to sell themselves into slavery to keep from starving (10–11). As Tuan notes, weather and anxiety over the dependability of harvests are universal causes of fear (*Landscapes* 56), and Africa's severe climate is a factor that makes African settings hostile places where nature humbles humankind.

African animals can also direct attention to nature's hostility toward humankind. Africa is justly famous for its wildlife, and African animals have frequently been employed in American and British fiction to dramatize the challenges, dangers, and difficulties of life in Africa. For example, in one of the early works of British fiction set in Africa, Daniel Defoe sends Robinson Crusoe down the African coast in an attempt to escape slavery at the hands of North African Moors. After sailing for five days, Crusoe and Xury, his companion, land on shore with the intent of exploring the countryside. They are discouraged, however, by "dreadful noises of the barking, roaring, and howling of wild creatures of we knew not what kinds" (20). Later, Crusoe and Xury go ashore for water only to encounter a "dreadful monster," which in fact is a "terrible great lion" (23). A few pages farther into the story, Crusoe befriends some natives by slaying an attacking leopard.

American fiction—perhaps because America too was once the home of magnificent and dangerous animals that challenged humans for dominance of the land—is especially concerned with the wildlife found in Africa. Cape buffalo, lions, leopards, rhinoceroses, and elephants provide American characters with opportunities to prove their manhood. Examples of African animals used as challenges that test a character's courage can be found in such stories as Ernest Hemingway's "The Short Happy Life of Francis Macomber" as well as in such novels as *Something of Value* by Robert Ruark and *Three Hunters* by William Harrison. With the demise of African wildlife in recent decades, American authors have sometimes employed African animals as tools of revenge for characters wishing to strike back at the West for destroying the natural legacy of Africa. For instance, in *Savannah Blue* by William Harrison, an African cobra is an agent of death against "those who had brought the new century" to Africa (24). Harrison's cobra is only one of the many African animals that serve as symbols in American fiction set in Africa. Hemingway employs the leopard as a symbol in "The Snows of Kilimanjaro," and Harrison uses the leopard for symbolic purposes in both *Africana* and *Three Hunters*.

While Africa's remoteness, topography, climate, disease, and wildlife offer many challenges for characters in American and British fiction with African settings, it is the people of Africa that Western characters fear most. Africa has been a favorite literary setting for primitivistic adventure (Lutwack 29), and, in both

British and American fiction, Africans are frequently described as being savage and hostile.

The tendency of British and American fiction to portray Africans as savage primitives is a tradition that is several centuries old; however, Europeans did not always presume that Africans were primitive beings. The Greeks and the Romans appear to have held mixed feelings toward Africa and Africans (Atkinson 9). Appiah observes that while the Greeks believed that "both the black 'Ethiopians' to the south and the blond 'Scythians' to the north were inferior to the Hellenes, there was no general assumption that this inferiority was incorrigible" (11). Joseph E. Harris reports that a late fourteenth-century European atlas includes a picture of Mansa Musa, the enormously wealthy king of Mali who traveled through Egypt on his way to Mecca in 1324 (60). Clearly, educated Europeans living in the Middle Ages knew that Africa was home to highly developed cultures.

Even as late as the eighteenth century, it was still possible for Europeans to describe Africans in positive terms. Mary Louise Pratt notes that one of the early explorers of South Africa, Peter Kolb, found the Hottentots to be cultural beings possessing religion, industry, government, and laws (44). By the end of the eighteenth century, however, "as modern racist categories emerged," the Hottentots ceased to be described as cultured people "capable of such things as government, professions, opinions or genius" (45).

Referring to Conrad's portrayal of Africans as savages, Chinua Achebe theorizes that for Westerners, Africa is a "metaphysical battlefield devoid of all recognizable humanity," a place where Americans and Europeans enter at their own peril (*Hopes* 12). Novels such as Frank Yerby's *The Dahomean*, Alex Haley's *Roots*, and Barbara Chase-Riboud's *Echo of Lions* have done much to improve the image of Africans in American literature, but literary and popular conceptions about African peoples have been slow to change. Appiah maintains that it may be hard for Africans as well as Westerners "to recover from the overwhelmingly negative conception of Africans that inhabited the mainstream of European and American intellectual life by the first years of Europe's African empires" (22).

Alex Haley admits that as he began research for what would become *Roots*, he was embarrassed to discover that his images about Africa had largely been "derived or inferred from Tarzan movies" (675). Haley's experience is not atypical; many Americans have a conception of Africa and Africans that has been shaped by the enormously popular novels of H. Rider Haggard and Edgar Rice Burroughs, as well as by numerous film versions of the works of these two authors. Africans in the novels of Haggard and Burroughs are usually portrayed as savage beings, and little attempt is made to understand the complexities of African cultures in these works. In *Tarzan of the Apes*, for example, the orphaned Tarzan discovers more humanity in his family of gorillas, especially his ape-mother Kala, than in the black Africans who move into his domain.

In novels featuring African settings, African characters commonly perform terrible acts of cruelty, and these cruel acts frequently involve the torture of a white victim. The torturers can be black, as in *Tarzan of the Apes* when D'Arnott is tied to a stake and repeatedly jabbed with spears (197), or the torturers may be Arab, as in *Beau Geste* (398). Of course, the victims of torture are not always whites. British and American novelists also frequently describe Africans torturing other Africans.

Moreover, Africans, particularly black Africans, are pictured as cannibals at least as far back as Defoe and in such diverse twentieth-century works as *Heart of Darkness*, *Tarzan of the Apes*, *Black Mischief*, *Something of Value*, *Congo*, and *White Man's Grave*. In *Robinson Crusoe*, Crusoe escapes from slavery by sailing south, along the African coast where no one would ever expect him to go because "we could ne'er go on shore but we should be devoured by savage beasts, or more merciless savages of human kind" (19). Portraying Africans as cannibals is a tradition that Alice Walker comments upon (and attempts to explain via Miss Lissie's story of her past life in prehistoric times) in *The Temple of My Familiar* (85–86), and Milbury-Steen notes that in British fiction, native cruelty—especially human sacrifice and cannibalism—is frequently offered as justification for British imperialism (16).

Beginning with Joseph Conrad, a number of novelists writing before World War II suspected that Europe was not as civilized as it pretended to be; for these writers, African settings provide a testing ground where the myth of Western civilization can be exposed. A list of pre–World War II authors who employ African settings to deflate the myth of presumed Western civilization includes Conrad, Edgar Rice Burroughs, and Joyce Cary.

Consider, for example, *Tarzan of the Apes*. Numerous critics have commented on Burroughs's depictions of black Africans, and several have maintained that Burroughs's writings are racist (Holtsmark 5). Few critics seem to have noticed, however, that Burroughs does not credit whites or Europeans—as a group or a race—as being especially civilized. In fact, writing about the black Africans who live in a village not far from Tarzan's tree house, Burroughs notes that the "pitiful remnant of what once had been a mighty tribe" had learned something of cruelty from Europeans: "To add to the fiendishness of their cruel savagery was the poignant memory of still crueler barbarities practiced upon them and theirs by the white officers of that arch hypocrite, Leopold II of Belgium" (196).

In this brief example, Burroughs follows Conrad's precedent and uses the presumed savagery of Africans to comment upon the savagery of Europeans. After World War II, writers such as Robert Ruark, Philip Caputo, William Harrison, Michael Mewshaw, and Richard Dooling continue the tradition of employing African settings to indicate that Western civilization is a myth and that Western culture is just as savage as any African culture. For these authors, the beast lurks within all people; Africans may indeed be savage, but Westerners are under the illusion that their culture is free from barbarity. African-American authors such as Frank Yerby, Alex Haley, and Barbara Chase-Riboud also directly compare African cultures to Western culture to demonstrate that African cultures are highly developed and that Western barbarity can equal or surpass that of Africa.

The irony of the belief that the West is more civilized than Africa has not been lost on Africans, and African novelists frequently cite the world wars as evidence of the barbarous nature of the West. Indeed, the world wars changed the African conception of self and forced Africans to rethink their attitudes toward Westerners. For example, in *Weep Not Child*, Kenyan novelist Ngugi wa Thiong'o directly compares the effects of World War I and World War II on Africans when one of the characters in the novel summarizes the difference in the two wars: "That war [World War I] was like a baby's war. . . . Those Africans who went to that one were only porters. But [in] this one [World War II] we carried guns and shot white men. . . . They are not the gods we had thought them to be" (9). And in his study concerning Africa's role in the philosophy of culture, Appiah makes this observation about the effect of World War II on Africans: "The lesson the Africans drew from the Nazis—indeed from the Second World War as a whole—was not the danger of racism but the falsehood of opposition between a humane European 'modernity' and the 'barbarism' of the nonwhite world. We had known that European colonialism could lay waste African lives with a careless ease; now we knew that white people could take the murderous tools of modernity and apply them to each other" (6).

Appiah notes that the African identity is, at least in part, the product of a "European gaze" (81). The European—and American—gaze as represented in fiction has not been kind to Africans. While individual African characters may be intelligent, educated, brave, and noble, Africans—at least in the works of several white American authors—have been pictured as savage beings. Therefore, while the physical and climatic features of Africa make African settings landscapes of difficulty, African peoples provide the greatest challenges for American and British characters in fiction with African settings.

Chapter 2

Antecedents: African Settings in British and American Fiction Before World War II

African settings have appealed to English authors since the very beginnings of the English novel, and the early examples of English novels with African settings establish a tradition that associates specific thematic concerns with Africa. These concerns—slavery and the slave trade, the conflict between humans and the natural world of Africa, and the notion that Africa is the home of lost cities and civilizations capable of harboring mysterious peoples and creatures—continue to interest contemporary American authors who feature African settings in their novels. Early examples of English fiction with African settings include *Oroonoko: or, the Royal Slave* (1688) by Aphra Behn, *Robinson Crusoe* (1719) and *Madagascar; or, Robert Drury's Journal* (1729) by Daniel Defoe, and *The History of Rasselas, Prince of Abissinia* (1759) by Samuel Johnson. In these narratives, Behn takes up the topic of slavery and its effects, Defoe discusses both slavery and the conflict between humans and the natural world of Africa, and Johnson describes a timeless African valley that is the forerunner of the lost cities in the novels of Haggard, Burroughs, and Crichton. Furthermore, because Behn, Defoe, and Johnson depict Africans as cultured, civilized beings, their works highlight the shift in Western attitudes concerning Africa and Africans that took place in the eighteenth and nineteenth centuries.

Behn's attitude toward Africans in *Oroonoko* demonstrates that in the late seventeenth century Europeans had not yet completely accepted racist notions about African and Africans; indeed, in *Oroonoko*, the Europeans are far more savage than the Africans. The story of *Oroonoko* involves two lovers who are taken as slaves and transported from Africa to South America. The lovers, Oroonoko and Imoinda, are reunited in Surinam, where Oroonoko leads a slave rebellion that fails, resulting in his and Imoinda's violent deaths. The protagonists of *Oroonoko*—Oroonoko and

Imoinda—are both black. Oroonoko's skin is "perfect Ebony, or polished Jett" (8). Imoinda is a "Beauty," a "fair Queen of the Night" (9). Oroonoko and Imoinda are attractive, intelligent, cultured, and heroic characters. Oroonoko is also something of a linguist; he has mastered English, French, and Spanish so that he can better conduct business with the slave traders who visit the coast of his nation.

Oroonoko comes from Coramantien, a "Country of Blacks" that has a highly developed social order and an economy based on war and the slave trade (5). At the beginning of the novel, Oroonoko excels at trading slaves, usually prisoners of war, and he gives a gift of slaves to Imoinda (9). At the conclusion of the novel, Oroonoko's views about slavery have changed because of his experiences as a slave. Hoping to inspire a slave revolt, Oroonoko tells his fellow slaves—many of whom he himself has sold into servitude—"of the Miseries and Ignominies of Slavery" (60). Moreover, Oroonoko observes that the institution of slavery dehumanizes its victims; slaves "suffere'd not like Men . . . but like Dogs" who had "lost the divine Quality of Men" (60).

William Atkinson maintains that Behn objects to a prince's being a slave, not to the institution of slavery; he claims that for Behn, "there is no intrinsic difference between Africa and Europe, only between the well-born and the lowly-born" (21). Atkinson has incorrectly assessed Behn's attitude toward slavery; the novel focuses on the transformation that Oroonoko undergoes during the course of the narrative. Oroonoko does not find slavery wrong when he sells his fellow Africans, but by the conclusion of the story, he can no longer deny the evils of the slave trade. *Oroonoko* is the first work to establish slavery and the slave trade as thematic concerns inherent in novels with African settings. The tradition established by *Oroonoko* is continued in contemporary American novels by African-American authors such as Frank Yerby, Alex Haley, Barbara Chase-Riboud, and Charles Johnson, all of whom make slavery and the slave trade concerns central to their works set in Africa.

Furthermore, Oroonoko's nobility is directly contrasted with the savagery of the European settlers of Surinam, where most of the narrative unfolds. In much American and British fiction concerned with Africa, it is Africans who prove their savagery by committing acts of torture, but in *Oroonoko*, Behn devotes the final pages of the novel to a description of European savagery against an African. After his first escape, Oroonoko is tricked into surrender by his English owner, Trefry, who offers Oroonoko amnesty. Not trusting the English, Oroonoko demands that Trefry's offer be put in writing, and it is (66). As soon as Oroonoko surrenders, however, he is taken to the "Place where all Slaves receive their Punishments of Whipping" (67). After Oroonoko has been whipped to the point of "almost fainting with loss of Blood, from a thousand Wounds all over his Body," he is put in irons and his wounds are rubbed with "*Indian* pepper, which like to have made him raving mad" (67).

As terrible as these acts of torture are, they only foreshadow the concluding scene of the novel, when, after another attempted escape, Oroonoko is again taken prisoner:

He had learn'd to take Tobacco; and when he was assur'd he should die, he desir'd they would give him a Pipe in his Mouth, ready lighted; which they did: And the Executioner came, and first cut off his Members, and threw them into the Fire; after that with an ill-favour'd Knife, they cut off his ears and his Nose, and burn'd them; he still smoak'd on, as if nothing had touch'd him; they then hack'd off one of his Arms, and still he bore up, and held his Pipe; but at the cutting off of the other Arm, his Head sunk, and the Pipe dropt and he gave up the Ghost, without a Groan, or a Reproach. (77)

By featuring cultured, intelligent, and courageous black Africans as major characters and by presenting the English slave owners in a savage light, *Oroonoko* is in direct opposition to the traditions established in later British and American fiction, traditions that frequently identify Africans as savage and Europeans as civilized. Moreover, while the European partition of Africa would not become inevitable until the Berlin Conference of 1884–1885 (Harris, *Africans* 165), Behn's description of Oroonoko's dismemberment can be seen as a symbol for the carving up of Africa by European powers.

Daniel Defoe is another early explorer of African settings in fiction. A small but important portion of *Robinson Crusoe* (1719) takes place in Africa, and most of the action in *Madagascar; or, Robert Drury's Journal* (1729) unfolds on the island off Africa's east coast. Slavery is an important concern in both. However, in Defoe's novels it is Englishmen who are enslaved by Africans; slavery is simply one of many woes that can befall those who leave the safety of home in search of adventure or fortune. In addition to his concern with slavery, Defoe also outlines the conflict between humankind and the natural world of Africa, and in *Madagascar* he provides English readers with their first detailed description of a complex African culture.

The African section of *Robinson Crusoe* occurs early in the novel. Captured by pirates, the young Crusoe is taken to the city of Sallee, "a port belonging to the Moors," and is sold into slavery (15). Although Crusoe has immediate thoughts of escape, he finds his position as a slave "not so dreadful as at first I apprehended" (15). Crusoe remains a slave for two years until he escapes in a fishing boat and travels down the coast of Africa with a Moor named Xury. Crusoe and Xury have a number of adventures along the African coast, including the encounters with the lion and the leopard already mentioned in Chapter 1. These encounters with the dangerous animals of Africa establish a literary precedent; to this day novels with African settings often comment on the wild animals that inhabit Africa and use these animals not only as challenges that characters must overcome in the pursuit of their goals but also as symbols for Africa itself.

Like Behn, Defoe challenges popular European conceptions about Africans. Crusoe notes that he and Xury sailed along the African coast, rather than sailing north toward Spain, because "who would ha' supposed we were sailed on to the southward to the truly barbarian coast, where whole nations of Negroes were sure to surround us with their canoes and destroy us" (19). However, the Africans that Crusoe and Xury encounter are not at all savage. After sailing for five days, Crusoe is forced to land in search of food and water. The natives he encounters are "black and stark naked" (24), but they are definitely friendly, providing Crusoe and his companion with food and water. Finally, after the Africans have given him provisions, Crusoe puts back to sea, "leaving my friendly Negroes" and setting sail for the coast of Guinea (24). The black Africans of *Robinson Crusoe* may not be as sophisticated as Oroonoko, but they are neither savage nor subhuman.

The African settings of *Crusoe* are limited to the early section of the novel, but Defoe's concern with the relationship between slave and master permeates the entire work, as does his interest in the conflict between man and nature that begins with the killing of the lion and the leopard. In fact, Crusoe must battle wild animals—packs of wolves—when he returns to Europe after many years of life on his island. Crusoe's encounters with the wolves in Europe and the lions and leopards in Africa show that the difference between life in Europe and life in Africa—at least in terms of the relationship between humans and nature—was not nearly so dramatic in Defoe's time as it is today.

Madagascar; or, Robert Drury's Journal (1729) is set almost entirely on the African island that gives the book its name. For much of the eighteenth century, *Madagascar* was accepted as fact (Oliver 15), but scholars have since determined the volume to be the work of Defoe (Secord 1). Like *Robinson Crusoe*, *Madagascar* is an account of an Englishman who is enslaved by Africans; while most of Drury's companions are murdered by the blacks who inhabit the island, Drury is spared and "reserved for the king's grandson" (74). Drury's story of his fifteen years of captivity on the island provides a detailed picture of an African culture with a well-developed agrarian economy, a sophisticated political system, and a complex religion. Drury's journal also describes the flora and fauna of Madagascar.

Drury is the first of many Westerners to "go native," and his story begins a long tradition of writing about Western expatriates living in Africa. In general, Drury is treated well by the indigenous people of the island. At one point he explains that his "mistress was very kind to me" (82), and, later during his stay on the island, he takes a native woman for a bride. Testifying to the state of European attitudes toward Africans in Defoe's time, Drury describes his wife as being as "fine as any ladies in Europe," adding that "We white people have a very contemptible and mean opinion of these blacks, and a great one of ourselves . . . but if an impartial comparison was to be made of their virtue, I think the Negro heathen will excel the white Christians" (172). Drury's account also demonstrates the difference in slavery as traditionally practiced in Africa and slavery as practiced in the Americas. By the time Drury is rescued, he is thoroughly integrated into Madagascar society. At the end of his fifteen years on the island, he is no longer a slave, having become the owner of a herd of cattle as well as a slave named Anthony (294).

In fact, Drury's attitude toward slavery after having himself been a slave is opposite that of Oroonoko in Aphra Behn's novel. After returning to England and finding his family deceased, Drury embarks once more for Africa on a venture to secure slaves. He buys many slaves from the Africans he visits on this second voyage, briefly lands in Madagascar to check on his cattle, then sails to Virginia, "where we sold our slaves, took in tobacco, and sailed for England" (312).

After *Madagascar*, the next notable use of African settings in English fiction occurs in Samuel Johnson's *The History of Rasselas, Prince of Abissinia* (1759). Johnson never tells us that Rasselas is a black African, but his place of birth is where the "Father of waters begins his course" (7). When *Rasselas* was published, Europeans had no real knowledge about the origins of the Nile. Schama notes that Europeans living in the eighteenth century often imagined the source of the Nile as being a "cascade forcing its way through a cleft in a solid wall of rock" (374), but it would be another hundred years after the publication of *Rasselas* before Burton, Speeke, and other British explorers would locate the origins of the great river. However, Johnson clearly intends for his readers to understand that Rasselas is from a nation deep in the heart of black Africa. Like Oroonoko, Rasselas is an intelligent, cultured character of royal birth. While Rasselas's race is not central to the plot or the theme of the novel, Johnson's book shows that as late as 1759 Europeans could still accept a black African as a suitable hero for fiction.

In terms of the literary use of African settings, it is the place that Rasselas comes from, not Rasselas himself, that is of primary interest. By creating the "happy valley" of Amhara, Johnson begins a long tradition of locating lost cities and civilizations in the heart of Africa. Rasselas's Amhara is a timeless place; it is a utopia where there is little change (Atkinson 22). Amhara is "surrounded on every side by mountain" and can only be entered through a "cavern that passed under a rock" (8). Johnson describes the valley in these terms:

The sides of the mountains were covered with trees, the banks of the brooks were diversified with flowers; every blast shook spices from the rocks. . . . All animals that bite the grass, or browse the shrub, whether wild or tame, wander in this extensive circuit, secured from the beasts of prey by the mountains that confined them. . . . All the diversities of the world were brought together, the blessings of nature were collected, and its evils extracted and excluded. The valley, wide and fruitful, supplied its inhabitants with the necessaries of life. (9)

Rasselas's valley is an African Eden hidden from the outside world and devoid of the harsh realities of nature.

Africa was not a popular setting for British fiction in the first half of the nineteenth century, but Africa was an important part of the English national consciousness during that period. For instance, the young Brontës—Charlotte, Emily, Anne, and Branwell—relied heavily on the Reverend J. Goldsmith's *A Grammar of General Geography* and its descriptions of the African nation of Ashantee for the details used in the setting of much of the Brontë juvenilia (Ratchford 11). The Brontës also modeled some of their tales after articles about Africa that appeared in *Blackwood's Magazine* (Azim 115). For the Brontës, the African setting is equated with distance, enchantment, romance, and the supernatural (Azim 116).

In *The Twelve Adventurers,* written by Charlotte Brontë when she was twelve years old, twelve heroes are shipwrecked on the coast of Guinea near the mouth of the Niger River (Ratchford 11). In the Brontë narrative, African landscape is described in the following terms: "Grain of a peculiar sort grew in great abundance, and there were large plantations of palm-trees, and likewise an immense number of almond-trees. There were also many olives and enclosures of rice" (6–7).

The narrator of *The Twelve Adventurers* is "greatly surprised at these marks of the land being inhabited," and the adventurers soon discover that the inhabitants are hostile (7). The first natives they encounter deny the adventurers shelter, and a battle ensues. The adventurers are victorious and take the king of Ashantee as their prisoner (7). Further exploration of Africa by the adventurers reveals a desert skirted "by a long line of gloomy forests. . . . To the north the Mountains of the Moon seemed a misty girdle to the land of Dahomey; to the south the ocean guarded the coasts of Africa" (11). For the young Brontës, as for many other writers, African settings are fantasy lands where strange people and creatures provide challenges that can be overcome.

The Brontë juvenilia also anticipate the later use of African settings as battle-grounds for warring colonial powers. As Ratchford notes, "Branwell, having read the story of the early struggle between the English and the Dutch for colonies and trade," develops a story in which the twelve adventurers battle the Dutch for possession of Ascension Island, off the west coast of Africa (11). After the Brontës, African settings serve as battlegrounds in the conflicts between the English and the Portuguese (*The Gorilla Hunters*—around 1860—by R. M. Ballantyne), the English and the Germans (*The African Queen*, 1935, by C. S. Forester), the Americans and the Soviets (*The Horn of Africa*, 1980, by Philip Caputo), and the Americans and the Chinese (*Fong and the Indians*, 1968, by Paul Theroux).

In the 1850s, Dickens refers to the British interest in Africa via the character of Mrs. Jellyby in *Bleak House*. Jellyby is obsessed with supporting missionary work in Borrioboola-Gha, on the left bank of the Niger (53). As Jellyby explains, the "African project . . . employs my whole time" (53). Although she has no accurate knowledge of Africa, claiming for instance that Africa "has the finest climate in the world" (53), Jellyby is described as being able to "see nothing nearer than Africa" (52). In fact, Jellyby's overwhelming interest in developing a mission in Bor-rioboola-Gha causes her to neglect the welfare of her family. Jellyby is a symbol, a warning from Dickens that England would do well to focus on its own problems at home before attempting to cure ills abroad.

The possibility of finding (and killing) exotic wildlife in Africa is the basis for the plot of R. M. Ballantyne's *The Gorilla Hunters*, an action-adventure novel that was first published in the 1860s and saw numerous printings during the closing decades of the nineteenth century. Ballantyne's novel is the first in which African wildlife plays a central role. Ralph Rover, Peterkin Gay, and Jack Martin are the gorilla hunters. They are wealthy young Englishmen who travel to Africa in search of adventure and encounters with exotic animals: leopards, lions, elephants, rhinoc-eroses, buffaloes, and gorillas. While the hunters will shoot most any animal, they are particularly interested in killing gorillas. As one of Ballantyne's hunters explains, the gorilla is the "man monkey that we've been hearing so much of for some years. . . . I'm determined to shoot a gorilla, or prove him to be myth" (12). After numerous adventures, including encounters with tsetse flies that destroy their horses (138) and armed natives who turn out to be friendly (141), the hunters finally face their quarry.

In *The Gorilla Hunters*, the gorilla is described in especially frightful terms; the roar of the gorilla is more ferocious than a lion's (146), and the gorilla is a "monster . . . calculated to strike terror into the hearts of beholders" (147). Ballantyne's use of the African setting is significant because he anticipates the writing of Edgar Rice Burroughs by locating his story in the jungles of Africa and by introducing readers to the great apes. *The Gorilla Hunters* is also the first in a long line of safari novels that includes works by Ernest Hemingway, Robert Ruark, and William Harrison.

During the second half of the nineteenth century, narratives of exploration—such works as David Livingstone's *Missionary Travels and Researches in South Africa* (1858), Richard Burton's *Two Trips to Gorilla Land and the Cataracts of the Congo* (1876), and Henry Morton Stanley's *In Darkest Africa* (1891)—were quite popular. Indeed, some African explorations, especially those by Stanley, were conceived as literary expeditions designed to produce marketable accounts (Atkinson 35). The popularity of these nonfiction accounts sparked a renewed interest in Africa as a literary setting. Furthermore, toward the end of the nineteenth century, many Britishers traveled to Africa and some settled in Africa. Olive Schreiner, the child of British missionaries, produced one of the more influential nineteenth-century novels with an African setting: *The Story of an African Farm* (1883).

Schreiner, who published under the name of Ralph Iron, is a realistic writer who takes great care to render the African setting accurately and to make setting a fundamental part of her narrative. Her contributions to the literary use of African settings, however, go far beyond her descriptions of the South African topography. Numerous modern critics have been harsh in their assessment of Schreiner's attitude toward native life and some have accused her of racism (Bristow xxvii), but Schreiner is the one of the first novelists to comment upon the destructive influences of Europeans on Africa and Africans.

For example, at the very beginning of *The Story of an African Farm*, Waldo—one of the principal characters—comments on some figures that bushmen living long ago had painted on a rock overhang. The paintings are of the bushmen and of the animals that once lived on the land that has been homesteaded and farmed by the Boers and the British. Waldo appreciates the beauty of the paintings and notes that the bushmen are gone, the "Boers have shot them all, so that we never see a little yellow face come peeping out among the stones. . . . And the wild bucks have gone, and those days, and we are here" (16). Waldo—like Schreiner herself—is an African, and he has a natural appreciation for the land and the animals of the continent. Later in the novel, for instance, Waldo will recall the beauty of the African "out-span," South Africa's wild country.

Schreiner's novel might be called an "African Western." *The Story of an African Farm*, for all its feminism and philosophical commentary, is essentially a picture of life on a frontier similar to that of the American West. As is the case of the literature of the American West, the indigenous population has been eliminated or subjugated, the settlers live on isolated ranches separated by vast spaces, and, in order to survive, they struggle with the land and the weather—especially drought. In *The Story of an African Farm*, the characters maintain their sense of community at special events such as weddings. The chapter titled "A Boer-wedding" features riders and wagonloads of families assembling from miles around for a night of dancing and drinking in a fashion similar to descriptions of community celebrations in the literature of the American West. "A Boer-wedding," for instance, has much in common with the barn raising scene in Frank Norris's 1901 novel *The Octopus* when "ranchers from the remoter parts of the county" appear for a night of music, feasting, and drinking at Annixter's farm (171).

While Schreiner makes no overt comparison of Africa and the frontier of the American West, other authors, most notably P. C. Wren, do make such direct comparisons. Wren, writing about North Africa in his 1924 novel *Beau Geste*, notes that African settings have much in common with the American West. In Wren's novel, the Americans—Hank and Buddy—have had experiences in the deserts of California that prepare them to survive in the Sahara among the Arabs. As Hank suggests, if he and his friends want to live, they must "turn Injun. . . . Get Injun glad rags and live like they does" (372).

Schreiner was a great inspiration to another writer who knew South Africa well: H. Rider Haggard. When writing about books that had influenced him, Haggard consistently mentions *The Story of an African Farm* (Etherington 21). Indeed, Etherington implies that Haggard turned to writing romances after failing to create realistic novels that could rival Schreiner's classic (22). Today, few readers know Haggard's works of realism; it is his stories of adventure and romance that have made him one of the most popular authors of the last 100 years.

In such novels as *King Solomon's Mines* (1886), *She* (1887), and *Allan Quatermain* (1887), Haggard resurrects Johnson's lost-city motif, provides detailed descriptions of the topography of South Africa, and establishes hunting as an important part of fiction set in Africa. Haggard also develops African settings as appropriate locales for science fiction, a use of African settings that influences the works of Edgar Rice Burroughs. Perhaps the best example of Haggard's interest in science fiction occurs in *She*, in which Ayesha (She) experiments with eugenics.

In *King Solomon's Mines*, Haggard manages to incorporate lost civilizations, bizarre topography, and big game hunting into one story. An early chapter of the novel describes an elephant hunt, another details a march across the desert, and, finally, Quatermain and his companions discover Kukuanaland, a lost civilization similar to Rasselas's Amhara.

Like Amhara, Kukuanaland is a paradise isolated both by desert and mountains. Coming out of the desert and approaching Kukuanaland, Allan Quatermain, the narrator of *King Solomon's Mines*, observes that the "country before us must lie at least three thousand feet higher than the desert we had crossed" (80). As he and his companions climb these mountains and descend into their valleys, Quatermain notes that "the atmosphere grew softer and balmier, and the country before us shone with a yet more luminous beauty" (82). Stopping for lunch by a stream, Quatermain describes the scene as a "paradise" (84). The lovely setting by the stream only prepares the reader for the greater beauty of Kukuanaland proper: "The vegetation was luxuriant, without being tropical; the sun was bright and warm, but not burning; and a gracious breeze blew softly along the odorous slopes of the mountains. Indeed, this new land was little less than an earthly paradise" (97).

Following Haggard's cue, American authors also place lost civilizations in Africa and employ African setting as mysterious places where science fiction tales are especially likely to unfold. For instance, in Edgar Rice Burroughs's *Tarzan and the Lost Empire*, von Harben and his native friend Gabula discover a remnant of the Roman empire walled off in a deep valley of the Wiramwazi mountains.

The fiction of Haggard and Burroughs reflects the shift in Western attitudes about Africa that occurred between the publication of *Oroonoko*, *Crusoe*, *Madagascar*, and *Rasselas* and the late nineteenth century and early twentieth century. In the works of Haggard and Burroughs, African peoples are not capable of supporting highly developed cultures. Indeed, the lost civilizations of Haggard and Burroughs are usually not African at all; they are remnants of European civilizations. In *King Solomon's Mines*, the natives of Kukuanaland are black Africans, but just barely. Haggard describes them as having hair that is "curly" rather than "woolly" and having features that are "aquiline." Moreover, the people of Kukuanaland have "lips [that] are not unpleasantly thick, as is the case among most African races" (100). In *She*, Ayesha is Persian, in *Allan Quatermain* the Zu-Vendis are whites, and the inhabitants of Burroughs's lost civilization in *Tarzan and the Lost Empire* are of Roman descent.

British and American authors writing at the turn of the century do, however, present us with minor characters who are both black and admirable. For instance, in *Allan Quatermain*, Haggard creates Umslopogaas, a brave and noble Zulu, and in Burroughs's *Tarzan and the Lost Empire*, Gabula is a loyal warrior who refuses to abandon Erich von Harben when all the other Africans flee. However, black Africans will not regain the roles of major characters that they enjoyed in such works as *Oroonoko* and *Rasselas* until the 1930s when Joyce Cary publishes his novels about colonial Nigeria.

Joseph Conrad's *Heart of Darkness* begins a new line of development in the use of African settings. The novel has sparked a great deal of literary criticism and controversy. Among the harshest critics of Conrad's portrayal of Africa and Africans is Chinua Achebe, who, in the essay "An Image of Africa," notes that Conrad places Africa in binary opposition to the West and maintains that *Heart of Darkness* questions the very humanity of black people and "parades in the most vulgar fashion prejudices and insults from which a section of mankind has suffered untold agonies and atrocities" (*Hopes* 15). The controversy surrounding *Heart of Darkness* is beyond the scope of this study, but the impact of Conrad's work in terms of the use of African settings in fiction is enormous. Conrad's most important contribution lies in his turning away from employing African settings as exotic places where strange beings and lost cities can be found and turning toward a concern with the effects of African settings on the interior lives of Western characters.

Heart of Darkness is the first work with an African setting in which Europeans "come to Africa to learn about themselves as well as to escape 'civilization' " (Gruesser 9). By placing Kurtz in the heart of Africa, Conrad tests not only Kurtz's character but also the very character of European culture (Goonetilleke 111). The Africa we encounter in *Heart of Darkness* symbolizes a lack of restraint (Gruesser 9), and this lack of restraint allows Western characters to come to a greater understanding of themselves and of European culture.

In *Heart of Darkness*, both Kurtz and Marlow come to a deeper knowledge about themselves and their culture via a direct comparison of Africa and Europe. However, the result of this direct comparison does not establish that Conrad is "a thorough-going racist," as Achebe maintains (*Hopes* 11). Instead, Conrad's direct comparison of Europe and Africa suggests that Europe is as savage as any African culture and that there is a potential for savagery in all people. Goonetilleke maintains that the crucial scene in *Heart of Darkness* occurs not in Africa but in Brussels when Marlow—who hates a lie more than anything—lies to Kurtz's intended. The descriptions of Brussels in this scene are characterized, according to Goonetilleke, by images of death and darkness; the implication is that European prosperity is based on inhumanity (116).

Conrad's use of African settings as a way of getting to the heart of the matter—whether that matter be the nature of a character's true self or a character's greater understanding of history and imperialism—is continued in the works of P. C. Wren, Joyce Cary, and Ernest Hemingway before World War II, and, after World War II, in the novels of Graham Greene and such American authors as Paul Bowles, Saul Bellow, Michael Mewshaw, William Harrison, and Philip Caputo. Conrad's direct comparison of European and African cultures also establishes the clash of Western and African cultures as a theme inherent in novels with African settings; this theme remains of interest to contemporary American authors such as John Updike and Richard Dooling.

In British literature, serious attempts at an examination of cultural clashes and their results come in the 1930s with the writings of Joyce Cary and Karen Blixen—who is "British" in the sense that she wrote in English while residing in a British colony. The focus on cultural interaction requires a more complete picture of African peoples than that provided by authors such as Haggard and Burroughs, and it is in the works of Blixen and Cary that developed, rounded African characters are encountered after a long hiatus.

Karen Blixen—who published *Out of Africa* in 1937 under the name of Isak Dinesen—draws loving pictures of a number of Africans she meets while living and working on a coffee plantation in Kenya. She also describes the native culture, particularly its legal system (100), and details native reaction to European technology, specifically the book (48) and the airplane (245). While Blixen's account of her years in Kenya is more philosophical journal than novel, many writers of fiction working after Blixen return to the theme of the interaction—and clash—of African and Western cultures.

Joyce Cary is foremost among those who examine the results of culture clash; in Cary's novels, the clashing of cultures always teaches Westerners something about themselves as well as something about Africans. In terms of his use of African settings, Cary is definitely Conrad's heir. Cary explains the appeal of Africa as a literary setting in these terms: "The attraction of Africa is that . . . basic obsessions, which in Europe hide themselves under all sorts of decorous scientific or theological or political uniforms, are there seen naked in bold and dramatic action" (prefatory note to *Aissa Saved* 10). Cary, like Conrad, uses African settings as ways to strip away illusions and uncover essential truths. Graham Greene's Africans novels, all published after World War II, continue the tradition established by Conrad and Cary of using African settings as places that force characters to achieve insights about substantial themes such as religion and war.

During the 1930s—a decade that saw a great interest in Africa as a literary setting—Joyce Cary published several novels about Africa: *Aissa Saved, An American Visitor, An African Witch,* and *Mister Johnson.* Like many British and American authors who have used African settings in their novels, Cary had direct experience with Africa, having spent a number of years in Nigeria as a civil servant. All of his African novels are set in colonial Nigeria during the early decades of this century. While Cary does comment on the introduction of Western materialism in Africa, his major concern is with the cultural impact of moral values (Goonetilleke 200).

In *Aissa Saved,* for example, Cary's basic theme is the nature of faith, and Cary directly relates the plot of *Aissa Saved* to a feature of the African setting: harsh weather. A drought afflicts the land, and both the pagans and the Christians turn to their respective deities to bring rain. As Goonetilleke explains, this drought "brings out the conflicting values of the Europeans and the Africans" and allows readers to understand the clash of Nigerian and Western cultures (207).

Cary is also adept at observing that there is, in fact, a clashing of cultures within African society. He is one of the first to note that Africa is home of three competing religions: Islam, Christianity, and animism, and Cary is the first novelist since Johnson to feature Africans as main characters in his work. In *Aissa Saved,* readers witness Aissa's conversion to Christianity, and in *An African Witch,* they follow the British-educated Loius Aladai as he struggles with racial prejudice and fights to win a future for his nation, Rimi. Cary's Africa is a place where the best intentions of the West—in *Aissa Saved,* for example, Bradgate's desire to build a bridge—meet with determined opposition from Africans who find Western ways foolish, wasteful, and sometimes dangerous.

With the story of the political uprising led by Louis Aladai in *An African Witch,* Cary establishes African politics as a subject worthy of literary consideration. Another British writer of the 1930s—Evelyn Waugh—shares Cary's interest in African politics and with the struggle for political power. Waugh details his interest in political themes in two novels, *Black Mischief* and *Scoop.* Like Cary, Waugh had extensive personal experience in Africa, and, like Cary, Waugh employs the clashing of Western and African cultures to satirize both African and Western societies. Waugh's most interesting contribution to fiction set in Africa is his invention of an imaginary nation as the setting for his work. *Black Mischief* is set in the mythical country of Azania—an island nation based loosely on Abyssinia, where Waugh had worked for a time as a newspaper correspondent (Doyle 574). The imagined African nation of Azania allows Waugh to incorporate the traits of a number of African cultures into one locale that represents the entire continent.

Ironically, one of the last British novels with an African setting to be published prior to World War II is a book about World War I. *The African Queen* by C. S. Forester was first published in 1935; however, Forester's publisher "did not like the end of the book" and "docked" its last two chapters (Forester ii). In 1940, *The African Queen* was reissued in the form the author intended. Forester's novel contains many elements essential to the literary use of African settings: a concern with climate, wildlife, disease, and the struggle between humans and the natural world; a detailing of an important feature of African topography (the Ulanga River); and the use of African settings as war zones for colonial powers.

The central theme of *The African Queen*, despite the plot's concern with the struggle between the British and the Germans for control of central Africa, is the conflict between humans and nature. By testing themselves against the rapids and the marshes of the Ulanga River, Rose and Charlie grow into characters who are strong and whole, strong enough even to fall in love with each other. Indeed, Africa as presented in *The African Queen* is a testing ground where humans battle nature (the river), the machine (the steam engine on the *Queen*), and each other (the Germans and the English). What is most unusual about *The African Queen* is the absence of Africans in the novel. There are very few African characters in Forester's work, and those characters play extremely brief and minor roles in the story. Indeed, the only important African character in *The African Queen* is the Ulanga River, and the Ulanga, like Rose and Charlie, changes its nature as it descends from the highlands of the Rift Valley into German-controlled Lake Witelsbach.

While Africa has been used as a literary setting in British fiction since the birth of the novel, American writers of the eighteenth and nineteenth centuries rarely set their works in Africa. In the late eighteenth and early nineteenth centuries, a number of slave narratives, for example, *Olaudah Equano or Gustavus Vassa, the African* (1789), that contain accounts of life and culture in West Africa were published. However, these narratives are works of autobiography, not fiction. Herman Melville, the only nineteenth-century American writer of note to have personal experience with non-Western cultures, had a deep interest in African customs and myths, and he makes extensive use of African traditions in *Moby Dick* and "Benito Cereno" (Fishkin A48). However, Melville does not actually place any of his fiction in Africa. In fact, one of the few nineteenth-century American novels to employ African settings is the 1853 "propaganda" novel, *Liberia; or, Mr. Peyton's Experiments* by Sarah J. Hale.

In *Liberia*, Hale concludes that "the Negro is constitutionally unable to cope with American society" and that the solution to the slavery problem is to return the Negroes to Africa (Gohdes [ii]). The early sections of *Liberia* present black American characters with a number of alternatives to slavery, including life in a northern city and life in Canada, but none of these alternatives proves suitable. Only by returning to Africa will black Americans truly be free. As a character named Dr. Durbin puts it, "transport these people [American blacks] to Africa, with our religion, our civilization, though in a low degree, and our political institutions, and experience has shown that there they become men" (227). Hale implies that the African in Africa is degenerate, and former slaves who settle Liberia have as one of their main goals the conversion and civilization of Africans. Hale does a credible job of describing the weather in Liberia (158) and the court of King Gezo in neighboring Dahomey—"All around the king's residence the ground was paved with human skulls" (237). But Hale's early, realistic descriptions of Liberia and the struggles of the first settlers quickly degenerate into utopian fantasy. Indeed, *Liberia* is important for only two reasons: the novel is a rare example of the use of African settings in nineteenth-century American fiction, and it is also an African "Western" in that it details the adventures of a pioneer community on the edge of a great frontier.

Even in American fiction from 1900 to World War II, the use of African settings is rare. In fact, only two American writers of note working during these decades— Edgar Rice Burroughs and Ernest Hemingway—employ African settings in their works, and no two authors better demonstrate the shift in the thematic uses of African settings. Burroughs follows the precedent established by Haggard, creating a fantasy Africa complete with Edenic landscapes (*Tarzan of the Apes*), time travel (*The Eternal Savage*), lost civilizations (*Tarzan and the Lost Empire*), and bizarre creatures that owe their existence to science (*Tarzan and the Ant Men* and *Tarzan and the Lion Man*). Hemingway follows the precedent established by Conrad in that Hemingway employs African settings as testing grounds that spark epiphanies and interior changes in his characters, for instance, the change that Francis Macomber experiences in "The Short Happy Life of Francis Macomber."

Burroughs is the greatest popularizer of African settings in American fiction. Like Haggard, Burroughs views African settings as particularly appropriate to the development of science fiction writing. Like Haggard, Burroughs considers Africa a mysterious, largely unexplored region that might be the home of mysterious creatures and people. And, like Haggard, Burroughs uses African settings as locales where time can be defeated and where genetic experimentation can change nature. In *Tarzan and the Lion Man*, for example, the agent of science fiction is genetics; the "god of England" has achieved immortality by mixing ape and human cells. In doing so, he creates a community of humanoid apes similar to that found in Jules Verne's 1901 novel *The Village in the Treetops*.

Hemingway, however, rejects Africa as a fantasy setting and follows Conrad's example of using African settings as testing grounds. That Hemingway always considered Africa a potentially productive literary setting is apparent as early as

The Sun Also Rises when Jake and Robert Cohn discuss their escape from Paris. Robert wants to go to South America. Jake suggests instead that they go "to British East Africa to shoot" (10). In a number of ways, Hemingway uses African settings for the same reason he uses Spanish settings. As Edward Stanton notes, for Hemingway "Spain is the land of the ancient truths—nature, the body, fertility, religion, ritual" (87). For Hemingway, Spain was the last good country. Spain had escaped the ravages of World War I, Spain had not yet become industrialized, and, most importantly, Spain offered access to ritual. The Spanish ritual that most appealed to Hemingway was the celebration of courage and death found in the bullring (Stanton 15).

Like Spain, Africa had escaped World War I, had not been industrialized, and offered a ritual of courage and death: big game hunting. Hemingway's Spain is in binary opposition to the modernism and industrialization of Paris just as Africa is in binary opposition to the West in much of contemporary American fiction. If in Spain Hemingway found the last good country, in Africa he found the last great continent.

Hemingway has a real affection for the physical topography of Africa. About the African land he writes "I loved the country so that I was happy as you are after you have been with a woman that you really love" (*Green Hills* 72), and in "The Snows of Kilimanjaro," Harry, the story's narrator, notes that "Africa was where he had been happiest in the good times of his life" (10).

Hemingway, then, uses African settings for three principal reasons, reasons that continue to attract contemporary American authors to African settings. First, Hemingway employs African settings to criticize the emptiness of life in the industrial nations. Second, he uses African settings to provide challenges that characters can meet in order to change their lives, the best example being "The Short Happy Life of Francis Macomber" in which Macomber proves his courage—much to his wife's dismay—by confronting nature in the form of the buffalo. Third, Hemingway considers African settings to be places where fundamental assessments—including assessments about literature—can be made. Examples of Hemingway's use of African settings as places that trigger assessments can be found in *Green Hills of Africa* and in "The Snows of Kilimanjaro." And it is no accident that Hemingway delivers his judgment about American literature, including the famous comment that "All modern American literature comes from one book by Mark Twain called *Huckleberry Finn*," at the beginning of *Green Hills of Africa*.

In summary, British and American novels written before World War II associate a number of thematic concerns with African settings: slavery, the conflict between humans and nature, and the notion that Africa harbors mysterious creatures and lost civilizations. The early examples of British fiction with African settings depict Africans as cultured, civilized beings; much of the later fiction featuring African settings depicts Africans as savage barbarians. Moreover, the use of African settings has evolved into two ways of writing about Africa. One branch is best represented by Haggard and Burroughs. This branch centers on the old notions that Africa is a strange and mysterious place where anything, including time travel, is possible. The other branch in the use of African settings is represented by Conrad, Cary, Forester, and Hemingway. This second branch assumes that Africa is a testing ground for characters, a place where characters can come to terms with themselves and their cultures. Both of these ways of thinking and writing about Africa have been carried over into contemporary American fiction with African settings.

Chapter 3

Filling in the Blank Space: Contemporary American Novels Set in Invented African Nations

Several American authors have set their novels in invented African nations, imaginary countries meant to represent the characteristics, values, and conflicts of the entire continent. Contemporary American novels set in invented African nations include *The Seersucker Whipsaw* by Ross Thomas, *The Tangent Objective* and *The Tangent Factor* by Lawrence Sanders, *The Coup* by John Updike, *Land Without Shadow* by Michael Mewshaw, and *Horn of Africa* by Philip Caputo. For the most part, these novels conform to the traditional Western notions about Africa outlined in Chapter 1. Among these conventions are the ideas that the West and Africa are in binary opposition, that Africa is a mysterious "blank" space, and that Africa is a testing zone where Westerners can experience epiphanies or gain rewards.

American novels with invented African settings are largely didactic. These works relay information about actual African cultures by including features of actual Africa in descriptions of invented settings. The use of an invented African nation as the setting for a novel allows authors to focus on the relationship between the West and Africa without being critical of any single African country. Like actual African nations, invented African countries are frequently divided by political, tribal, and religious conflicts; these divisions are often the result of different peoples being grouped together under a single flag by their former colonial masters. Again and again, novels set in invented Africas note that political upheaval in Africa is the legacy of imperialism. These novels are also reminders that imperialism, in the guise of Cold War conflicts in which the superpowers use Africa as a battleground, is still a powerful force in contemporary Africa.

Some readers may assume that the invented African nations they encounter in contemporary American fiction are actual countries. Most authors of these novels acknowledge the imaginary nature of their settings, usually in a disclaimer stating that characters and locations in their narratives are fictitious; however, some do not bother with such disclaimers, allowing readers to make their own assumptions about the nature of a novel's setting. For instance, Michael Mewshaw's *Land Without Shadow* is set in an invented North African nation called Maliteta, yet Mewshaw nowhere indicates that he has created Maliteta. Moreover, giving the invented setting a realistic quality, novels set in invented African nations usually provide a wealth of detail about the nation's geography, culture, and history. An emphasis on realistic detail is part of the didactic nature of these works. Frequently, the invented African nation is a vessel containing information about actual African nations and cultures.

It is also understandable that readers might confuse invented African countries with actual African nations when one considers the degree to which national boundaries have changed in Africa since World War II. In fact, boundaries in Africa have shifted several times since the last half of the nineteenth century. The Berlin Conference of 1884–1885 formalized European dominance in Africa and led to the drawing of boundaries that divided historically contiguous African societies and precisely defined the areas claimed by European powers (Harris, *Africans* 185). By the outbreak of World War I, the French, British, Belgians, Germans, Portuguese, and Spanish had succeeded in subjugating all of Africa except Liberia and Ethiopia. (Liberia, which was established in 1822 as a colony of freed slaves from the United States, became an independent republic in 1847.) After World War I, German holdings in Africa were divided among Britain, France, and Belgium, and once again boundaries were redrawn and names of African territories were changed. Ethiopia, which expelled all foreigners in the mid-seventeenth century and repelled an Italian invasion in the 1890s, fell to Italy in 1935 and remained part of Italian East Africa until 1941 when it was liberated by British troops.

Prior to World War II, a map of Africa consisted of more than forty nations and territories; a map of contemporary Africa features more than sixty nations. In a veiled reference to the frequently changing map of Africa, Ross Thomas prefaces *The Seersucker Whipsaw* with this disclaimer: "All of the characters and events in this novel are as imaginary as the country of Albertia, which did not exist the last time the author looked at a map of Africa" (i). Thomas implies that he would not be terribly surprised, if, glancing at a map of Africa produced at some date after the publication of his book, he were to discover a country named Albertia.

Many of the concerns associated with invented African settings can be traced to Evelyn Waugh's *Black Mischief*, a novel that satirizes both African and Western cultures by comparing the West to Africa. In *Black Mischief*, Waugh describes an imaginary island nation called Azania. Azania lies off the coast of what, in Waugh's time, was Italian Somaliland. For the most part, *Black Mischief* conforms to traditional Western conventions about Africa; for instance, Azanians are portrayed as being primitive, savage, cruel, and cannibalistic.

As Gruesser notes, Azania is a microcosm for the African continent geographically, historically, and politically (18). Azania is a composite Africa, populated by

Indians, Arabs, the native Sakuyu, and the "Wanda-Galla immigrants from the mainland who, long before the coming of the Arabs, had settled in the north of the island" (11). Over this diverse population rules Seth, the Oxford-educated, but incompetent, Emperor of Azania. An interest in African politics is part of what Gruesser terms the "political assessment tradition" of writing about Africa (xii), and political affairs—especially the struggle among Western powers for control of African resources—are significant concerns that Waugh associates with his invented setting.

Like *Black Mischief*, American novels featuring invented African settings often focus on political events—especially elections, coups, and revolutions—and these novels frequently satirize life in the West and comment on life in Africa by comparing the two. Like Azania, the invented nations found in contemporary American novels are generalized, composite countries that are intended to represent large regions of—if not all of—Africa. For instance, *The Coup, Land Without Shadow*, and *Horn of Africa* unfold in invented nations or provinces located somewhere in the Sahara. *The Seersucker Whipsaw, The Tangent Objective*, and *The Tangent Factor* feature invented settings that are similar to several actual West African nations.

Novels set in invented African nations or provinces tend to emphasize that, despite the presence of widespread poverty, many African nations possess enormous wealth in the form of mineral resources such as oil, diamonds, and copper. These novels also frequently note that Africa is split along urban/rural lines as well as tribal and religious lines. Power struggles within these invented African nations are usually battles between different tribes or fights between Islamics and Christians.

As Gruesser notes, American and British novels published in the 1970s often subject Africa to harsh criticism for the failure of African nations to "provide adequate education, health care, and other services; and to create diversified, competitive economies" (44). Most of the American novels set in invented African nations were published in the 1970s, and most of these novels are critical of African political and social affairs. However, Gruesser goes too far in maintaining that when the political and economic failures of African nations became impossible to ignore, "Western writers began to look for someone or something to blame" and accepted a "pre-existing 'analysis' of postcolonial Africa's problems" that maintained that "political freedom released the darkness, blankness, and nightmarish aspect of Africa that colonialism had sought but failed to control" (45).

In fact, American novelists simply subject African politics and cultures to the same sort of scrutiny that writers have always applied to the politics and culture of the United States. After all, many significant American novels—one need only recall the works of John Dos Passos and John Steinbeck, for example—are heavily critical of American politics and of America's failure, as Gruesser might phrase it, to "provide adequate education, health care, and other services" to its population. Furthermore, American writers who set works in African nations, be they real or invented countries, are more interested in describing conditions in Africa than in placing blame. When blame is placed in these works, it usually falls not upon African cultures but upon the legacy of imperialism and corrupt African leaders who deserve censure.

The creation of an invented African nation as the setting of a novel is a risky literary undertaking. Recalling his childhood love of maps, Marlow—the narrator of Conrad's *Heart of Darkness*—says, "At that time there were many blank spaces on the earth" (33). One of the largest blank spaces on young Marlow's map was Africa, and some critics fault writers who fill Marlow's blank map with invented nations and peoples. For instance, Malini Schueller maintains that John Updike's *The Coup* "functions to legitimate an imperialist discourse that denies the political existence of the Third World" (115), and Gruesser insists that *The Coup* projects a "white Western male fantasy" of Africa (103). Novelists themselves sometimes feel uneasy about inventing African nations or provinces as settings for their narratives. Commenting about the invented setting of *Horn of Africa*, Caputo explains: "I had considered creating an entire country in which to set this story, but decided that that would be carrying literary imperialism too far. No doubt there are people who will feel I've gone too far as it is; what arrogance to place a nonexistent province on the map of one of Africa's oldest nations, and then populate it with an imaginary black-Arab tribe" ([vii]).

It would be a mistake, however, to level charges of arrogance and "literary imperialism" against American authors who have set novels in invented African nations. Although these novels do, for the most part, reflect traditional Western notions about Africa, these works are mainly didactic, seeking not to invent an Africa that suits Western conventions but to inform Western readers of conditions and problems shared by many African nations. These novels are usually more critical of Western culture than of African cultures, and they are generally anti-imperialist, frequently pointing out that many of the problems of contemporary Africa are the result of colonialism. Indeed, most of the contemporary American novels set in invented African nations are highly critical of American as well as British, Russian, Cuban, and Chinese meddling in Africa. Writers who create invented African nations as settings for their narratives are taking a literary gamble, but the rewards of such risk taking, as American novels set in invented African nations demonstrate, can be great.

PART I: NOVELS SET IN INVENTED WEST AFRICAN NATIONS

The Seersucker Whipsaw: Election Time in Albertia

Ross Thomas's *The Seersucker Whipsaw*, a political thriller set in the 1960s, explores the possibility of establishing a Western-style democracy in a postcolonial African nation. Thomas's Albertia is a British colony on the verge of independence. American political advisors Clinton Shartelle and Peter Upshaw are hired to manage the presidential campaign of Chief Sunday Akomolo, who is given the code name *Scarface* because of his tribal markings. As Shartelle's employer—a public relations advisor named Padraic Duffy—explains, Shartelle has been brought in "to help out Africa" (21). The election in Albertia is an opportunity "to carve out a bastion of democracy in Africa," and a victory for Akomolo will establish Shartelle as "one of the world's foremost political strategists" (24).

Chief Akomolo is a Christian from Albertia's largest tribe. His competition for the presidency includes Sir Alakada Mejara Fulawa, an Islamic from northern Albertia whose campaign is managed by a prestigious British firm, and Dr. Kensington Kologo, a medical doctor from eastern Albertia who has support from the U.S. CIA. Of all the developing nations south of the Sahara, Albertia "is almost alone in its readiness and ability to accept the full challenge that self-rule imposes" (55). Thomas's intention in *The Seersucker Whipsaw* is to show, via the example of his invented nation, why democracy will be difficult to achieve in postcolonial Africa.

Like most contemporary American novels set in invented African nations, *The Seersucker Whipsaw* filters African life through the eyes of a Western narrator, in this case the political writer and advisor Peter Upshaw. Like many American characters in fiction set in Africa, both Shartelle and Upshaw come from the American heartland (New Orleans and North Dakota, respectively), and both find something of value in Africa. Africa rewards Shartelle and Upshaw by giving them a cause worth fighting for and an opportunity to find love.

As they manage Akomolo's presidential campaign, Upshaw and Shartelle learn a great deal about life in Albertia and in West Africa. Thomas provides details about typical Albertian dress (long, flowing robes worn over loose trousers) and food (soups made with peanuts and dishes flavored with peppers). Albertians are very generous and hospitable, traits common in many African cultures, and, like many Africans, the Albertians frequently express their thoughts and feelings in proverbs. In addition to these details about Albertian culture, Upshaw and Shartelle soon discover that the Albertians do not care for their former colonial masters, the British. About the British, Chief Akomolo says, "In my heart, I try not to hate them. . . . Yet they are a cold people . . . cold and unfeeling and vengeful" (36).

Albertia is a nation of twenty million people with one of the best harbors in West Africa. In some ways, Albertia resembles colonial Nigeria in that Albertia has a solid agricultural economy, an efficient civil service system established by the British, and a wealth of untouched oil reserves (8). However, Albertia is similar in shape and size to the actual West African nations of Togo or Benin. Thomas describes his invented nation in terms that make the economic divisions in Albertia (and Africa) apparent:

Albertia is shaped like a funnel and its spout is Barkandu, the capital city. Along the thirty-three mile strip that forms its claim to the sea are some of the finest white sand beaches in the world and some of the most treacherous undertows. In the middle of the strip of sand is a natural deep sea harbor that divides the city geographically and economically. To the north, toward the interior, are the city's fifty-six miles of squalor where the Albertians live on their ninety-six dollar-a-year average incomes. To the south are the broad boulevards, the neat green lawns, the Consulates, office buildings, hotels . . . night clubs, foreign-owned shops, department stores, and the Yacht Club. (39)

Beyond the coast, conditions in Albertia are best described as undeveloped. There are only two roads from the capital city of Barkandu to the interior. One is the ninety-six miles of "patched asphalt" running from Barkandu through the rain forest to Ubondo, "the second largest all black city in Africa. It's a million people living in a sea of tin-roofed houses" (89). Looking out over Ubondo, Shartelle says, "Now boy, that's what I call Africa. Look at all that squalor" (90).

Albertia's other highway leads north to the Sahara, to Timbuktu, and although Thomas provides Albertia with a neighboring, French colony so that Shartelle and Upshaw can take their women friends, the wealthy Widow Claude and an American Peace Corps worker named Anne Kidd, on vacation (247), few details about the French territory are offered.

Albertia is a hot, humid nation where the afternoon temperatures frequently near 100 degrees Fahrenheit. Taking advantage of Albertia's climate, the savvy campaigner Shartelle orders three million fans, each labeled with a political slogan, for distribution to voters (59). Albertia is also a place that seems to exist out of time, and this sense of timelessness is related to Albertia's climate. Upshaw observes that "West Africa dulls any sense of time. . . . It's always July in West Africa. A hot July" (229).

One message of *The Seersucker Whipsaw* is that there are many Africas and that sometimes these various Africas exist within the borders of a single nation. In Albertia, rival tribes struggle for power, and political loyalty is often determined by religion. In Albertia, as in actual Africa, there are three competing religions: animism, Christianity, and Islam. At one political event, Shartelle and Upshaw are stunned by the appearance of a juju man whose job is to get rid of evil spirits. The juju man wears a lion skin, a mask, and a hat made of a plastic model of a destroyer named *Ft. Worth, Texas* (103).

There is also an urban/rural division in Albertia that is characteristic of Africa at large; a trip to Koreedu, a small village in the interior, provides a picture of Africa that is far different from the city slums of Barkandu or Ubondo. Koreedu lies where the rain forest gives way to cultivated palm groves and fields of rough grass (223), and it is in Koreedu that Shartelle encounters the old, traditional Africa with all its charms and all its problems. The people of Koreedu are extremely generous and hospitable, but they are also superstitious. For instance, when Shartelle cures a baby of colic by using an American folk remedy, the people of Koreedu believe he is using magic (227). Indeed, like much of *The Seersucker Whipsaw*, the Koreedu scene is didactic; Thomas wants to demonstrate that the urban/rural split—as well as conflicts along lines of tribe, class, and religion—makes democracy difficult to achieve in newly independent African nations.

Although Thomas incorporates many Western conventions about Africa into his novel, he also shatters a number of stereotypes. For example, he notes that women, particularly the women traders who operate the mammy wagons, have considerable economic and political power in West Africa. He also observes that not all of Africa is blessed with vast, untamed space and plentiful wildlife. At one point, Shartelle—who always seems to be trying to convince himself that he is actually in Africa—asks about the animals in the rain forest. William, Shartelle's African driver, explains that there are no wild animals because they have all been eaten (88).

In addition to using the invented nation of Albertia as a way to inform readers about conditions in postcolonial West Africa, Thomas also uses the setting of *The Seersucker Whipsaw* to comment on the culture and political system of the United States by comparing the United States with Albertia. Thomas frequently reminds his readers that political violence, especially the assassination of presidents, occurs in America as well as in Africa. Furthermore, Shartelle, who comes from New Orleans and jokingly claims he is part Negro (11), uses the occasion of a trip to Africa to comment upon the race problem in 1960s America. Blacks in America, Shartelle explains, should be given equal rights, but he worries that black Americans may loose their culture even as they gain legal equality (11).

Postcolonial Africans are also in danger of losing their cultures, but, ironically, the greatest threat of cultural imperialism in *The Seersucker Whipsaw* comes not from the former colonial ruler, Britain, but from the United States. Thomas is one of the first to note that Africa, like most of the Third World, is greatly affected by American culture. At the same time the Albertians are gaining independence from the British, they are succumbing to American television. The programming on Albertian TV consists of shows such as *Highway Patrol, Dragnet, The Lone Ranger*, and *Gunsmoke*; some leaders are concerned that American television may be too violent for African audiences (143). This concern is highly ironic considering the Western stereotype of Africa as a violent, savage place.

Thomas also turns his attention to problems within Albertia; these are problems shared by many African nations. Wages are low, and poverty is widespread. There is a fair amount of corruption in Albertian politics, and the rival political parties are known to employ gangs of toughs to harass opponents. Foreign powers, the British and the Americans, attempt to influence and control Albertia in order to exploit its natural resources. The population of Albertia is largely uneducated and superstitious, and Shartelle takes advantage of their ignorance. At one point in the campaign, he learns that the opposition intends to advertise with a skywriting plane and a blimp. Exploiting a combination of old and new threats, Shartelle dispatches "poison squads" to travel from village to village spreading the rumor that the smoke from the skywriting will prevent the birth of sons and that the blimp actually carries an American A-bomb (173–74).

Although Thomas highlights the differences between Albertia and the United States, he also notes that elections in democracies have many constants. For instance, after attending a meeting of Albertia's political elite, who, for the most part, are professionals educated in Europe or the United States, Shartelle insists that "It's sure the same all over" (193). The most important constant is that given a choice, people will vote for policy that hurts them the least (153).

Yet despite Shartelle's faith in universality, Albertian politics are different from politics in the United States. Early in the novel, Chief Akomolo points out that American politics, like African politics, can be violent; however, in making his point, Akomolo highlights an essential difference in African and Western political traditions. Akomolo asks Shartelle why Mr. Hoover and the FBI, in conjunction with the military, did not arrest Lyndon Johnson after the assassination of President Kennedy. In Africa, Johnson's arrest would be expected. As Akomolo tells Shartelle, "who's to say that Johnson didn't hire this Oswald? After all it happened in his home state of Texas" (39).

Soon after he wins the election, Akomolo is assassinated by military leaders who take control of Albertia. The coup, however, is far more violent than the assassination of President Kennedy; it is savage, and in this respect Thomas conforms to the convention of associating savage actions with Africans. After being shot six times while going for his revolver, Akomolo is beheaded (258). Shortly after Akomolo's decapitation, a character named Major Chuku appears on the scene and has the Corporal and his squad shot.

After the coup, Shartelle stays in Africa, working underground with Akomolo's tribe to help Albertia obtain democracy. Although Upshaw is expelled from Albertia, he returns to help Shartelle and to be with his new-found love, Peace Corps teacher Anne Kidd. Considering the political reality in Albertia, the odds are against Upshaw and Shartelle. Unfortunately, as *The Seersucker Whipsaw* predicts and recent history has proved, the chances of establishing Western-style democracies in postcolonial African nations are also slim.

The Tangent Objective and *The Tangent Factor*: The "Little Captain" and Dreams of a United States of Africa

Like Thomas's *The Seersucker Whipsaw*, *The Tangent Objective* and *The Tangent Factor* by Lawrence Sanders are political thrillers set in an imaginary West African nation. Like Thomas, Sanders incorporates many Western conventions about Africa into his work, especially the notions that political affairs are more likely to be settled by bullets than by ballots in Africa and that Africa is a place where Western characters can change their lives.

Sanders calls his invented nation Asante. Asante is a former French colony with a vast, untapped oil reserve. Peter Tangent, a political advisor with U.S. CIA connections, has been hired by Starrett Petroleum of Tulsa, Oklahoma, to extend Starrett's lease on Asante oil. During the course of *The Tangent Objective*, Tangent and his colleagues join forces with Captain Obiri Anokye—the "Little Captain"—to overthrow the ruler of Asante, King Prempeh IV. Tangent's reward for aiding Captain Anokye in his coup is a new, and generous, lease agreement for Starrett Petroleum that will assure Tangent a fortune in stock profits. In addition to winning him material wealth, Tangent's experiences in Africa cure him of impotence by offering him an opportunity to prove his manhood in combat situations.

Early in *The Tangent Objective*, Tangent describes Asante: "Third-smallest country in Africa in land area. . . . A population of about eight hundred thousand. . . . It's a thin, wedge-shaped sliver of land between Ghana and Togo. Runs north-south. About thirty miles wide on the coast. On the west is Lake Volta. On the east is the Mono River. South is the Atlantic Ocean. At the northern tip, Asante, Ghana, Togo, and Upper Volta all come together at a map position called Four Points" (4–5). This attention to geographical exactness is important because in *The Tangent Factor*, the sequel to *The Tangent Objective*, geopolitical concerns come into play when Anokye invades actual African nations from his base in Asante.

In addition to information about the geography and political system of Asante, Sanders provides a wealth of detail about Asante's topography and economy. Asante "is at a break in the West African rain forest" where the savanna meets the sea (*Objective* 4). The economy is mainly agricultural; the main crops are cotton, wheat, coffee, and yams. Asante has some limited light industry, a brewery and a few textile mills, and there is one gold mine in the nation (*Objective* 4). The capital city of Asante is Mokodi, a clean, modern city with tree-lined boulevards, public gardens and parks, an electric power works, and drinkable water. There is a reliable telephone system, one daily newspaper, but no radio or television stations (*Objective* 4–5).

Like Albertia in *The Seersucker Whipsaw*, Asante is a nation divided along religious, economic, and urban/rural lines. While the streets of Mokodi are lined with nightclubs, theaters, restaurants, and sidewalk cafes, "in the small villages of the uplands and the grasslands, kids paw through dungheaps looking for undigested nuts" (*Objective* 5). King Prempeh and his relatives are all Islamics; they "own everything" and have a brutal, secret police force to quell dissent (*Objective* 5). However, as Tangent explains, "As African countries go, it's not as good as the best, not as bad as the worst" (*Objective* 6).

Peter Tangent (like so many other Americans in novels set in Africa, Tangent is from the American heartland—Crawford, Indiana) has considerable knowledge about Africa. He has "visited 39 of Africa's 61 nations" (*Objective* 39), speaks several African languages, is familiar with African cultures and arts, and, in general, likes Africa and Africans. In these respects, Tangent is unusual; in most American novels with African settings—real or imagined—American characters know little about Africa and are usually on their first visit to the continent.

Although Sanders filters many observations about Africa through Tangent's eyes, the most interesting character in Sanders's African novels is Captain Anokye. Indeed, Anokye is one of the few important African characters in the African novels of contemporary white American authors. Anokye is a composite "great African leader" somewhat like Egypt's Gamal Abdel Nasser. Like Nasser, who always maintained that he was a black African (Early 36), Anokye is a strong proponent of Pan-Africanism. Anokye comes from a poor family and rises to power via military service. Anokye is an intelligent, educated character who, although his formal schooling is limited, "has continued to study on his own" (*Objective* 24). One of his colleagues details Anokye's intellectual abilities: "He speaks French, of course, and English very well. Some German and Italian. Several African languages. He likes history, biography, and political science" (*Objective* 24).

Technically, Anokye is a Christian: "his family were members of the small Mokodi Baptist community" (*Objective* 34). However, Anokye retains his connections with traditional Africa and is drawn to the traditional beliefs. "Perhaps," Anokye thinks, "the old beliefs were best. . . . Many, many beliefs and many, many gods." Anokye believes that Africa is large enough to accommodate all deities, "Africa's and those of every nation on earth" (*Objective* 34).

Anokye initially sees his mission as that of savior of Asante. After all, in Asante, the "land was fertile, rainfall was plentiful, the people were prudent and hardworking. With proper management, there was no reason why Asante should not prosper" (*Objective* 85). In addition to these economic strengths, Asante possesses vast oil reserves and a growing tourism industry. Willi Abraham, one of Anokye's political advisors, believes that Asante has the potential to become a model African nation where citizens can enjoy freedom and prosperity (*Objective* 85).

It is notable that Abraham's dreams for Asante's future are similar to the American dream of life, liberty, and the pursuit of happiness because, in a number of ways, Anokye is an African George Washington and his revolution is somewhat similar to the American revolt against the British. Asante is attempting to free itself from the shackles of a corrupt king just as colonial America was attempting to free itself from George III. Like colonial Americans, Anokye and his colleagues must write a constitution in order to govern after the rebellion has been successful. As is the case under the constitution of the United States, the chief executive of the newly formed Asante government will also be its commander in chief (*Objective* 208).

Anokye's coup is successful, and, after killing King Prempeh and installing a new government, Anokye turns his attention to the rest of the African continent much as the early political leaders of the United States turned to the American West and dreamed their dreams of manifest destiny. At the conclusion of *The Tangent Objective*, Anokye, Tangent, and the other revolutionaries meet and survey a huge map of Africa:

"So many weak nations," said Sam Leiberman. "Many small, poor, and weak nations," President Anokye repeated slowly. . . . "With governments as evil as Prempeh's—and worse. With ignorant and greedy rulers torturing the land and the people. Africa, my Africa. . . . I see Africa, one land, one great continent unified and strong. . . . I say to you we can create *one* Africa. . . . Think of it! One land, one government, one people. The world's second-largest continent becomes the world's first nation!" (311)

So ends *The Tangent Objective*, and so begins *The Tangent Factor*, in which Anokye starts to transform his Pan-African dreams into reality. In *The Tangent Factor*, Anokye attempts to heal the divisions that plague Africa by marrying his sister, Sara, to the son of a Togolese general whose family is Islamic, by promoting negritude, and by downplaying the importance of tribalism.

As Anokye and his advisors discuss their plans for a Pan-African federation, *The Tangent Factor* takes on a futuristic quality. The African federation will consist of semi-sovereign nations. Each nation will have "its own chief executive appointed by Anokye, but with national legislatures elected by popular vote" (*Factor* 304). The federation will have one law code, but it will be elastic enough to allow for local traditions and tribal customs. There will be a single monetary system, and the federation will have only one army, one uniform, and one flag. Anokye will become the president of the federation; the chief executive of each member nation will actually be a governor, not a president.

In *The Tangent Factor*, Anokye continues to be a compelling, admirable character; however, Sanders hints that power may corrupt the captain who would became a great Africa leader. Anokye is not above employing violence and treachery to accomplish his goals. He finds it necessary to develop a secret army complete with domestic spies and agents who are sent to numerous African nations including Nigeria, Zaire, Angola, Kenya, Chad, and South Africa (*Factor* 208). He also dispatches Sam Leiberman, a white mercenary, to Benin to burn the Musée Ethnographique, "an awesome treasure house of African culture" (*Factor* 90). Leiberman makes the fire appear to be the work of the Togolese government. Later, Anokye manufactures a war between Togo and Benin and uses the Togo-Benin conflict as an excuse to invade and occupy both nations. The occupation of Benin gives Anokye's army land access to Nigeria, the next country Anokye plans to invade. The occupation of Nigeria will be the most important step toward the creation of what Anokye hopes will become the "United African States" (*Factor* 293).

Sanders closes his Tangent novels with the implication that Anokye's dreams of a united Africa may turn out to be a nightmare vision. In *The Seersucker Whipsaw*, Ross Thomas points out that the divisions left by imperialism may make democracy impossible to achieve in contemporary Africa. In his Tangent novels, Sanders implies that the conditions that frequently lead to political violence in Africa might someday give rise to a leader, such as Captain Anokye, who can heal the rifts that divide Africa. However, Sanders warns that such a leader may forget his good intentions and be corrupted by power; the great African unifier may become the great African dictator.

PART II: NOVELS SET IN INVENTED SAHARAN NATIONS

The Coup: Ellelloû vs. the United States

John Updike's *The Coup* is an ambitious satire that critiques contemporary America and contemporary Africa through the voice of Colonel Hakim Felix Ellelloû, the president of the invented African country of Kush. Updike names his invented nation after the ancient African kingdom of Kush, a kingdom mentioned by several classical writers, including Herodotus. Ancient Kush developed a written language that, unfortunately, remains undeciphered, limiting knowledge about Kush's history (Harris, *Africans* 42). However, Kush is believed to have been an "urban, materially advanced, literate" kingdom that "existed in the interior of the continent for a thousand years" (Harris, *Africans* 45). The historical Kush, then, is in binary opposition with Updike's invented nation, a country that is mostly rural, mostly poor, and mostly illiterate.

The Kush of *The Coup* is a Saharan nation that suffers from prolonged drought and famine. Ellelloû calls Kush "a land of delicate, delectable emptiness," separated from the Mediterranean and the northern border by an "ocean of desert" (4). On the map, Kush resembles "an angular skull whose cranium is the empty desert." The irregular line of the skull's jaw is "carved by the wandering brown river" (16).

Because Ellelloû is an unreliable narrator, his observations cannot always be trusted (Markle 285). However, since he claims that he copies information about Kush from an "old *Stateman's Year-Book*" (6) and because he has no cause to lie about the geography and economy of Kush, it seems reasonable to accept Ellelloû's details about the country. Ellelloû's *Statesman's Year-Book* describes Kush in these terms: "In area Kush measures 126,912,180 hectares. The population density comes to .03 per hectare. . . . There are twenty-two miles of railroad and one hundred seven of paved highway. . . . In addition to peanuts are grown millet, sorghum, cotton, yams, dates, tobacco, and indigo. . . . The natives extract ingenious benefits from the baobab tree" (5–6). Ellelloû notes that Kush also has an "ample treasury" of diseases (6). The average life expectancy in Kush is thirty-seven years, the literacy rate is 6 percent, and the per capita gross national product is seventy-nine dollars (7).

Kush has been called a composite of Chad and Mali (Eiland 318), and Lathrop notes that Kush is very similar to Niger, a nation that some have described as "a perpetual disaster area" (250). However, Kush is actually a composite of many African nations and many traditional Western notions about Africa; Kush is an arid, poverty-stricken, disease-ridden, "empty" country ruled by a raving despot who comes to power via a coup. Just as Kush is a composite African nation, Ellelloû is a composite leader; he is an Islamic fundamentalist of the sort common in the Middle East, yet he resembles actual African rulers such as Idi Amin of Uganda, Bokassa of the Central African Republic, and Mobuto Sese Seko of Zaire. Like Ellelloû, Amin, Bokassa, and Mobuto were former non-commissioned officers who rose through the ranks (Chukwu 62).

In fact, some present-day African leaders sometimes sound hauntingly like Ellelloû. For example, before he immolates an American relief worker on a pyre of donated breakfast cereal, Ellelloû tells the American that the "people of Kush reject capitalist intervention in all its guises. They have no place in their stomachs for the table scraps of a society both godless and oppressive" (40). *The Coup* was published in 1978, but in the summer of 1995, Robert Mugabe, President of Zimbabwe, lashed out at U.S. lawmakers. According to wire service accounts, Mugabe said, "Let the Americans keep their sodomy, bestiality, stupid and foolish ways to themselves" ("Zimbabwean" A4).

Ellelloû's character has been interpreted as Updike's statement of doubt about the ability of men like Amin and Mobuto to "shoulder the responsibilities of government" (Chukwu 62). Updike makes his concern with the nature and problems of leadership clear when, discussing the drought and famine that plague Kush with imprisoned King Edumu, Ellelloû feels the "terror of responsibility" (14). Looking about him for someone with whom to share this terror, Ellelloû finds only an attendant, a "policeman" who will report what he has heard to Michaelis Ezana, the Minister of Interior who is Ellelloû's rival.

In choosing an invented nation as the setting for his satire, Updike follows a long literary tradition. Swift, for instance, sends Gulliver to a number of invented lands, Voltaire causes Candide to travel to the invented country of El Dorado, and Waugh sets his African satire in the invented nation of Azania. Indeed, while critics have pointed out allusions to Nabokov's *Pale Fire* (Oates 81) and the poetry of T. S. Eliot (Chukwu 66) in Updike's novel, few have noted the numerous parallels between *The Coup* and Waugh's *Black Mischief*. The most important of the similarities is the use of an invented African nation to satirize both African and Western cultures. Furthermore, Kush and Azania are both composite nations that attempt to capture numerous aspects of African life within their borders.

Moreover, both Seth, the Emperor of Azania, and Ellelloû, the President of Kush, have been educated at Western universities, and both Seth and Ellelloû are incompetent leaders. Seth's reaction to Western culture is, however, nearly opposite Ellelloû's reaction to the West. Seth wants to Westernize his nation, and he believes the quickest way to accomplish this goal is to consume Western goods. Ellelloû's exposure to American culture has led him to despise consumerism. Indeed, Ellelloû's hatred of American products even leads him to burn emergency food supplies that the United States has sent to alleviate the famine that plagues Kush. Finally, *The Coup* and *Black Mischief* are both concerned with political affairs and with the struggle among foreign powers for control of African resources. In *Black Mischief*, this struggle is a contest between the French and the English; in *The Coup*, this struggle is between the United States and the Soviet Union.

In addition to being a suitable vehicle for satire, the invented setting of Kush is also central to the plot and theme of *The Coup*. Much of the plot revolves around Ellelloû's concern with the drought that has plagued Kush for five years; much of the novel's parody of quest literature, as well as its satirical observations about the United States and Africa, takes place in the Balak, Kush's most severe desert.

In order to find the talking head of the dead King Edumu, Ellelloû must travel into the Balak, "the trackless northeastern quadrant that borders on Libya and Zanj" (90). The Balak, where "not even the *National Geographic* has been," consists of "weird mesas" and "geometrically perfect alkali flats" (90). In the Balak, "by day the desert is so blindingly hot and pure the sands in some declivities have turned to molten glass; by night the frost cracks rocks" (90). Deserts are special landscapes that have become archetypal symbols for deprivation, and they are usually associated with sterility in the "literary wastelands of the twentieth century" (Lutwack 48). The sterility of the desert can be seen as symbolizing Ellelloû's spiritual and physical sterility. Chukwu points out that Updike paints Ellelloû in images of sterility and barrenness; Ellelloû is born of a rape, governs a starving land, and husbands women whose children are not his own (66). Some maintain that the desert becomes a symbol of Kush's spiritual waste (Schueller 117), and in *The Coup* itself, the Soviets claim that Kush's "barren landscape, where children and cattle starve, mirrors [Ellelloû's] exhausted spirit" (213).

Ellelloû travels across the desert at night, and during the day, he recalls his other great quest journey, his trip to the United States where he attended college in Franchise, Wisconsin. (In *The Coup*, Updike frequently gives American places satirical names.) The physical setting of Franchise, with its cool lake and lush summers stands in opposition to the barrenness of the Balak just as the barrenness of American consumerism stands—at least in Ellelloû's mind—in opposition to the values of Islamic nationalism. On his quest to the United States, Ellelloû gains two rewards, a white wife and a renewed faith in Islam. On his quest to the Balak, Ellelloû gains the knowledge that he is not in control of his own country and that, in fact, the citizens of Kush do not even know who he is.

During the journey across the Balak, Ellelloû delivers, through flashback, his most cutting comments about American culture, especially the American culture of the 1950s. While in the United States, Ellelloû attends McCarthy College where he dates a white coed named Candy who resides in Livingston Hall. Candy's racist father thinks Ellelloû can "tell him the secret, of how the blacks can be the way they are" (186). At McCarthy College, Ellelloû is converted to Islam by Oscar X, a radical who considers whites the devil race (193), and challenged by professor Craven, who is jealous of Ellelloû's affair with Candy and who accuses Ellelloû of being "an American . . . from Detroit who affects a French accent" and a "prissy African manner" (201). The professor gives Ellelloû a B in African history because Ellelloû's exam has "so little feel" for Africa (201).

While in the desert, Ellelloû makes numerous comparisons between life in Africa and life in the United States. For instance, in a flashback, Ellelloû recalls how he explained the difference in African and American attitudes toward intimacy to Candy. The nature of village life means that Africans are always together, always touching each other, while Americans are isolated from one another because they are wealthy enough to have large houses in which each child often has a room (164).

In addition to employing the bleak landscape of Kush to trigger Ellelloû's comments about America, Updike uses a feature of Kush's climate, the prolonged drought, to promote the plot of *The Coup*. In fact, Updike's use of drought in *The Coup* is similar to Cary's use of drought in *Aissa Saved*. In *Aissa Saved*, the drought that affects colonial Nigeria is seen—at least by the Africans—as a sign of religious crisis: "Oke is the Kolua goddess of mountains and fertility, and every logical person in Yanrin saw at once that if Oke was indeed offended the bad rains, the bad harvest, the drought were easily explained" (31). In *The Coup*, the drought is seen—at least by Ellelloû—as a political and moral crisis; it is a crisis that is resolved only when Ellelloû falls from power. As numerous critics have observed, soon after Ellelloû's fall, the drought breaks and for two months, "rain continued to fall upon Kush" (261).

Updike, like Thomas and Sanders, knows that there are often many Africas existing within the borders of a single nation. Like Albertia in *The Seersucker Whipsaw* and Asante in *The Tangent Objective* and *The Tangent Factor*, Kush is a nation divided along economic and religious lines. While loyalties in Albertia and Asante are mostly determined by belief in Islam or Christianity, in *The Coup* the religious split is between those who are animists and those who are Islamic. The religious divisions in Kush are best represented by King Edumu who has led a divided spiritual life. Edumu lives most of his life as an animist, but after his overthrow by Ellelloû, he converts to Islam (6).

Like other invented African nations in contemporary American fiction, Kush is also a land split sharply along economic lines. Widespread poverty exists in Kush, as in Albertia and Asante, yet, Kush, like Albertia and Asante, is blessed with a wealth of natural resources in the form of oil. However, Kush's resources have not been developed, and the only way to gain wealth in Kush is to gain political power. For example, despite his ravings against materialism, Ellelloû lives well. Ellelloû keeps a grand apartment in the capital and maintains a villa for each of his four wives (9–10), and he owns one of the few Mercedes cars in Kush. Kutunda, Ellelloû's mistress, also demonstrates that the way to wealth in Kush is via political power; she rises from beggar to government minister on the wave of political change.

While their rulers live lavishly, the people of Kush starve. The economic divisions in Kush, and the ruling elite's approach to dealing with these divisions, are apparent at the Kush International Airport. Kush's airport is "a single runway" where a six-foot high aluminum fence separates foreign visitors from a refugee camp. As the privileged arrive in Kush via air-conditioned 747s, behind the aluminum fence, children fight rats for morsels of food (204–5).

Like Kush, Ellelloû is also rent by divisions. Updike neatly symbolizes the internal conflict that plagues Ellelloû through his four wives; each represents a different aspect of his character (Chukwu 62). Ellelloû's four wives can also be seen as symbols for the forces that divide Kush and, by implication, Africa.

Ellelloû, like the majority of the citizens of Kush, is Islamic, yet the population of Kush retains a strong attachment to the old, animistic ways. Ellelloû's first wife, Kadongolimi, "is an embodiment of tradition and continuity" (Chukwu 62). She stands for the values of precolonial Kush, and it is Kadongolimi who tells Ellelloû that he should have never abandoned the old ways for Islam (107).

Kadongolimi is the opposite of Candy, Ellelloû's white wife from the United States; Candy represents what Chukwu calls Ellelloû's "unconscious attraction to the western way of life" (62). Updike, like other contemporary novelists, knows that Western culture and wealth hold enormous appeal for Africans. Kush's attraction to American ways are satirized, as is American consumerism itself, when Ellelloû visits the American town that has been built in the dessert near a petrochemical factory. The American town in the desert has a strange affect on Ellelloû's driver and bodyguard who "had never before seen . . . ice-cream stands in the shape of a sundae cup. . . . Or the golden parabolas of a MacDonald's" (236).

Sittina, Ellellou̇'s third wife, is perhaps the most symbolic of all his women. She is a black-African who has been educated at an all-black university in Alabama (59). Ellellou̇ notes that Sittina is caught between two worlds, between the Western way and the African way (Chukwu 63); she is symbolic of both Ellellou̇'s divided personality and of Africa in general, for, as Ellellou̇ observes, "who, in the world, now does not live between two worlds" (62). Barthold notes that Sittina fits Ellellou̇'s "spiritual identity" and that both Ellellou̇ and Sittina are representative of "a state of temporal" flux that exists in present-day Africa (8).

Kutunda, Ellellou̇'s most recent female acquisition, represents Ellellou̇'s political ambitions and is symbolic of the political turmoil that has swept Africa since World War II. She is an African Lady Macbeth who convinces Ellellou̇ to execute King Edumu. Ironically, Kutunda, who rises to power in the government that overthrows Ellellou̇, later suggests that Ellellou̇ also be beheaded.

Another woman who also plays a symbolic role in *The Coup* is Angelica Gibbs. She comes to Kush to find out what has happened to her husband, an American relief worker who has been killed on Ellellou̇'s order. As Angelica spends more time in Kush, she finds much about the country appealing. She takes to wearing African clothing, gets a dark tan, and asks Candy, Ellellou̇'s American wife who plans to return to the States, "How can you bear to leave? The smells! The pace! For the first time in my life, I'm one with my blood. God, how I hated America" (265). Through the character of Angelica, Updike satirizes the old notion that Africa puts Westerners more in touch with themselves and with nature.

The Coup has attracted more critical attention than any other contemporary American novel set in an invented Africa nation. Unfortunately, the composite nature of Kush has been ignored by several critics who fault Updike for creating a nation that is a "physical impossibility" (Markle 283). Critics such as Joyce Markle and Barry Amis are mistaken to hold Updike to a realistic standard in a novel that intentionally exaggerates actualities for the sake of satire. For instance, Markle complains that *The Coup* suffers from "massive problems of plausibility" because, among other things, Ellellou̇'s Mercedes drives all day in a country said to have only one hundred and seven miles of paved road (283). Apparently, Markle doesn't believe that a Mercedes is capable of negotiating unpaved streets. And in a paper presented to the 1979 MLA convention in San Fransciso, Barry Amis faults Updike for such inaccuracies as placing Indian shops (a feature of East Africa) and *souks* (a feature of North Africa) in Kush. Amis also objects to Updike's mentioning that some Africans own and trade slaves and that some Africans believe in magic or juju (qtd. in Markle 283). To criticize Updike for including features of East and North Africa in his descriptions of Kush is to deny the composite nature of Updike's invented nation and to ignore the fact that in both British and American fiction invented African settings are traditionally composite creations.

Land Without Shadow: Hollywood Goes to Maliteta

Michael Mewshaw's *Land Without Shadow* is set in the invented nation of Maliteta; Maliteta lies deep in the Sahara "east of the High Atlas Mountains" (24). Like Kush, Maliteta suffers from political upheaval, drought, and famine; like most invented African nations in contemporary American fiction, Maliteta is a nation divided. Mewshaw symbolizes Maliteta's divisions by splitting the nation with an invented river, the Kimoun. North of the Kimoun, where *Land Without Shadow* takes place, Maliteta is a vast desert inhabited by tribes of Berber nomads; south of the Kimoun, the population is black and there are "water and trees and jungle and elephants" (112). The northern capital is Tougla; the southern capital is Morburka. Morburka is like Tougla, "only bigger with black faces and jungle instead of brown ones and desert" (131).

In *Land Without Shadow*, Mewshaw echoes several traditional Western notions about Africa and challenges at least one Western stereotype about the continent. Mewshaw observes that political corruption, poverty, and violence are conditions of everyday life for many Africans, and he describes Maliteta as a blank space—an empty land. As they fly over Maliteta, one of the American characters who is looking out the plane window is asked what he sees. The answer is "Nothing. I've never seen so much nothing" (24). Yet Mewshaw is also one of the few American authors writing about Africa to note that ancient African cultures produced great works of art equal or superior to Western art. Like other contemporary American novels set in invented African nations, *Land Without Shadow* is heavily didactic. Mewshaw wants to inform his readers about a large region of Africa, and he comments upon African and American cultures by comparing the United States to his invented nation.

Mewshaw also points out that multinational business interests and the government of the United States are not above making deals with corrupt African leaders. In *Land Without Shadow*, the Malibetan government, a Hollywood studio, a French corporation, and the United States embassy in Maliteta conspire to keep the rest of the world from learning about a famine that threatens to wipe out an entire people. The lives of thousands of Malitetans depend on the efforts of a few individuals determined to get information about the famine to the outside world so that the wealthy Western nations can provide relief.

Most of the action in *Land Without Shadow* is filtered through the eyes of Jack Cordell, a middle-aged artist who has quit his teaching job and divorced his wife. In a number of ways, Cordell is the conventional American in Africa. He is from the American heartland (Odessa, Texas), the trip to Maliteta is his first visit to Africa, and the journey comes at a low point in his life. In Africa, Cordell finds a battle worth fighting—the struggle to save the starving Berbers—and a new love—film and stage star Helen Soray.

Cordell is living in the south of France, painting "anything to convince himself he was an artist," when he gets a letter from an old friend, Tucker Garland (4). Garland is a movie producer who wants to hire Jack as art director on a new film called *Terms of Peace*. The movie, which deals with the adventures of a Peace Corps worker, is to be shot in Maliteta. Because he is broke and behind on his child support, Jack reluctantly accepts Garland's offer. The movie's title neatly summarizes Jack's and Helen's dilemma; they cannot be at peace with themselves if they go along with the official cover-up of the Malitetan famine.

Throughout *Land Without Shadow*, Mewshaw uses the Hollywood film crew and movie stars as symbols of American excess. The stars of the film are Barry Travis and Lisa Austin. In the 1960s, Travis "had played high-strung, hollow-cheeked rebels; Barry had been on speed back then" (19), but he has taken to drinking Coors beer and has put on a lot of weight. Lisa Austin is a "living billboard. For years before she went into films she had been in all the ads for hair spray, shampoo, lipstick, toothpaste, and bathing suits" (19). Lisa is accompanied by Roberta, her hairdresser, and Phil, her pistol-packing bodyguard. Helen Soray, an Obie-winning actor, is the only intellectual among the Hollywood types; she spends her time reading *The Sheltering Sky* (20). With heavy irony, Mewshaw lands the film crew and the pampered movie stars in the middle of a starving African nation. Indeed, the novel frequently contrasts poverty-stricken Maliteta, where the oppressive government wants to cover-up the famine and a policy of genocide against nomads, with the material excess of the United States.

The Americans in Garland's film crew know little or nothing about Maliteta, but even as their plane lands at the Tougla airport, they realize they are in for trouble. Moments after a smooth landing, the plane comes under rocket attack from Malitetan rebels. The rockets miss, but bullets riddle the plane's fuselage, "ripping out wads of paneling and upholstery" (26). Jack and the other Americans eventually learn that Berber insurgents are attempting to overthrow the president of Maliteta, who is from the southern part of the nation. The president's picture is featured on numerous billboards; he is a "black man in uniform with tinted glasses and scarred cheeks" whose motto is "unity and sacrifice are the first steps to national strength" (44). There is, however, little unity in Maliteta, a nation divided by race, religion, language, and geography.

Jack, the movie stars, and the film crew are housed in the finest hotel in Tougla, but the establishment is ugly and uncomfortable. The hotel, however, is a paradise compared to the native quarter. In the hotel there is plenty of water, and the food for the crew is flown in from London. Tougla, like many African cities both real and invented, is a town divided; there is a small European section and a walled native quarter. The Catholic church is padlocked and the "sidewalk out front was an obstacle course of beggars, of the old, the ill, and the malformed" (47). Jack thinks the medina would make a good location for shooting the film; he finds it odd "how fascinating certain spots were to look at and how awful they must be to live in" (51). In the medina, the restaurants are closed because there is no food to serve, and in the market the "grain bins were empty, the spice bowls low" (48).

Bleak as they are, conditions in the city of Tougla are far better than in the nearby refugee camps where "bodies are laid out, covered with white cloth" and starving children suffer from trachoma (109). In an attempt to save national pride and eliminate the nomadic Berbers, the president of Maliteta wants to keep the outside world from knowing about the famine that afflicts his nation.

While the citizens of Maliteta starve, the movie stars battle their weight problems. For instance, Lisa Austin has regular injections of hormonal extracts refined from horse urine. " 'You ought to try it,' she explains to Barry Travis. 'It's the best way to lose weight' " (59). Barry fights the pounds the old-fashioned way; he jogs. Running across the desert in a green rubberized suit, Barry is an odd sight. The Malitetans don't understand why anyone would want to lose weight because in "Maliteta only rich people are fat and they're proud of it" (99).

One of the interesting landmarks in Maliteta is an outcropping of volcanic rocks that have been painted by prehistoric tribesmen. The rock paintings show "leafy trees and lush fields of grains with rivers running through them. Naked hunters ten feet tall, their bodies striped with bright geometric designs, stalked elephants and hippos" (101). Jack's guide, a young Malitetan filmmaker named Moha, explains that this part of Africa had been fertile thousands of years ago. The rock paintings provide a setting for the final scenes of *Land Without Shadow*, and they also permit Mewshaw to make some observations about the nature of art in Africa. Jack, who is himself an artist, sees the prehistoric African rock paintings as being equal to any great work of Western art, and he compares the rock paintings to the Sistine Chapel (102).

While scouting the Painted Rocks as a setting for a scene in the movie, Jack discovers the refugee camp and realizes that Maliteta is suffering from a massive famine in which thousands will die if the outside world does not rush to provide aid. Moha has produced a movie detailing the extent of the famine and its effect on the Berber tribes, and Jack decides to quit working for Garland's company and smuggle Moha's film to the West on one of the weekly flights that bring supplies from Europe to the film crew.

In American fiction set in Africa, the good intentions of Western characters often lead to disaster, and when Jack attempts to help the starving Berbers in Maliteta, he only causes trouble. He meets with Berber leaders to give them money for food, only to discover that they plan to buy weapons with the money. The rebels threaten to kidnap Jack and the movie stars if he doesn't help them hijack a plane. Before Jack can agree or disagree, government troops raid the house where the meeting is taking place, and Jack is lucky to escape unharmed after a fierce gun battle ensues (166). That night, rebels blow up the power lines that link Tougla with the southern capital, Morburka.

The conclusion of *Land Without Shadow* symbolizes the moral dilemma presented to the West by Africa. Is the continued filming of a movie—and by implication the making of money–more important than taking humanitarian action to save a starving people whose government would eagerly let them perish? Is it acceptable for Western nations to consume the natural resources of Africa and look to Africa as an emerging market while ignoring corruption and poverty on the continent?

Following the suggestion of the Berber rebels, Moha kidnaps Jack and Helen and drives them to the Painted Rocks where he plans to hold them hostage until international news crews arrive to publicize the famine in Maliteta. Jack and Helen are actually more coconspirators than hostages; they want to alert the outside world to the famine, yet they would prefer to avoid violence and bloodshed. Moha plans to escape and take his film to Algeria, but he is shot by a sniper.

After Moha's death, the film crew is flown to France. In contrast to Maliteta, the French countryside looks "eerily like America, the dual-lane highway, kaleidoscopically bright, was lined by gas stations—Mobil, Shell, Esso—used-car lots, motels, supermarkets, miniature golf courses, and a gocart track" (221). Fortunately, Moha has given Helen a copy of his film, and she and Jack quit the movie and make plans to publicize the famine.

Land Without Shadow, like other novels set in invented African nations, is highly critical of Western actions in Africa as well as of corrupt African leaders. Using his film crew to provide examples of American values, Mewshaw is able to contrast American excess with an African nation rent by poverty, drought, famine, and political divisions inherited from colonialism. For Maliteta's corrupt president, as well as for most of the Americans in the film crew and the representatives of the U.S. government working in the Malitetan embassy, business as usual is more important than saving African lives.

Horn of Africa: Killing Time in Bejaya

The principle setting of Philip Caputo's *Horn of Africa* is Bejaya, an invented province located in northwestern Ethiopia. Of all the invented African settings in contemporary American fiction, Bejaya is the most remote, most primitive, and most violent. Bejaya is a country of "dry plains and gray mountains bounded by the scorching brilliance of the Red Sea" (41). Bejaya has a "thought destroying" landscape (300), a landscape so harsh and otherworldly that it is compared with the surface of the moon (230). A trip to Bejaya is not only a journey off the map it is also a voyage back in time to "the ages of man's beginnings" (254). Life in Bejaya is as harsh and brutal as the desert, and, with the exception of automatic rifles, the Bejayans have no machines of any kind. Bejaya is so primitive, so remote, and so untouched by time that it "isn't even [in] the Middle Ages" (257).

Indeed, even the actual African settings featured in *Horn of Africa* have a changeless quality. As Moody, a British character in the novel, explains: "[It's] as if nothing's changed in Africa. . . . Now instead of . . . the British . . . and the French and the Portuguese, it's the Americans and the Russians and their Cuban gurkhas" (128). Imperialism, then, is one of the things that makes Africa a changeless zone that exists outside of time. The effect of imperialism on Bejaya mirrors situations in many actual African nations; imperialism has left Bejaya divided along political, religious, and tribal lines. Indeed, Caputo's invented province has a history that neatly symbolizes Africa's colonial past; Bejaya has been subjugated by one outside power after another throughout its history. First, Arabs displaced Bejaya's original inhabitants, and, in more recent history, the Turks took the land from the Arabs. The Turks were then forced out of Bejaya by the Italians, who controlled the territory until World War II when the British invaded. After the war, the British gave Bejaya to Haile Selassie and the Ethiopians. The Bejayans then revolted against Selassie, and, with Soviet help, came close to winning independence (43–44).

Horn of Africa opens in the months after a group of leftist officers calling themselves the Dergue, which means *committee*, deposes Haile Selassie and appeals to the Russians for aid. Moscow then switches sides in the civil war and supplies the Dergue with weapons, as well as Cuban pilots and Russian advisers, for use in the war against the Bejayan independence fighters (44).

Disillusioned by the Russians, a new rebel faction calling itself the NIIF—the National Islamic Independence Front—splits from the Revolutionary Command Council. The NIIF is a devout Muslim group led by a sheik named Muhammad Jima (44). Jima is a Beni-Hamid, and the core of NIIF is the Beni-Hamid tribe, a highland people "whose men never went anywhere without guns in their hands and knives in their belts" (45). Jima's people are known for Islamic fanaticism and ferocity in battle.

Jima realizes that after Bejayan independence is won, there will be a civil war between the rebel factions. Hoping to secure rulership of all Bejaya, he allies the Beni-Hamid with the United States. In exchange for weapons and training, Jima agrees to allow America to maintain control of an important military base (46). *Horn of Africa*, then, follows the tradition established by the Brontë juvenilia, Ballantyne's *The Gorilla Hunters*, and Forester's *The African Queen* by portraying Africa as a battleground where Western superpowers challenge one another. Bejaya is a hot zone in the Cold War.

Jima's political officer is a Beni-Hamid named Murrah, a character who—like the fractured independence movement—symbolizes the divisions in Bejaya that have been brought about by imperialism. Murrah's father was a Beni-Hamid warrior who died in the early battles of the civil war, and Murrah loses the rest of this family to disease and starvation (173). Murrah's entire life has been determined by the three great curses that plague Africa: war, disease, and famine. After he is rescued by a UN relief team, Murrah is placed in a Christian orphanage. Later, American soldiers stationed in a nearby military base train him to work as a copyboy on the base newspaper. Instead of learning to be a warrior, he learns to read and speak English (173).

Murrah resents Americans because they are wealthy, but what really makes him hate Americans is the behavior of the soldiers stationed in his country. The American soldiers revolt Murrah by "swaggering down the streets as if they owned the city, their faces flushed, their white hands caressing the black flesh of Bejayan whores" (174). Because the Italian colonials never acted in such a manner, Murrah decides that Americans are a brutal, disgusting people (174).

Murrah's dislike for American soldiers soon turns into open rebellion; he makes a speech arguing that "they should go, all of them. . . . They are an arrogant and shameless people" (175). A Russian agent recruits Murrah, and the young Bejayan is trained in Moscow. The Russians woo Murrah away from Islam and teach him the fine points of warfare (179).

When he returns to the desert to fight for Bejayan independence, Murrah is shocked to discover that the "creed of revolution" cannot keep the Islamics and Christians from warring against one another (182). His next shock comes when Russian planes, manned by Cuban pilots, attack the Bejayan rebels. After many of his men are slaughtered in a Russian air attack, Murrah rejects Marxism and joins Jima, but although he is an officer under Jima's command, he dreams of the day when he will lead his own faction.

Murrah is a contradiction created by imperialism; he is a Muslim raised by Christians, a Marxist who sees the failure of Marxism, and a Beni-Hamid who hates his own people. Imperialism—both American and Russian—has turned Murrah into a monster who rejects his own culture. Finally, Murrah, who wants to move Bejaya from the "Middle Ages into the twentieth century" in a single generation (179), suggests that the only reasonable action is to practice revolutionary methods that "erase what is written" (259). Particularly, Murrah wants to erase the nomadic way of life that is embraced by more than a third of the Bejayan population (260).

The solution to the problems of nomadism is not forced settlement, a failed policy that had been tried by the Italians and the British. Murrah says that the "nomads are our kulaks. We should solve their problems as the Soviets solved the problems of the kulaks. . . . *Annihilate them*" (260). Through Murrah, *Horn of Africa* implies that imperialism is such a corrupting force that it naturally leads to a genocidal self hatred. In some ways, Murrah's genocidal attitude is similar to that of the government of Maliteta in Mewshaw's *Land Without Shadow*. Like Maliteta's president, Murrah would be happy to see the nomads exterminated either by famine or by force.

Caputo is not the only American author to invent an entire African people. In *Henderson the Rain King*, for instance, Saul Bellow creates two African tribes, the Arnewi and the Wariri. However, Caputo's Beni-Hamid are by far the most primitive and violent of all the African peoples—invented or actual—in contemporary American fiction. The tribe's initiation ceremony is an example of the Beni-Hamid's violent culture. Tribal manhood among the Beni-Hamid is acquired by killing a man in battle (349). In fact, a Beni-Hamid becomes a man when he kills and skins another man. The skin of the slain enemy is an important part of the manhood ritual (397) and a feature of the Beni-Hamid wedding ceremony because a husband must bring to his wife a "certain gift to demonstrate his manhood" (258).

By creating a land as brutal as Bejaya and a people as violent as the Beni-Hamid, Caputo is not simply bowing to the old notion that Africa is a harsh place populated by savages. Caputo compares the Ben-Hamid with his Western characters in order to explore the depths of Western depravity, not African savagery. To show that Westerners are capable of limitless violence, Caputo places his characters in an environment that has a culture based on violence and the warrior code. In fact, there are three important Western characters in *Horn of Africa*, and each of these characters is on a quest; each sees Africa, especially Bejaya, as a testing zone.

The narrator of the novel is an American named Charlie Gage. Like many other American characters in novels with African settings, Gage is at a low point in his life when he has his adventure in Africa. Gage is a hashish-smoking Vietnam veteran who has recently divorced his wife and quit his newspaper job. Gage's experiences as a soldier in Vietnam and as a reporter in war-torn Beirut have left him cynical. He explains that his ex-wife is a graduate of a small woman's college that had taught her that humans were rational beings who, with effort, could solve all their problems. Everything Gage has seen in the world teaches him otherwise (19).

At the beginning of *Horn of Africa*, Charlie Gage is drifting along in Cairo, disoriented by cynicism and hashish. Caputo uses the first section of his novel to make numerous comparisons between life in urban Africa and life in the West. For example, Gage compares life in Paris with life in Cairo, noting that the many of eight million people who live in Cairo suffer from disease and malnutrition. Even the poorest resident of Paris lives much better than the average resident of Cairo (85).

Because Gage has firsthand knowledge of Bejaya—he has traveled there and has written a news account of the war—he is recruited by an American CIA agent named Colfax for the mission to Bejaya. Colfax intends to send a team to train and arm Jima and the Beni-Hamid. Colfax tells Gage that his job is to turn Bronze Age "savages" into a twentieth-century army (128). Colfax meets Gage in the shadow of the great pyramids, and he explains to Gage that the mission to Bejaya is necessary because Gage and Colfax are like the cobras on the Egyptian friezes. The cobra symbolized Buto, protectress of the Northern Kingdom in ancient Egypt, and Colfax refers to himself and his fellow agents as protectors of the American way of life (52–53).

In fact, Gage is blackmailed into the job, and Caputo uses an element of the African setting to convey Gage's ill feelings about the mission. When Gage is given the choice of working for Operation Arotrops—as the mission is called—or being responsible for the death of a friend, a sandy wind known as the *Khamsin* darkens the sky around Cairo (21). The *Khamsin*, a dirty, ill wind that can blow for weeks, symbolizes the dirty deal that Gage is dealt and sets the tone for the story that follows. Moreover, near the conclusion of the story, another natural phenomenon inherent in the setting—a dust storm—foreshadows one of the novel's most dramatic moments (473).

Although Gage is blackmailed into joining the mission to Bejaya, the operation gives him an opportunity to fulfill his dreams. Gage explains that even as a very young man he had always wanted to be a hero (440), and the war in Bejaya allows Gage to became a hero because he risks his life to stop a mass murder—the slaughter of prisoners planned by Nordstrand, another American on the mission—and because he successfully struggles for survival in the African desert.

The leader of the commando squad is a cashiered British officer named Moody. The Beni-Hamid speak a language called *To-Bedawyi* (121), and Moody is the only

Westerner on the mission who can translate *To-Bedawyi* into English. Moody has been discharged from the British army after losing control and executing Arab prisoners during a revolt in Oman (279). Moody joins the mission to Bejaya because it will give him a chance to test himself in a situation similar to that he faced in Oman (282). He hopes to regain his honor in Bejaya. Before departing Khartoum for Bejaya, Moody assembles supplies of tinned food and "vials of tetracycline, enteroviaform, halizone, iodine, and penicillin" (190); he knows that in Africa disease is often a more deadly enemy than the opposing army.

Moody gets his wish for a second chance; the circumstances that led to the shooting of the Arab prisoners in Oman are almost exactly replicated near the conclusion of *Horn of Africa*. Moody exchanges insults with two Beni-Hamid warriors, and one of the men spits in Moody's face. Moody loses control and shoots both men at point blank range (476). Realizing that he has failed his test once again, Moody shoots himself in the head. As Gage explains, Moody's flaw was his failure to accept that violence was an essential part of his nature (477).

The third member of the commando team is Jeremy Nordstrand, the most important character in the novel. Nordstrand plays a dual role; he sees Africa, especially Bejaya, as a testing zone that will allow him to discover himself, and he also symbolizes some of the worst aspects of imperialism. Nordstrand is from the American heartland: Walton, Minnesota. He is part Norwegian, part German, part English, part Swedish, and part Chippewa Indian; he is "as all-American in his bloodlines as he was in his inclination toward violence" (307).

The problem for Nordstrand is that it is impossible for him to sound the depths of the violence in his soul while living in the United States. Indeed, Nordstrand has found even the violence of the Vietnam War too controlled (122), and he looks forward to the fighting in Bejaya because there will be no limits; it will be war "in an empty place" (122). Nordstrand admits that he has come to Bejaya to find freedom, the "freedom to discover myself, to explore my limits" (121). Bejaya is the logical place for Nordstrand to discover his limits—or his lack of them—because Bejaya is an "empty place, one of the very last empty places left" (121).

For Nordstrand, Bejaya (and by implication Africa) provides a setting in which he can resolve a moral debate. Specifically, Nordstrand is intrigued by the notion of killing for no reason at all other than the desire to kill. When asked why a sane man would want to kill for no reason, Nordstrand replies that he wants to be God, but since he can't create life as God can, he will have to destroy life (263).

At first, Nordstrand thrives in the harsh environment of Bejaya. While Moody and Gage struggle to go on across the desert where there is nothing but "sand, sun, stars, and wind," Nordstrand draws a "vitality from that lifeless land; it was as if he had found a spiritual home in its limitless reaches" (252). Throughout the novel, Nordstrand insists upon conditioning himself so that he can live on the land just as the Beni-Hamid do. For instance, he throws away all the medicine and tinned food that was so carefully assembled in Sudan, and he eats the gruel that is the staple of the Beni-Hamid diet. Being a warrior people, the Beni-Hamid respect Nordstrand because he too is a warrior. The Beni-Hamid make Nordstrand their hero after he downs a Russian MIG (332) and executes a group of prisoners from a rival tribe (340).

In fact, it is Nordstrand's desire to go native, to be initiated into the Beni-Hamid tribe, that leads to his downfall. After killing and skinning an enemy, Nordstrand undergoes ritual scarification. Nordstrand is Murrah's American counterpart. Like Murrah, he has rejected his own culture, and like Murrah, he is bent on mass murder. Ironically, Nordstrand's insistence on living like the Beni-Hamid causes his fall; the infection he contracts as a result of being ritually scarred with a dirty blade will eventually weaken him and contribute to his death (422).

Since Nordstrand's demise is caused by disease, he is like numerous other American characters who come to Africa to test themselves only to be destroyed by the elements inherent in the African landscape. In some ways, for example, Nordstrand resembles Port, the American who dies of typhoid in Paul Bowles's *The Sheltering Sky*. Like Port, Nordstrand hopes to find in Africa an alternative to the safe and sanitized way of life in found in the West. Like Port, Nordstrand proves that one can never be what one is not—a Westerner can never be an African; both Port and Nordstrand reject American culture to embrace African culture, and the price of such rejection of their heritage is their lives.

In addition to being yet another American who sees Africa as a testing zone, Nordstrand also personifies imperialism in a number of ways. Nordstrand's moral and ethical system is based on brute force just as imperialism was based on military and technological might. Imperialism was a racist institution, and Nordstrand, despite his desire to join the Beni-Hamid tribe, is a racist who frequently refers to Africans as "niggers" (110) and believes that "wogs" can be pushed around.

Perhaps the best example of Nordstrand as symbol of imperialism occurs in Khartoum when he plunges into the "crush of humanity" in the market, shoving the Sudanese aside, "his combat boots making corrugated tracks over the imprints of the barefoot crowds" (124). It is almost as if Nordstrand were the personification of imperialism, leaving the imprint of his occupation for all to see.

Horn of Africa is similar to other contemporary American novels with invented African settings in that it conforms to the traditional uses of African settings by portraying Bejaya as a flash point in a war between imperialistic superpowers and by using Bejaya as a testing zone for Westerners. In *Horn of Africa*, Western—especially American—culture is critiqued by comparing the West to an invented setting as well as to actual African places. Caputo also compares Western characters to members of an invented tribe, the Beni-Hamid, in order to demonstrate that Westerners can be just as violent as any African people.

Most importantly, however, Caputo makes his invented setting a symbol for all of Africa; Bejaya—like such other invented settings as Albertia, Asante, Kush, and Maliteta—is a land suffering from divisions that are the direct result of imperialism. Like much of actual Africa, Bejaya has long been occupied by foreign powers; like much of actual Africa, Bejaya is a country forced into a union with a neighboring people by imperial powers that had no regard for ethnic, tribal, and religious differences. The results of such forced unions are frequently political corruption, war, famine, and genocide—factors sadly present in actual Africa as well as in contemporary American fiction set in invented African nations.

Ross Thomas, Lawrence Sanders, John Updike, Michael Mewshaw, and Philip Caputo are all white males who have used invented African nations as settings for their novels. Alice Walker has also invented an African place (Olinka) and an African people (the Olinkans) for use in three of her books: *The Color Purple*, *The Temple of My Familiar*, and *Possessing the Secret of Joy*. Works by Walker and other African-American novelists are the subject of Chapter 4.

Chapter 4

Black on Black:
African-American Novels with
African Settings

For many decades, African Americans were reluctant to embrace their African heritage because they had adopted the traditional Anglo-Saxon view that placed Africa and Africans in an inferior light; however, in recent years many African Americans have included Africa as a conscious, positive element of their culture (Berghahn 31–32). Contemporary fiction by African Americans reflects this reassessment of Africa, and several well-known novels by African Americans make reference to Africa and to myths and legends about Africans. For instance, Toni Morrison's *Song of Solomon* alludes to a slave who could fly and who one day "stood up in the fields . . . and was lifted up in the air. Went right back to wherever it was he came from" (323). And Paule Marshall's *Praisesong for the Widow* uses as a motif the legend that Ibo slaves newly arrived in America turned and walked "right on out over the river. . . . And when they got to where the [slave] ship was they didn't so much as give it a look. Just walked on past it [toward Africa]" (39).

Yet despite this interest in Africa and Africans, relatively few novels by black Americans are actually set in Africa. When African-American authors do set their stories in Africa, they—like their white colleagues—often write about Africa in a didactic manner; however, the lessons, themes, and African settings presented in novels by African Americans differ greatly from those found in novels by white Americans.

For example, African novels by white authors are usually set either in East Africa or the Sahara; African novels by African-American authors are usually set in West Africa. Few of the important characters in African novels by white authors are African; most of the important characters in African novels by black authors are African. White novelists often portray Africa as a changeless, timeless place without a history; African-American novelists who set works in Africa usually write historical novels about African cultures and events. Indeed, the histories presented in novels by African Americans are often searches for identity and challenges to stereotypes about Africa and Africans.

These different ways of using African settings are the results of different ways of thinking about Africa. White authors have traditionally seen Africa as a mysterious unknown, a testing zone where (white) characters can achieve greater self knowledge by shedding the conventions of civilized culture and by encountering hostile natural environments and peoples. As Barthold notes, for "Joseph Conrad's Kurtz and Saul Bellow's Henderson, Africa is where a person's past is lost and where the true self emerges" (4). For African-American novelists, however, African settings are frequently employed as a way of discovering a lost past and recovering a lost heritage.

For white authors, as demonstrated by novels set in invented African nations as well as in such works as Bellow's *Henderson the Rain King*, Africa is often a symbolic—not a real—place. African-American authors, however, tend to see Africa and its history in realistic—not symbolic—terms. Specifically, African-American novelists seek to remind readers that Africa is the home of many great cultures and the scene of one of the greatest crimes against humanity in all of history: the slave trade to the Americas.

Most African novels by black Americans contain accounts of Africans being enslaved and taken from West Africa during the late eighteenth or early nineteenth centuries. Among these novels are *The Dahomean* by Frank Yerby, *Roots* by Alex Haley, *Echo of Lions* by Barbara Chase-Riboud, and *Middle Passage* by Charles Johnson. These works provide descriptions of varying detail about African cultures and about how life was lived in Africa before enslavement. By showing readers that African cultures are developed and complex, these descriptions counter the familiar notions that Africans are primitive peoples lacking civilization.

The only notable exceptions to the use of historical West African settings in contemporary African-American fiction set in Africa are three novels by Alice Walker: *The Color Purple*, *The Temple of My Familiar*, and *Possessing the Secret of Joy*. While Walker briefly describes the workings of the nineteenth-century West African slave trade in *The Temple of My Familiar*, her main focus is on Africa of the long ago past and on twentieth-century Africa. Moreover, Walker's novels are not set in actual Africa; the African scenes in these novels unfold in an invented place called Olinka. However, Walker's use of African settings is heavily didactic, especially in the case of *Possessing the Secret of Joy*, a novel that calls attention to a tradition still practiced in many African cultures: female genital mutilation.

The choice of subject matter and the didactic intent of most African novels by black Americans can be traced to the writings of Africans who were enslaved and taken to America during the late eighteenth and early nineteenth centuries. The best known and most detailed of these early narratives is the autobiographical *Olaudah Equiano or Gustavus Vassa, the African*, a frequently anthologized work. Other examples of early narratives with African settings have been collected in *Steal Away: Stories of the Runaway Slaves*. What links these early stories to contemporary African-American fiction set in Africa is that each of these narratives provides a picture of life in Africa as it was lived before enslavement, a story of capture that details the operation of the slave trade in West Africa, and information about the horrors of the passage from Africa to America.

Like contemporary African-American fiction set in Africa, slave narratives with African settings are openly didactic. Autobiographical accounts of enslavement "had a mass impact on the conscience of ante-bellum Americans" (Andrews 8), and "nineteenth-century whites read slave narratives . . . to get a first-hand look at the institution of slavery" (Andrews 9). The early narratives also gave whites their first glimpses of how life was lived in Africa.

Equiano makes his intent clear at the beginning of his story, noting that he is motivated to write not by desire for immortality or literary reputation, but to promote the "interests of humanity" and bring about the end of the slave trade (4). Equiano was born in 1745, in a place called *Essaka* deep in the interior of the West African kingdom of Benin. He observes that the "distance from this province from the capital of Benin and the sea coast must be very considerable, for I had never heard of white men or Europeans, nor of the sea" (5).

Equiano provides a great deal of information about his culture, discussing its systems of religion, law, and family life. He also gives much attention to affairs of war. Equiano writes that "[W]e have fire-arms, bows and arrows, broad two-edged swords and javelins. . . . All are taught the use of these weapons; even our women are warriors, and march boldly out to fight along with the men. Our whole district is a kind of militia" (11–12). In *The Dahomean*, Frank Yerby dramatizes similar methods of warfare, giving special attention to the role of women warriors who served King Gezo, an absolute monarch who ruled Dahomey in the early nineteenth century and who built a "nation to be feared" on the fortunes of the slave trade (Harris, *Africans* 118).

Equiano notes that African chiefs conduct war to gain slaves who are traded for European goods (11) and that his father owned many slaves (19). However, Equiano maintains that slavery as practiced in Africa is far different from slavery in the Americas: "Those prisoners which were not sold or redeemed, we kept as slaves; but how different was their condition from that of the slaves in the West Indies. With us, they do no more work than other members of the community, even their master; their food, clothing, and lodging were nearly the same as theirs (except that they were not permitted to eat with those who were free-born); . . . some of these slaves have even slaves under them as their own property, and for their own use" (12). This interest in detailing the differences in African slavery and slavery in the Americas is a concern featured in Yerby's *The Dahomean*, Haley's *Roots*, and Chase-Riboud's *Echo of Lions*.

Armstrong Archer, an early writer whose works are included in *Steal Away*, records that in 1784, when he was fourteen years old, he and his father were taken from Africa. Archer is from a place called *Kamao*, "which derived its name from a certain delicious fruit found abounding most plentifully in that province" (39). Archer's father, Komasko, is a member of the royal family who has been heavily involved in the slave trade; however, after recognizing the destructive nature of the trade, Komasko seeks to establish a treaty banning its practice. In a manner similar to that in which Oroonoko is enslaved in Behn's 1688 novel, Archer and his father are taken captive while negotiating with European slavers. Archer recalls that "[M]y father remarked to one of his shackled neighbors that this was a doom they long ago deserved, for having, on former occasions, betrayed so many of their country-men into the hands of their present oppressors. But this observation threw their afflicted souls into still deeper despair" (42–43). Since a concern with describing the slave trade that involved European, African, and American nations is at the heart of most contemporary African-American novels with African settings, it is not surprising that these novels are similar to nonfiction accounts of life and enslave-ment in Africa.

While contemporary African-American fiction set in Africa looks back to early authors such as Equiano and Archer, black American authors setting works in Africa have also written in a didactic manner similar to that found in contemporary African literature. There is a clear connection—both in theory and in execution—between such works as Chinua Achebe's *Things Fall Apart* and African-American novels set in Africa. In his essay "The Writer as Teacher," Achebe provides a theoretical background for both African literature and African-American literature set in Africa. Achebe notes that "it would be foolish to pretend that we [Africans] have fully recovered from the traumatic effects of our first confrontation with Europe" (*Hopes* 44). He then relates the following example to prove his point and to demonstrate why teaching is perhaps the most important function of African fiction:

Three or four weeks ago my wife, who teaches English in a boys' school, asked a pupil why he wrote about winter when he meant the harmattan. He said the other boys would call him a bushman if he did such a thing! Now, you wouldn't have thought, would you, that there was something shameful in your weather? But apparently we do. How can this great blasphemy be purged? I think it is part of my business as a writer to teach that boy that there is nothing disgraceful about the African weather, that the palm tree is a fit subject for poetry. (*Hopes* 44)

Achebe's theory, which is similar to Frank Yerby's statement of purpose in *The Dahomean*, is applied in *Things Fall Apart*. Achebe uses the Nigerian setting, particularly that of an Ibo village at the time of the European conquest, to dramatize his thematic concerns. As Simon Gikandi notes, Achebe's fiction is an attempt to rewrite and to correct history by offering a narrative that counters the colonial version of events (3). Achebe's objective—an objective shared by African-Ameri-can authors such as Yerby, Haley, Chase-Riboud, Johnson, and Walker—is to write fiction that enables people to regain knowledge of their cultural heritage.

Achebe's picture of life in precolonial Nigeria is similar in several ways to the accounts of life in Africa offered in contemporary African-American fiction. Achebe wants his readers to understand that colonialism destroyed a noble people with a sophisticated culture. African-American novelists placing their stories in

Africa also want to demonstrate that the slave trade destroyed many peoples; these writers want to correct a historical record that has failed to adequately detail the horror inflicted upon those who were taken into bondage in Africa and transported to the Americas.

Contemporary African-American fiction set in Africa also asks readers to compare Western and African cultures so that stereotypes about Africa can be shattered. Indeed, in much of this fiction, common Western stereotypes about Africans are reversed when Africans describe Europeans. For instance, one notion that many whites held about Africans is that Africans frequently practice cannibalism; yet in *Roots*, Haley's Africans believe that the whites are cannibals who eat the Africans they capture (56). Furthermore, in Chase-Riboud's *Echo of Lions*, the African characters assume that they will be eaten by the Europeans (24); and in Johnson's *Middle Passage*, the white captain of the slave ship has practiced cannibalism (32), and late in the novel, the crew of the *Republic* resorts to cannibalism.

PART I: SETTING THE RECORD STRAIGHT

The Dahomean: What It Was Like Back There

The contemporary African-American novel that makes the most extensive use of African settings is Frank Yerby's *The Dahomean*; nearly all of the action in *The Dahomean* unfolds in Africa. To some extent, Nyasanu, the main character of *The Dahomean*, resembles Okonkwo, the main character of Achebe's *Things Fall Apart*. Both are highly respected members of their societies whose personal downfalls are brought about—at least in part—by the tragic flaw of pride. Both Nyasanu and Okonkwo are deeply influenced by their fathers and deeply troubled by some aspects of their cultures.

In *The Dahomean*, Yerby presents the African section of his story in a long flashback sandwiched between a brief prologue and a concluding scene that are set in America. Like *Things Fall Apart* and Equiano's autobiography, *The Dahomean* details numerous aspects of an African culture, and, like Achebe, Yerby writes with the intention of correcting the historical record. In a note to the reader, Yerby declares: "The purpose of *The Dahomean* . . . is admittedly to correct, so far as it is possible, the Anglo-Saxon reader's historical perspective. For among the countless tragedies caused by North American slavery . . . was the destruction of the high, and in many ways, admirable, culture of the African" (n.p.).

The Dahomean opens in America when two brothers are returning to their plantation after buying a slave at an auction ([v]). Monroe Parks berates his brother Matt for buying a slave "Straight out o' Africa. . . . Got the tribal scars on his temples and his chest. And you won't even put the cuffs on him" ([iv]). But Matt Parks is curious about his new slave; Matt asks his brother if "you ever wonder what he was like—back there? in Africa, I mean?" ([v]). The next 380 pages of *The Dahomean* answer Matt's question.

The Dahomean provides the most detailed description of an African culture in contemporary American fiction. As the reader follows the life of Nyasanu, who was born in 1820 and whose name means "man among men" (4), layer after layer of information about life as it was lived in King Gezo's Dahomey is presented. In the first chapter alone, for instance, Yerby releases information about religion, magic, economics, and family life among the Dahomeans. Nyasanu's people are technologically advanced, having mastered iron making and having developed an efficient system of taxation despite the fact that they lack a written language (19). They possess firearms that they have purchased from Europeans, and they have made alliances with neighboring powers such as the Ashanti. In addition to detailing the many accomplishments of the Dahomeans, Yerby notes two major problems that exist in Dahomean culture: polygamy and rule by an absolute monarch.

Yerby's interest in the practice of polygamy—a practice that is perhaps the most striking example of how African cultures differ from Western culture—is apparent from the very beginning of his novel. Nyasanu, who is seventeen when the story opens, will soon be circumcised and marry his true love, Agbale. He is upset by Agbale's demands that he defy his culture and agree not to marry any other women (8). Nyasanu is the son of Gbenu, a great chief, and Nyasanu's noble birth obligates him to take numerous wives for political, economic, and religious reasons. Gbenu, for instance, has more than forty wives and many sons and daughters to "establish his worship among the ancestors once he has crossed the river, gone to Them" (8). And from an economic point of view, polygamy is a wise practice because in Dahomean culture "children—especially girl children—were wealth. The gifts the prospective son-in-law had to make to the father of the bride was one of the sources of a man's fortune" (8). Yet Nyasanu realizes that when a man has many wives—his father has forty-three and the king has hundreds—that some of the wives will be unfaithful (9).

Yerby also comments on the practice of female genital mutilation, a subject that Alice Walker takes up in *Possessing the Secret of Joy*. Agbale recalls the "intensely painful things [done] to her female genitalia" in a procedure so severe that it is taboo to discuss it in Dahomey. Genital mutilation and ritual scarification are just two of the ordeals that must be endured by females in *The Dahomean*.

The absolute rulership of King Gezo is also a topic of the early pages of Yerby's historical novel, and Yerby implies that power is the same everywhere. In effect, all Dahomeans are property of Gezo. As Nyasanu's father explains, the people are taxed from birth to death "so that the princesses and princes may live in licentious idleness—that is if our lives are not required of us . . . because the kings need a certain kind of worker . . . to be sent to the ancestors to . . . [serve] the royal dead" (20). Indeed, Nyasanu notes that human sacrifice is common in the court of King Gezo; Gezo is said to sacrifice a man and woman each morning as a greeting to his ancestors (43).

In *The Dahomean*, Yerby frequently frames descriptions of the unsavory aspects of life in Dahomey with a comment meant to show that life in the West also has its faults. The point is to demonstrate that examples of so-called "barbarism" on the parts of Africans can be matched by examples of "barbarism" on the parts of Westerners. This example, counter-example approach to comparing Western and African cultures is also a feature of Richard Dooling's *White Man's Grave*. At one point in *The Dahomean*, for instance, Nyasanu must travel to the capital city of Ahomey to receive an honor from the king. While in the capital, Nyasanu witnesses a series of executions. The male prisoners are executed in public, but the women are led into an inner court because Gezo, unlike European leaders of the time, thinks it "unseemly" to execute women in public (269).

While he acknowledges the numerous problems within Dahomean culture, it is the practice of slavery and slave trading that Yerby finds to be the most objectionable feature of Gezo's nation. In his discussion of the West African slave trade, Yerby establishes a precedent by detailing the workings of the trade so that his readers will obtain a better understanding of its nature and scope. The economy of Gezo's nation is based on the capture and trading of slaves. The Dahomeans themselves own slaves, and every year or two a war is initiated against neighboring peoples in order to obtain slaves that can be traded to whites for European goods.

Indeed, one of the more powerful chapters of *The Dahomean* details a campaign to capture slaves and describes the Dahomean methods of war. Dahomey has a draft (115), the king dresses like a common soldier to avoid capture (123), and women fight in a special unit that serves as the king's guards (148). What the king wants, one character explains, is slaves to "sell to the Furtoo [whites] for more gunpowder, cloths, rum, gold" (128). The three-continent nature of the slave trade in which manufactured European goods were traded to African rulers for slaves who were exported to the Americas is detailed in varying degrees in nearly all of the contemporary African-American novels set in Africa, but Yerby is the first to focus on the African role in the slave trade.

The war to obtain slaves marks the beginning of Nyasanu's rise to power, a rise that, ironically, leads to his eventual enslavement. As a reward for his courage in battle, Gezo makes Nyasanu a governor of a province and gives him his daughter, Princess Taunyinatin, for a wife (262). Nyasanu makes a fine governor—after his appointment he is called *Hwesu*—but his marriage to the princess brings discord to his compound. His wives feel threatened by a newcomer, especially one of royal birth, and tension mounts (127). Furthermore, as a member of the royal family, Taunyinatin is exempt from many of the taboos—including the taboo against adultery—that regulate the behavior of ordinary Dahomean women. Taunyinatin's favorite lover is her brother: Prince Atedeku.

When he marries Taunyinatin, Nyasanu tells her that if she betrays him, he will kill both Taunyinatin and her lover (348). The cost of such actions on Nyasanu's part could only be a slow, but certain, execution. One evening Nyasanu returns to his compound to discover Taunyinatin in Atedeku's embrace. In the fight that ensues, Nyasanu wounds Atedeku and banishes him to the savanna (362). In the scene that finds Atedeku hurt and alone in the savanna, Yerby emphasizes the dangers of wild Africa. As Atedeku sees the jackals "slinking in, behind the hyenas," he realizes that he still lives only because the lions and leopards have not yet found him (370). Atedeku survives his ordeal in the savanna only because his rescuers locate him by spotting the carrion birds that are circling in anticipation of Atedeku's death.

After his rescue, Prince Atedeku seeks revenge, and that revenge is to capture Nyasanu and his family and either kill them or sell them into slavery. Caught by surprise, Nyasanu is quickly subdued while Prince Atedeku and his men execute Nyasanu's children and rape his wives (376). A crowd appears at Nyasanu's compound, but Atedeku pacifies the citizens with a royal scepter that the king entrusts only to messengers on official business. Atedeku had stolen the scepter long ago, and the misuse of Gezo's absolute authority makes Nyasanu's enslavement possible (379).

The conclusion of *The Dahomean* briefly summarizes the mechanics of the slave trade. Nyasanu is branded and loaded along with "three hundred and fifty men, women and children into a schooner not big enough to hold one hundred in any comfort. He lay in that steam scald of urine and human excreta for the thirty-six days it took . . . to get to a nameless island in the Florida reefs" (382). For six months, the "breaking-in period," Nyasanu is taught rudimentary English and basic farm work. Nyasanu does not bother to tell his captors that their agricultural technology is inferior to that of his people in Africa (382). *The Dahomean* closes with Naysanu riding in the back of the Monroe brothers' wagon, thinking that the "black men who sold other black men to white slavers . . . couldn't even imagine how slavery in America differed from the rather gentle and indulgent variety of it practiced at home" (383).

Although traditional African slavery as described in *The Dahomean* seems neither "gentle" nor "indulgent" since slaves are routinely sacrificed to the ancestors (119) and female slaves are forced to share their sexual favors with whomever their masters command (343), Yerby is largely successful in achieving the goals he sets for his novel. Yerby wants to enlighten readers about the complexities of African cultures and to inform them about the nature of the slave trade. *The Dahomean* is convincing not only because of the wealth of detail provided by Yerby, but also because Yerby is willing to describe some of the less appealing aspects of Dahomean culture in Gezo's time.

Roots: You Can Go Home Again

Alex Haley's *Roots*, the best known of contemporary African-American novels set in Africa, was published just five years after *The Dahomean*. Because of its enormous popularity both as a novel and as a television movie, *Roots* has been called part of America's "national consciousness" (Pinsker 185). Like *The Dahomean*, *Roots* is a didactic novel. Indeed, *Roots* is said to have changed the very nature of African-American literature precisely because it purported "unashamedly and old-fashionedly to 'instruct and delight' black Americans about the historical truth" (Pinsker 184).

Although Haley returns to Africa at the conclusion of his saga, the most important African portion of *Roots* is at the beginning of the story. Haley devotes the first thirty-three chapters of *Roots*—one hundred and fifty pages—to an account of Kunta Kinte's life in a West African village during the late eighteenth century. Like Achebe and Yerby, Haley details various aspects of African culture, describing the economic, religious, and family life of the people of Juffure.

Haley's Africans, however, differ somewhat from the characters presented in *Things Fall Apart* and *The Dahomean*. One difference is that the people of Juffure have rejected traditional African religion and have converted to Islam. Furthermore, the African culture presented in *Roots* is strangely devoid of technology—iron making, for example—that West Africans had mastered many centuries before Kunta Kinte's birth, and Haley's Africans are also oddly isolated from European influences that were common in late eighteenth-century West Africa (Courlander 295). Indeed, Courlander believes that Kunta Kinte's "primitive being" is disturbing because it derogates both Kinte and the level of development achieved by his tribal culture (295). However, while it is true that Haley romanticizes some aspects of African culture so that he can better contrast the old ways of life in Africa with the new ways of living introduced by Europeans (Courlander 295), the people of Juffure are in no way primitive beings.

For instance, in addition to a well-developed system of agriculture, religion, family life, and law, the people of Juffure have an oral history that is preserved by *griots*, and at least some of Kunta Kinte's people are literate in that they are able to read "Koranic verses and write with grass-quill pens dipped in the black ink of bitter-orange juice mixed with powdered crust from the bottom of the cooking pots" (24). Indeed, a traveling religious leader called a *moro* visits Juffure and brings headbundles that "Kunta knew would contain treasured Arabic books and parchment manuscripts such as those from ancient Timbuktu" (104). The *moro* teaches the young men of the village not only about the Koran, but also about the "Christian Koran, which was known as the Holy Bible" (105).

Furthermore, while it is true that Kunta Kinte's people do not possess firearms and other Western goods, they do know about Europeans and Western technology. Kinte's people call whites *toubobs*, and, as a youth, Kinte is warned to be on guard against them. He is told that a white man smells "like a wet chicken" and "often shoots his firesticks, which can be heard far off" (58). And while some have called *Roots* "badly written" and termed Haley's view of African life a "hackneyed vision" (Pinsker 188), *Roots* is actually very successful in describing one African culture's struggle with a hostile natural environment and in providing details about the West African slave trade as it existed in the late eighteenth century.

For example, Haley is careful to describe the natural world that surrounds the people of Juffure and that governs the cycles of their agricultural system. Early in *Roots*, Haley describes some of the flora and fauna found in West Africa as well as the land itself, which consists of "marshy faros where generations of Juffure women had grown their rice crops" (5). During one dry, lean season of Kinte's youth, the "savanna's waterholes had dried to mud and the bigger and better game had moved into the deep forest—at the time the people of Juffure needed all their strength to plant crops for the new harvest" (7). The lean season is so severe that illness and starvation soon stalk the people of the village. Even as the life-giving rain begins to fall, people begin to die, and Kinte himself is stricken by disease (13). The struggle against nature continues as the village must guard its crops from wildlife such as baboons and birds. In addition to determining the cycle of planting and harvesting, the weather in West Africa also affects the mental health of the people of Juffure. Describing the harmattan, a dusty wind that can blow for weeks during the dry season, Haley explains that the constant wind sets families on edge and causes many to be short tempered (45).

Haley also details the nature of the West African slave trade and its effects on Kinte's people. Kinte's father, Omoro, has traveled down the Kamby Bolongo River and has seen "great toubob canoes . . . moored in the river, each big enough that its insides might hold all the people of Juffure. . . . Nearby was an island, and on the island was a fortress" where slaves are processed (57). Omoro explains to Kinte that Africans are deeply involved in the selling of slaves to the whites: "[T]he King's personal agents now supplied most of the people whom the toubob took away— usually criminals or debtors, or anyone convicted for suspicion of plotting against the king—often for little more than whispering. More people seemed to be convicted of crimes, said Omoro, whenever toubob ships sailed in the Kamby Bolongo looking for slaves to buy" (58). And later in the novel, an elder of the village explains that "Toubob could never do this [enslave Africans] without help from our own people. . . . For toubob money, we turn against our own kind" (120).

However, Haley clearly details the differences in slavery as traditionally practiced in Africa and slavery as practiced in the Americas. For example, the relationships between slaves and masters in Kinte's society are strictly regulated. Slaves can charge their masters with cruelty or "with taking more than half share of what the slaves' work had produced. Masters, in turn, accused slaves of cheating by hiding some of their produce or . . . of deliberately breaking farm tools," and slaves may marry into their master's family after first obtaining permission (137). Therefore, *Roots* presents a much more convincing case that traditional African slavery was a "gentle" and "indulgent" institution—as Yerby calls it—than does *The Dahomean*, and, of course, Haley details the nature of traditional African slavery in order to contrast it with the harsher form of slavery that Kinte will endure in America.

In *The Dahomean*, Yerby deals with the middle passage in a few sentences near the end of his story; in *Roots*, Haley spends nearly fifty pages detailing the terrors of the passage. It is Haley who, despite what some have called his "hackneyed" diction and a prose style that is "perfect fodder" for television (Pinsker 187), provides images of the middle passage that are employed again and again in later works such as *Echo of Lions* and *Middle Passage*. For instance, Haley gives graphic descriptions of Kinte's branding and of the numerous beatings and whippings that Kinte receives at the hands of his captors (154). Haley is also among the first to describe in detail the horrible conditions on the slave ships. Kinte and the other

Africans are packed together so tightly that they cannot move, and the "urine, vomit, and feces that reeked everywhere . . . spread into a slick paste covering the hard planking of the long shelves on which they lay" (168).

In fact, *Roots* marks a turning point; after *Roots*, African-American novelists become progressively less interested in describing life as it was lived in Africa before enslavement and more interested in detailing the nature of the slave trade and the horrors of the passage to the Americas. Barbara Chase-Riboud's *Echo of Lions* provides an excellent example of this shift in thematic focus.

Echo of Lions: You Must Remember This

While Yerby subtitles *The Dahomean* "a historical novel" and the publisher of *Roots* "stoutly proclaimed that *Roots* was history, not fiction" (Courlander 294), *Echo of Lions* is historical fiction in the truest sense because it is based on an actual event: the 1839 *Amistad* rebellion in which Africans were successful in taking control of a slave ship, and, after lengthy trials in the United States, were able to return to Africa. Like Yerby and Haley, Chase-Riboud uses the first pages of her novel to describe the culture of a West African village; like Yerby and Haley, Chase-Riboud wants to demonstrate that Africans had reached a high state of development before the European occupation of Africa.

Chase-Riboud's main concern, however, is not African culture but the nature of the slave trade to the Americas—a trade that continued well into the 1840s and 1850s despite laws that made the importation of slaves into the United States illegal. In addition to describing the slave trade, *Echo of Lions* details the ways in which the sensational legal case concerning the *Amistad* rebels influenced American history and the struggle to abolish slavery in the United States. At one point, for instance, Chase-Riboud takes readers into the mind of John Quincy Adams, the former president who represents the Africans before the Supreme Court. Adams speculates that the "trial of Joseph Cinque [the leader of the Africans] was front page news" and that "Joseph Cinque had cost Martin Van Buren the election" (326).

Most of *Echo of Lions* is set at sea or in the United States, but the pages Chase-Riboud dedicates to African settings, pages that occur mainly at the very beginning and the very ending of her novel, convey a wealth of information about Africa and about the culture of the Mendeland people. For example, the first pages of *Echo of Lions* provide details about agriculture, religion, and family life in a small West African village. Chase-Riboud also describes the system of justice and law practiced in Mendeland in the 1830s. The African setting at the beginning of *Echo of Lions* establishes a point of reference that allows readers to compare and contrast African justice and law with American justice and law.

Although Chase-Riboud provides little information about the legal case that requires Sengbe Pieh—later called Joseph Cinque—to leave his wives and his compound and travel to a neighboring village for a court hearing, the reader is told that it "was a matter of *ndewe*, a cousin. And it was a matter of honor" (19). The "trial had dragged on for many moons, for it had been appealed twice and was now before a Council of Paramount Chiefs" (20–21). At the hearing, charges and counter-charges are made, and the loser of the case will have to pay damages in the form of slaves and livestock. In at least a few ways, the Mendeland legal system resembles the American legal system. In Mendeland, as in the United States, a case can go on for many months, and the system of appeals that leads to a hearing before the Paramount Chiefs is somewhat similar to the appeals that must be heard before a case can go to the U.S. Supreme Court.

On the way home from the trial, Sengbe Pieh and his companion are captured by slavers. The slavers are whites, and Sengbe Pieh's first impression of a white man is frightening. The white who captures Pieh is described as a "monster" whose red beard and hair cause Pieh to think that the man has snakes growing from his face and head. The white also has a "rancid" smell than sickens Pieh (23).

Like Yerby and Haley, Chase-Riboud is careful to differentiate between slavery as traditionally practiced in Africa and slavery as practiced in the Americas. One of the other captives, a man named Grabeau, explains to Pieh that the whites will not respect Pieh's rank or negotiate with his village for ransom. The whites, Grabeau says, "will kill you, or eat you, or sell you to other white men who own giant houses topped with many roofs of cloth which swim across the waters" (24–25). The whites are "ignorant, yet our nations trade with them, make war for captives for them" (25).

The next step in the slaving process requires that Pieh and his fellows be moved to the coast, and many die along the way. Chase-Riboud catalogues some of the diseases that weaken and kill the captives: dysentery, typhoid, malaria, and yellow fever (29). Strong men who might be able to resist the whites are lost by the dozens.Finally Pieh and the other captives arrive at the coast and are marched into a slave factory owned by Don Pedro Blanco, a slaver "whose bills on banks in England, France, or the United States were good as gold" and who had "lived nearly a lifetime amid the pestilential swamp and murderous climate, trafficking in human flesh, provoking wars, and bribing and corrupting native chiefs" (31). Blanco's barracoon "was the largest and most solid edifice Sengbe Pieh had ever seen. It loomed stories above him, the heavy log fortress seeming as impregnable and impossible to unlatch as the bolt-lock carbines of the caravan's guards" (32).

After an escape attempt, Sengbe Pieh is loaded onto a ship for the voyage to Cuba, a Spanish colony where the importation of slaves is legal. Highlighting her concern with the nature of the slave trade and the horrors of the middle passage, Chase-Riboud provides numerous details about the transportation of slaves to the Americas and about the British attempt to curb the slave trade. For example, slavers cannot be prosecuted if the British do not actually discover slaves on board the ships; therefore, many slavers simply dump their cargo when they see British ships approaching. In the early days of the trade, slaves were herded on deck and "bound by their ankles to one long chain, which [was] attached to the anchor" (37). When the British approached, the anchor was dropped and the "chain with its load of living bodies sank to the bottom of the sea" (37). Later, this system was refined. Chase-Riboud provides these details about the design of an efficient slave ship: "The slaves were all shackled to the same chain, which ran the length of the deck on both sides, and to which was attached a heavy iron ball. The trapdoor could be opened, and the iron weight falling into the sea would drag with it every human attached to the chain" (37).

After Sengbe Pieh and his companions are transported to Cuba, they are given new names (Sengbe Pieh becomes Joseph Cinque) and false passports. This renaming is one of the many ways in which the Africans lose their connections with their homelands. The slaves are then loaded upon the *Amistad*, a ship that is supposed to complete the final step of the slaving process by smuggling the Africans to the United States.

While aboard the *Amistad*, Cinque and his comrades revolt and take charge of the ship. They hope to sail back to Africa, but they land in New York. Although most of *Echo of Lions* unfolds in the United States after the *Amistad* runs ashore, information about Africa and Africans is released throughout the novel. For example, in order to relay to readers popular Western misconceptions about Africa, Chase-Riboud allows Cinque to overhear comments made by a professor at Yale. The professor insists that Africans have no culture, no poets, and no philosophers. According to the professor, Africans have made no contributions at all to world history (292). After hearing these comments, Cinque realizes that whites "dreamed of a whole continent of black people, neatly dressed in New England calico, each carrying a Bible, each with a Christian name" (202).

When Cinque finally returns to Africa, he discovers that his entire family, as well as most of his village, has been sold into slavery (370–71). However, Cinque's return to his homeland is a victory for the abolition movement in the United States and for all African Americans. As one character explains to Cinque, "you have proven that a round trip is possible" if not to Africa then "to *ourselves*" (367). Chase-Riboud's novel is a significant contribution to contemporary American fiction set in Africa because it educates readers about West African culture, informs readers about the nature of the slave trade, and artfully dramatizes an important event in American history.

Middle Passage: These Men Are Your Brothers

Like *Echo of Lions*, Charles Johnson's *Middle Passage* uses African settings sparingly and focuses more on the nature of the slave trade and the horrors of the middle passage than on life in Africa before enslavement. Like *The Dahomean*, *Roots*, and *Echo of Lions*, *Middle Passage* strives to inform readers about Africa and the slave trade; however, *Middle Passage* is unusual because its narrator, Rutherford Calhoun, is a free black American, not an African or an omnipotent narrator who enters the minds of numerous characters. And while *Middle Passage* is not an historical novel in the sense of *The Dahomean*, *Roots*, or *Echo of Lions*, Johnson's novel does concern itself with history. In fact, *Middle Passage* casts world history in an Afrocentric light.

One night in 1830, in order to escape his debts and a forced marriage to Isadora Bailey—a teacher who would like to reform him—Calhoun steals away aboard a ship bound out of New Orleans. He wakes the next morning to find himself far out into the Gulf of Mexico on a vessel named the *Republic*. The *Republic* is a slaver, and its mission is to pick up a cargo of mysterious tribesmen at a West African trading fort called Bangalang and transport them to America.

The name of the slave ship in *Middle Passage* is clearly symbolic. Writing in the ship's logbook, Calhoun notes that "The *Republic* was physically unstable. She was perpetually flying apart . . . during the voyage" (35–36). The voyages across the Atlantic in pursuit of slaves are shaking the *Republic* to pieces just as the slavery issue is ripping apart the United States during the first half of the nineteenth century; the republic is indeed unstable.

The captain of the *Republic* is a malformed man named Ebenezer Falcon. Calhoun is surprised to discover that Falcon, who is widely known for his success in enslaving Africans, is a dwarf (29). Although he is extremely short, Falcon has a huge shoulder span and a "long head" with a "great bulging forehead" (29). Falcon knows seven African dialects and thinks his mission on earth is to Americanize the planet (30). However, as Calhoun learns near the conclusion of *Middle Passage*, the *Republic* is owned not by Falcon but by a consortium of businessmen, including a free black American named Papa Zeringue. Naturally, Calhoun finds it repulsive that an American of color would seek to profit by enslaving Africans and importing them to the United States (203–4).

Forty-one days after leaving New Orleans, the *Republic* puts down anchor alongside the trading post at Bangalang, and Johnson uses the arrival in West Africa as an occasion to release information about the nature of the slave trade. The barracoons at Bangalang were constructed by the Royal African Company in the late 1600s (44). When Calhoun arrives in 1830, Bangalang is controlled by Owen Bogha. Bogha is a halfbreed—the son of an English slaver and a princess from a small African tribe. He has an English education and oversees the slave trade from his hilltop fortress (44).

That first night off shore in West Africa, Calhoun cannot sleep because "sharp cries such as only Negro women can make drifted on the wind from the warehouse, where Africans living, dying, and dead were thrown together" (58). The next morning, Calhoun goes ashore and gets his first glimpse of the *Republic's* cargo, the Allmuseri, when a caravan of slaves arrives at the barracoon. Like the *Republic*, the Allmuseri are symbolic. The Allmuseri represent all Africans, and many traditional notions about Africa are associated with them. The Allmuseri are a composite people, a merging of many tribes (61).

Like Africa, the Allmuseri are timeless and mysterious. Calhoun says that "they were a remarkably *old* people. About them was the smell of old temples" and lost cities (61). Moreover, Calhoun has been told that all Allmuseri have a "second brain, a small one at the base of their spines" (61). The Allmuseri are victims of the harsh African climate. Calhoun learns that a prolonged drought has weakened them and made the tribe easy victims for Arab slavers (62).

Like the Africans in *Roots* and *Echo of Lions*, the Allmuseri consider the Westerners to be barbarians; they fear that they are being shipped to America "to be eaten" by whites (65). And like Yerby, Haley, and Chase-Riboud, Johnson details the horrors of the slave ships. For example, when the Africans realize they are to be loaded into the ship's hole where they will be crammed together in filth for the long voyage across the Atlantic, several leap overboard in suicide attempts (66).

In addition to the slaves, a mysterious crate is loaded onto the *Republic*, and the ship sets sail for America. The members of the crew speculate that the crate might contain the "Missing Link between man and monkey" or something that "had fallen from the sky near the Allmuseri villages" (67). When a cabin boy is sent to investigate the crate, he returns crazed and speaking in "a slabber of Bantu patois, Bushman, Cushitic, and Sudanic tongues" (68). Falcon tells Calhoun that the crate contains an African god that "has a hundred ways to relieve men of their reason" (102).

Johnson employs the African deity and the suspected magical powers of the Allmuseri to question the basis for Western knowledge and to imply that Africans not only live differently from Westerners, they *see* and *know* differently from Westerners. For instance, when Ngonyama, the leader of the Allmuseri, views a portrait of Isadora that Calhoun carries with him, Ngonyama asks Calhoun "Why is her face splotched with smudges?" Cahhoun explains that Ngonyama is referring to the *"shadows* the artist had drawn under her chin and eyes, for his [Ngonyama's] tribe did not use our sense of perspective but rather the flat, depthless technique of Egyptian art" (75). Calhoun also implies that Ngonyama has conjured up a storm that nearly sinks the *Republic* (83).

This African way of understanding and seeing the world is also reflected in the Allmuseri written language—a language that consists of "pictograms." Calhoun speculates that such a language would be good for analyzing or "deconstructing things into discrete parts, which probably explained why the Allmuseri had no empirical science" (76–77). Their history is no less unusual than their language because Allmuseri history implies an Afrocentric view of the development of world culture. The Allmuseri had once been seafaring explorers who had visited India and sailed across the Atlantic, "bringing their skills in agriculture and metallurgy to the Olmec who, to honor these African mariners, stamped their likeness in stone and enshrined in song their prowess as warriors" (76–77).

Therefore, while Yerby, Haley, and Chase-Riboud are satisfied to demonstrate that Africans had achieved highly developed cultures before the coming of Europeans to Africa, Johnson implies that Africans are largely responsible for exploring the world and spreading skills such as "agriculture and metallurgy" to other, less developed continents such as Asia and the Americas.

Eventually, Ngonyama and the other Africans take over the ship. Some of the crew are executed, and some are spared. Calhoun is spared because, as Ngonyama explains, "No one will hurt you here, Rutherford. These men are your brothers" (131). Johnson uses the slave revolt to comment on recent American events when Falcon, who has been injured in the revolt, becomes crazed and begins to babble predictions that might be the ravings of a twentieth-century white supremacist (145).

After Falcon's death, the Allmuseri and the surviving crew steer the *Republic* back toward Africa. The Americans are forced to adopt African ways in order to exorcise the evil (Western) spirits that the Africans believe infest the ship. For instance, the Americans are told to speak to the Africans in Allmuseri, not English, and the Allmuseri forbid the crew to sing in English, the "oppressor's" tongue (55). The crew is also forced to learn Allmuseri stories, to feed the Allmuseri god, to use Allmuseri medicine to treat illness, and to eat Allmuseri food (155). In other words, the Americans are stripped of their culture just as enslaved Africans were forced to give up their languages, religions, and literatures. Because of hunger and illness, however, many of the rules set by the Africans are not enforced.

The climactic scene in *Middle Passage* occurs when it is Calhoun's turn to feed the African god. When he goes below deck to tend to the deity, he has a vision in which the African god takes the form of Calhoun's father: Riley. The African deity is a device that will reconnect Calhoun, "a Marginalized American colored man," with his lost heritage (169). Calhoun says that the deity stood "before me mute as a mountain. . . . Within its contours my father's incarnation was trapped like a ship in a bottle" (168). The African deity presents Calhoun with a "seriality of images." The Allmuseri god is a sort of groit who when asked for one item of tribal history can only proceed by "reeling forth the entire story of his people, could not bring forth this one man's life [Calhoun's father's life] without delivering as well the *complete* content of the antecedent universe to which my father . . . belonged" (169). What the African deity presents to Calhoun, then, is not only an image of his father but also an image of his entire African heritage. This overwhelms Calhoun; he passes out.

When he recovers consciousness, Calhoun discovers that fever and hunger have decimated the Africans and the Americans aboard the *Republic*. The sailors have, in fact, been forced to resort to cannibalism to survive (174). Finally, the *Republic* sinks in a storm, and Calhoun is rescued by a passing ship, a ship that is commanded by Papa, the Creole slave trader who is searching for the *Republic*.

Rutherford Calhoun has been changed by the middle passage. He has made peace with the ghost of his father and come to understand the importance of his African heritage. As he puts it near the conclusion of the novel, the long voyage across the Atlantic had "irreversibly changed my seeing, made of me a cultural mongrel" (187).

Middle Passage differs from such works as *The Dahomean*, *Roots*, and *Echo of Lions* because of Calhoun's first-person narration and because of Johnson's concern with Afrocentric history. However, *Middle Passage*, like *The Dahomean*, *Roots*, and *Echo of Lions*, describes the horrors of the slave trade and the journey across the Atlantic. Like other African novels by Black Americans, *Middle Passage* is a novel of discovery; the story connects Calhoun with his heritage—both in a personal and cultural sense.

PART II: THE WORLD ACCORDING TO WALKER

The Color Purple, The Temple of My Familiar, and *Possessing the Secret of Joy*

Alice Walker has made extensive use of African settings in three novels: *The Color Purple, The Temple of My Familiar,* and *Possessing the Secret of Joy.* In these works, Walker employs a wide range of African settings. Most of the African scenes unfold in a contemporary—but invented—nation called Olinka; some scenes take place in an ancient, unnamed region of Africa. Like much African-American fiction set in Africa, Walker's novels are frequently didactic, but the lessons offered by Walker are broader than those presented in other African novels by black Americans.

For instance, the African novels of Yerby, Haley, Chase-Riboud, and Johnson are mostly concerned with describing African cultures, detailing the West African slave trade, and recording the horrors of the middle passage. Walker, however, not only provides information about African cultures and about the slave trade, she also uses African settings to promote her feminist concerns. In writing about these concerns, she constructs a "history" of the world that explains the origins of patriarchal societies and the beginnings of such common African practices as the ritual scarification and the genital mutilation of women.

Olinka, Walker's invented African nation, is the locale for most of the African scenes in *The Color Purple, The Temple of My Familiar,* and *Possessing the Secret of Joy.* About Olinka, Walker writes: "I do not know from what part of Africa my African ancestors came, and so I claim the whole continent. I suppose I have created Olinka as my village and the Olinkans as one of my ancient ancestral tribal peoples" (*Possessing* 283).

Olinka, however, is much more than a village or a tribe. Olinka is a West African nation with an Atlantic coast and considerable inland territory. Like many actual African nations, Olinka is composed of several ethnic groups. In *The Temple of My Familiar,* for instance, an Olinkan character notes that "in our country we have many different tribes. . . . [W]e have the Olinka, the Ababa, the Mama" (187). Like actual African nations, Olinka has suffered from colonialism, and like many contemporary African nations, Olinka is ruled by a corrupt leader who has little regard for his people. Only the president, his relatives, and the army have enough to eat (*Temple* 180), and there is no free press (*Possessing* 194).

As time passes in Walker's African novels, Olinka changes, mirroring the transformations that have occurred in actual African nations during this century. For example, when Nettie, a major character in *The Color Purple,* first arrives in Olinka during the 1930s, the nation is a remote place—so remote that the women have never seen white people (128). Nettie writes her sister Celie and tells her that the march from the coast through the jungle to the inland village where Nettie and her family are working as missionaries takes four days (127). But as decades pass, Olinka—like actual Africa—becomes less and less remote; in *Possessing the Secret of Joy*, a novel with a contemporary setting, it is easy for journalists and photographers from every part of the world to attend a controversial trial in Olinka's capital city (245).

Walker first makes use of African settings in *The Color Purple*, an epistolary novel comprised mainly of letters written by two sisters, Celie and Nettie. Critics have noted that the novel follows a long tradition of didactic writing by adopting the epistolary form (Katz 187). Katz believes that *The Color Purple* is a lesson about the "nature of learning and enlightenment" as well as about the "nature of patriarchal oppression" (193). The novel also contains numerous lessons about African life, culture, and history. When Nettie and the missionary family leave the United States and move to Olinka in the 1930s, they are largely ignorant of African life and culture. Readers of the novel learn about Africa along with Nettie who relays what she discovers to Celie.

At the beginning of *The Color Purple*, Nettie admits that "I never dreamed of going to Africa. I never thought of it as a real place" (110), yet she has an emotional feeling that borders on religious sentiment when she first sees the coast of Africa, the "land for which our mothers and fathers cried—and lived and died—to see again" (120–21). Indeed, *The Color Purple* highlights the link between African Americans and Africans in a number of ways. Perhaps the most obvious, and most symbolic, of the links is the marriage of Adam—the son of black American missionaries—and Tashi—an Olinkan girl who lives in the village where Adam's parents have their mission. Walker specifically merges African-American and African cultures via Adam's scarification (236) and Tashi's immigration to the United States (243).

In fact, Tashi becomes a naturalized U.S. citizen and seems to have a high regard for her new country. Tashi is the major character of *Possessing the Secret of Joy*. In that novel, she finds herself in an Olinkan prison for the murder of M'Lissa, the Olinkan woman who has mutilated Tashi and hundreds of other young women in the name of tradition and patriotism. Tashi observers, "Sometimes I dream of the United States. I love it deeply and miss it terribly, much to the annoyance of some people I know. . . . The crime they say I committed would make no sense in America" (55–56).

Indeed, the linkage between African Americans and Africans that Walker begins in *The Color Purple* is continued in *The Temple of My Familiar* and in *Possessing the Secret of Joy*. In *Possessing the Secret of Joy*, for instance, Tashi's American family and one of her American friends travel to Olinka to protest her execution. The last thing that Tashi sees is the protest banner held by her American supporters (279). Walker's implication is that African Americans have an obligation to be concerned with political, as well as cultural, affairs in Africa.

In addition to establishing a connection between African Americans and Africans, *The Color Purple* provides a condensed history of Africa through Nettie's letters. The events of Olinkan history run parallel to events in many actual African nations. For example, Nettie describes Olinka's transformation from a village-based agricultural economy to a colonial, plantation economy. This transformation is characterized by the building of a road through the Olinka village so that a rubber plantation can be operated by an absentee European owner. The population of the village is relocated, and the people's culture is destroyed (192); the colonial experience of Olinka is, of course, symbolic of the colonial experiences of actual African nations.

The Color Purple also introduces readers to such African customs as ritual scarification and female genital mutilation. These customs will become the subject of *Possessing the Secret of Joy*. Numerous critics have pointed out that these African customs are described as a way of universalizing Walker's thematic statements about patriarchal oppression. Byerman maintains that Celie's oppression by males in America is mirrored by the oppression of women in Africa; he notes that the "African traditions, made available through the device of Nettie's letters, suggest the universality of oppression" (62). Moreover, Winchell writes that Nettie "compares the power the Olinka man has over his wife to the power their stepfather had over her and Celie, and the general desire of African society to keep women uneducated to the desire of American whites to keep blacks ignorant" (94).

The use of African culture and ritual to dramatize the universality of the oppression of women is the most significant manifestation of African settings in *The Color Purple*. Just as Celie and Nettie have been oppressed by males in America—Celie has been raped by her stepfather (3) and "sold" to her husband (12), and Nettie is forced to run away from home to avoid being raped (17)—women in Olinka are oppressed by men. Some Olinka women are "promised to old or middle-aged men at birth" and "among the Olinka, the husband has life and death power over the wife. If he accuses one of his wives of witchcraft or infidelity she can be killed" (142–43). Moreover, genital mutilation—a ritual that Olinkas require of all females—is an act of extreme violence against women. Tashi, whose struggle to come to terms with her own mutilation is the subject of *Possessing the Secret of Joy*, undergoes the ritual in *The Color Purple* (201).

While the main message of *The Color Purple* concerns the universal oppression of women by patriarchal societies, the novel offers a number of other lessons—lessons about the relationship of African Americans to Africans and lessons about the history of Africa in this century—that should not be overlooked.

Walker continues to employ African settings for didactic purposes in *The Temple of My Familiar*—a sprawling novel with many important characters and with settings that span the world and thousands of years of time. In *The Temple of My Familiar*, an African animal, the lion, comes to symbolize the nobility and strength of a major character, Lissie (417). In fact, in one of her past lives, Lissie had been a lion—a lion who mated with women—before men drove the lions and other animals away and "asserted themselves, alone, as the familiars of women" (367).

It is difficult to overstate the vastness of the scope of *The Temple of My Familiar*. Winchell writes that *The Temple of My Familiar* is "likely to remain a novel often begun and seldom finished. Any novel that attempts to provide a spiritual history of the universe hardly makes for light reading" (115), and Howard notes that the story "is about everyone and everything . . . almost since the beginning of time" (141).

Much of Walker's "spiritual history" takes place in ancient Africa. In *The Temple of My Familiar*, Walker explains how matriarchal societies gave way to patriarchal societies, how women throughout the world have come to find themselves oppressed by men, and how the way of life once followed by a lost, matriarchal African tribe might offer a solution to the conflicts between men and women. In *The Temple of My Familiar*, the univeral oppression of women is dramatized by the stories of Zede, a woman from South America, and by the past lives of Miss Lissie. Indeed, the African scenes are frequently punctuated by scenes in South America that "explain" the end of the worship of the South American goddesses and the beginning of the oppression of women in Native American cultures.

Lissie's stories are not the only African tales in *The Temple of My Familiar*. Walker presents readers with three different views of African events; three alternative "histories." One alternative is provided by Lissie's stories. Another "history" is presented by characters from *The Color Purple* who travel back to Olinka for what turns out to be an sort of African-American/African family reunion. A third account of African events is provided by the experiences and readings of Mary Ann Haverstock, a wealthy white radical who flees to Africa from the United States.

Like many African-American novels set in Africa, *The Temple of My Familiar* describes the capture and enslavement of Africans and the horror of the middle passage. Lissie explains that in one of her past lives in Africa she had been sold into slavery by her uncle (62) and taken to the coast by Arabs who then sold her to white men (62–63). Lissie says that among the slaves were "men sold into slavery because of their religious belief, which was not tolerated by the Mohametans. They carried on the ancient tradition of worship of the mother, and to see a mother sold into slavery . . . was a great torture for them" (63). According to Lissie, the slave trade was part of an organized drive to extinguish the worship of mothers (63).

In fact, Lissie explains much of world "history" through the stories of her past lives. She tells her tales to Suwelo, a member of the history department at a California university who meets Lissie when he travels to Baltimore to settle his uncle's estate. In *The Temple of My Familiar*, readers learn along with Suwelo as Lissie presents her feminist lessons, and Suwelo has a lot to learn about feminism. When he first appears, he is reading a pornographic passage from a novel, and, as Winchell points out, Suwelo has never read a book by a woman and doesn't care to (120). On a grand scale, Lissie teaches Suwelo how things became the way they are—how men replaced the old mother worship with patriarchal religions and societies. On a more personal level, Lissie teaches Suwelo to respect the women in his life.

Lessons about a more contemporary Africa are offered in Part II of *The Temple of My Familiar* in which Olivia—a character from *The Color Purple*—returns to Africa with her daughter Fanny. Olivia's appearance in *The Temple of My Familiar* is possible because her daughter Fanny is married to Suwelo. Like *The Color Purple*, *The Temple of My Familiar* presents a microcosm of African history through events in Olinka. In *The Temple of My Familiar*, these events are narrated by Olivia, who tells the story years after the events occurred.

Olivia offers this summary of African history:

"The Africa that we encountered had already been raped of much of its sustenance. Its people had been sold into slavery. Considering both internal and external 'markets,' this 'trade' had been going on for well over a thousand years. . . . Millions of its [Africa's] trees had been shipped to England and Spain and other European countries to make benches and altars in those grand European cathedrals . . . its minerals and metals mined and its land planted in rubber and cocoa and pineapples and all sorts of crops for the benefit of foreign invaders. . . . And Africa itself became—was made—an uninhabited region, except for its population of wild and exotic animals." (146)

A third view of African history is presented through the readings of Mary Ann Haverstock, a wealthy white radical who changes her name to Mary Jane Briden and moves to Africa where she becomes a famous playwright. Briden is one of many characters in American fiction who travel to Africa to reinvent themselves. Briden is inspired to go to Africa by the adventures of great aunts, Eleanora and Eleandra, whose writings and photographs concerning Africa are preserved by a college in England.

In these nineteenth-century writings, Briden discovers the story of M'Sukta, an African who is the last of her tribe. M'Sukta has been brought to England where she lives in a replica of an African village, constantly on display for visitors (*Temple* 225). While the story of M'Sukta might at first seem contrived, M'Sukta's experiences as a display in a museum are not that different from the real life experiences of Sartje Baartman, the so-called Venus Hottentot, who was displayed in nineteenth-century Europe as a curiosity because of her large bottom.

M'Sukta's tribe had always been a matriarchy, but all her tribe has been killed or sold into slavery. M'Sukta has been rescued by an explorer and moved to the Museum of Natural History where it is hoped she will pass on her people's way of life and preserve her tribe's language (*Temple* 233). M'Sukta's role in *The Temple of My Familiar* is to offer an alternative, matriarchal model that might some day replace the patriarchal systems that dominate the world.

At the conclusion of the novel, Fanny and Suwelo are reunited and are planning a new home. They will solve their problems by adopting a way of life they have learned about by reading stories concerning M'Sukta and her tribe. The house Fanny and Suwelo are building is "modeled on the prehistoric ceremonial household of the M'Sukta's people, the Ababa—a house designed by the ancient matriarchal mind and the first heterosexual household ever created. It has two wings, each complete with its own bedroom, bath, study, and kitchen. . . . After thousands of years of women and men living apart, the Ababa had, with great trepidation, experimented with the two tribes living, a couple to a house, together. Each person must remain free, they said" (396).

While Walker looks back to ancient African matriarchal cultures as a means of obtaining freedom from patriarchal control in *The Temple of My Familiar*, in *Possessing the Secret of Joy*, she attacks an ancient African tradition—the genital mutilation of girls and young women. *Possessing the Secret of Joy* is Walker's most African, and most didactic, novel. As Buckman observes, *Possessing the Secret of Joy* is a "text that acts as a revolutionary manifesto for dismantling systems of domination" (93).

The purpose of the book is to educate the world to the horror of female genital mutilation and to save young girls and women from being disfigured—simply because men say it should be so—in the name of tradition, religion, or patriotism. As Walker explains in a note to the reader, an "estimated ninety to one hundred million women and girls living today in African, Far Eastern and Middle Eastern countries have been genitally mutilated" (281). Walker has pledged to donate some of the royalties from *Possessing the Secret of Joy* to "educate women and girls, men and boys, about the hazardous effects of genital mutilation, not simply on the health and happiness of individuals, but on the whole society in which it is practiced, and the world" (282–83). The subject matter makes *Possessing the Secret of Joy* a difficult novel. As Howard puts it, "one does not want to read *Possessing the Secret of Joy*. Instead, clutching one's stomach . . . one wants to howl to the winds and the heavens in angry protest and despair" (143).

While some scenes in *Possessing the Secret of Joy* take place in Europe or the United States, the majority of the action unfolds in Walker's invented African nation, Olinka. The story is told from a number of perspectives—mainly those of Tashi, Adam, and Olivia—characters from *The Color Purple*. In fact, *Possessing the Secret of Joy* retells some events that have occurred in *The Color Purple*. For instance, in *Possessing the Secret of Joy*, Olivia recalls the day that she and her brother, Adam, arrived in the Olinka village where their parents had come to work as missionaries. Olivia's impressions of the remoteness of the village echo Celie's descriptions of the village in *The Color Purple*. Olivia recalls that "We had been weeks on the march that brought us to Tashi's village. . . . I remember looking up at my father and thinking what a miracle it was that we'd somehow—through jungle, grassland, across rivers and whole countries of animals—arrived in the village of the Olinka that he'd spoken so much about" (7).

Ironically, the evening that Olivia and her family arrive in Olinka, Tashi's older sister bleeds to death after being mutilated. This event sets the tone for the story that follows, a tale that is delivered piece by piece in bursts of brief commentary from Tashi and the people who love her.

Tashi is a character torn between different worlds: the tribal world of the Olinka and the Western way as presented by the black American missionary family that comes to Olinka. She becomes friends with the Americans and falls in love with Adam, the son of the missionaries. It is Adam who causes Tashi to rebel against her Olinkan culture. For instance, after Adam and Tashi fall in love, they break the most important of all the Olinkan taboos by making love in the fields (27).

Because of the influence of the missionaries, Tashi does not undergo mutilation, what the Olinka call the "bath," at the proper age. It is only later, when the war for Olinkan independence is under way, that Tashi submits to the ritual. Tashi undergoes the "bath" because of the teachings of an Olinkan revolutionary called "Our Leader." He is called "Our Leader" because the colonial rulers forbade anyone to speak his name (122). As Tashi remembers: "From prison Our Leader said we must keep ourselves clean and pure as we had been since time immemorial—by cutting out unclean parts of our bodies. Everyone knew that if a woman was not circumcised her unclean parts would grow so long they'd soon touch her thighs; she'd become masculine and arouse herself. No man could enter her because her own erection would be in the way" (119).

Tashi, then, undergoes mutilation as a way to get back in touch with the culture she had abandoned by accepting Christianity and breaking the taboo against love making in the fields. Tashi regrets her decision for the rest of her life, and she decides to strike back by killing M'Lissa, a woman who has become an Olinkan hero because she preserves the culture by mutilating hundreds of girls and young women.

Walker provides readers of *Possessing the Secret of Joy* with a great amount of information about genital mutilation and its history. At one point, an Olinkan creation myth is said to have been the origin of the practice (228). As a child, Tashi heard a group of men talking about the myth and its relation to the genital mutilation of women. She remembers the men saying that genital mutilation was god's way because "God liked it fighting" (Olinka men are said to enjoy forcing their way into women who have been sewn shut), and "God liked it tight" (232).

Tashi explains that there are three types of circumcision: "Some cultures demanded excision of only the clitoris, others insisted on a thorough scraping away of the entire genital area" (118–19). Tashi has experienced the most severe form of all, infibulation. Tashi's external genitalia have been removed and her vulva has been sewn tight, leaving only a small opening for the passage of blood and urine.

As Buckman notes, Tashi was once a woman who took pleasure in her body, but after the "bath," "Tashi is embarrassed by the shuffling walk and the odor that are characteristic results of the procedure . . . [and] neither she nor Adam, her husband, could ever again experience the sexual pleasure they had before the operation. The operation ensures that the woman will have no pleasure through vaginal intercourse, and Adam, a non-tribal American male, does not enjoy either the blood or the pain that result for Tashi from forcing the vaginal opening wider" (90).

Walker makes the point that Olinkan women must share the responsibility for their oppression. A special group of women, called *tsunga*, are empowered to perform the surgery, and many women pay the *tsunga* to resew them after the birth of each child (239). The novel implies that if the practice of genital mutilation is to be ended, women must take the lead and resist the procedure by any means necessary, just as Tashi resists by killing M'Lissa.

Complicating an already difficult novel, Walker presents readers of *Possessing the Secret of Joy* with a controversial observation about AIDS and Africa. While awaiting execution, Tashi is housed in a prison that also serves as an AIDS ward.

Tashi and her American family and friends begin working in the ward, and they discover a supposed "origin" of the disease from a character named Hartford.

Hartford was hired by white scientists to hunt monkeys and chimpanzees for medical experiments (259). Later he is paid to kill the captured monkeys and apes (260). According to *Possessing the Secret of Joy*, cultures grown on monkey kidneys were used to produce a tainted vaccine that "carried with it the immune deficiency virus that causes AIDS" (247). Buckman believes that the AIDS passage is linked to the concern with genital mutilation as an anticolonial statement on Walker's part: "The AIDS and genital mutilation narratives clearly posit the body, specifically male and female African bodies, as a site of both international and intranational colonization. Both Western and male ideologies posit the Other (African, female) as a commodity whose definition should be fixed by the power elite. . . . In discussing a ritual that is traditionally taboo and in verbalizing a creation myth for AIDS that is vehemently denied by dominant groups, Walker deconstructs the silence that helps to empower these groups" (92).

Walker has accomplished many of her objectives in *Possessing the Secret of Joy*. A brutal ritual that was once largely unknown in the West has became a controversial issue thanks to Walker and others. Only recently, for instance, the U.S. immigration system granted political asylum to a nineteen-year-old woman from Togo who fled her homeland to escape genital mutilation ("Togolese" A6).

In summary, African-American authors have employed African settings to historicize the experiences of Africans and to incorporate into fiction a number of lessons about Africa and the slave trade. Yerby recreates a lost civilization with all its glories and all its blemishes in *The Dahomean*. Haley recaptures his lost heritage and describes the horrors of the middle passage in *Roots*. In *Echo of Lions*, Chase-Riboud reminds readers of an important African event that influenced American history, and, in *Middle Passage*, Johnson gives Africans credit for "civilizing" most of the world. In her three African novels, Walker promotes her feminist agenda and urges an end to a brutal custom. Like their white colleagues, African-American novelists setting their works in African have learned that Africa is a history—a lesson waiting to be relayed—as much as it is a continent.

Chapter 5

Genre Africa

The use of setting in fiction is, of course, closely related to the type of story an author is telling. For instance, Lutwack notes that adventure fiction favors foreign and exotic settings because "intense action seems to be helped by unfamiliar scenes for its enactment," and he also observes that Africa has long been a favorite setting for adventure stories (29). Africa has become a fertile setting for authors writing genre fiction, especially science fiction and action-adventure fiction. However, although these novels may conform to the demands of a particular genre, these works frequently rise above genre expectations in terms of thematic concerns, and they often include a didactic element similar to that found in the larger body of contemporary American fiction set in Africa. For instance, novels such as Ruark's *Something of Value*, Michener's *The Covenant*, and Harrison's *Burton and Speke* can certainly be called action-adventure novels, yet they are also historical accounts that inform readers about African places and events. Crichton's *Congo*, while obviously a science fiction tale, contains passages that release a great amount of information about Africa and its history.

PART I: SCIENCE FICTION AFRICA

Considering the popularity of Africa as a setting for science fiction during the early part of the twentieth century—particularly in the works of H. Rider Haggard and Edgar Rice Burroughs—it is surprising that so few contemporary American writers have chosen Africa as a setting for their science fiction novels. Perhaps most science fiction authors assume that readers no longer expect Africa to be the home of exotic, strange, and previously undiscovered creatures and peoples. After all, most of Africa has been explored as well as exploited; in fact, outer space has replaced Africa as the great unexplored region that might be inhabited by unusual beings. However, two notable contemporary American science fiction novels have been set in Africa: *The Wild Boys* by William S. Burroughs and *Congo* by Michael Crichton. These novels follow different science fiction traditions. *The Wild Boys* is a work of futurism that uses African settings to paint a bleak picture of what the world might become; *Congo* makes use of many of the traditional notions about Africa that were popularized by science fiction writers working in the earlier decades of this century.

The Wild Boys: The Future Is Now

Much of the action in *The Wild Boys* takes place in North Africa. As one character in the novel, a control agent, explains, the "wild boys are an overflow from North African cities that started in 1969. . . . That spring gasoline gangs prowled . . . the city dousing just anybody with gasoline and setting that person on fire" (143). Stories about the wild boys spread and boys from every country run away to join wild boy tribes (150).

The first African scene in the novel takes place in Marrakech where the Chief—the head of some unnamed government organization—has gone undercover to discover more about the wild boy movement that is threatening to bring down the control machine that regulates the Western, developed world. However, it is not until the chapter titled "Le Gran Luxe" that readers get a full account of Burroughs's vision of the future.

"Le Gran Luxe" is set in Marrakech in 1989—twenty years after the actual publication of *The Wild Boys*—and Burroughs describes an over-populated world that is divided between the incredibly wealthy and the incredibly poor. Marrakech has "spread in all directions up into the Atlas mountains to the east, south to the Sahara, westward to the coastal cities, up into the industrial reservation of the north. There are fantastic parties, vast estates, and luxury such as we read about in the annals of the Roman Empire" (50–51).

However, there is also terrible poverty, and there are wild boys "in the streets packs of them vicious as famished dogs. There is almost no police force in operation and everyone who can afford it has private guards" (50). Gasoline has become almost impossible to obtain, so steam cars and "electrics are coming back" (52). The less wealthy resort to more primitive means of transport such as covered wagons, stage coaches, and mule trains (166). But while transportation in *The Wild Boys* is not highly developed, "Burroughs . . . projects an elaborate repertoire of advances in the biological sciences, including cloning" (McHale 66).

In Burroughs's view of the future, the division between the wealthy and the poor is obscene, and this split has led to the spontaneous development of wild boy tribes who see the rich as prey. One of the wealthy is a character named A. J. who hosts a fantastic party on his vast Moroccan estate. A. J.'s compound is protected by electric gates and thirty-foot-high walls. Every possible sort of food is served to A. J.'s guests (58). Outside the gate of A. J.'s estate, the poor assemble, eagerly awaiting leftovers.

However, these tasty leavings are presented to the poor in an unusual manner. Solid leftovers are scraped into one container and liquids into another. As his guests assemble on the balcony overlooking the main gate, A. J. speaks on the "importance of maintaining a strong benevolent image in the native mind" (59). After his speech,

a panel slides back in the wall on one side of the gate and a huge phallus slides out pissing Martinis, soup, wine, Coca-Cola, grenadine, vodka, bourbon, beer, hot buttered rum, pink gin, Alexanders, glog, corn whiskey into a trough forty feet long labeled DRINKS. From a panel on the other side of the gate a rubber asshole protrudes spurting out Baked Alaska, salted herring, duck gravy, chili con carne, peach melba, syrups, sauces, jam, fat bone and gristle into another trough labeled EATS. Screaming clawing drooling the crowd throws itself at the troughs scooping up food and drinks with both hands. The odor of vomit rises in the clouds. A. J. presses a button that seals the balcony over. . . . We all stay a month which isn't hard to do considering what is inside and what is outside. (59)

This is Burroughs's satirical version of the benevolence of the wealthy in the near future.

The development of the wild boys seems almost a natural reaction to the desperate world that Burroughs describes. In *The Wild Boys*, the youth of the Third World are considered to be born dead; they have no chance in life, and so they decide to strike back at the powers of control in any way they can. The wild boy objective is to destroy the control systems that keep them in a state of hopeless poverty while protecting the wealthy.

Moreover, wild boys are in touch with nature and derive some of their powers and fighting techniques from the natural world. They seem to have a special relationship with wildlife, especially African wildlife, that enables them to use wild creatures as weapons. For instance, toward the conclusion of the novel readers learn that there are a variety of wild boy tribes, including mamba boys who command legions of mambas and cobras and cat boys who have made weapons by sewing claws into leather gloves and filling the claws with cyanide (153). By linking the wild boys so closely with nature and the natural world, Burroughs implies that industrialization, capitalism, and the control machine that protects them has led to the separation of man and nature; therefore, only by reconnecting with nature can the wild boys hope to destroy the machine. The conclusion of *The Wild Boys* shows the wild boy tribes winning their war against the West.

Africa is a suitable setting for *The Wild Boys* because Africa is the poorest continent, a continent that has seen massive famine in recent decades; yet Africa is also the home of many wealthy elites who enjoy lifestyles only slightly less lavish than that of A. J. One need only recall the lavish weddings and coronations of a number of contemporary African leaders for examples of obscene wealth existing alongside terrible poverty. When *The Wild Boys* appeared in 1969, it must have seemed unlikely that Burroughs's bleak vision of an over-populated world ravaged by gangs of young men could ever become reality. However, in 1997, any reader familiar with the news and television accounts of children warriors fighting in

Africa's wars or of thousands of young men looting Los Angeles will find Burroughs's novel frighteningly prophetic.

Congo: Everything Old Is New Again

While Burroughs exaggerates actual conditions in Africa to create a futuristic vision of what life might be like in the closing years of the twentieth century, Michael Crichton's *Congo* looks back to the traditional features of science fiction set in Africa. One reason Africa was a popular setting for the science fiction of H. Rider Haggard and Edgar Rice Burroughs was that some areas of the continent remained unexplored by Westerners in the early decades of the century; therefore, Haggard and Edgar Rice Burroughs could invent lost civilizations and fantastic creatures for their African works while clinging to the notion that anything might be possible in the recesses of the dark continent. Crichton also makes use of the idea that some regions of Africa remain unknown and, therefore, might harbor the sort of lost civilizations and undiscovered species that are a part of the science fiction of Edgar Rice Burroughs and Haggard. As Crichton points out in the introduction to *Congo*, an introduction that presents the events of the novel as being actual, the "northeastern corner of the Congo basin, where the rain forest meets the Virunga volcanoes" remains unexplored (xi). Crichton also notes that like the early explorers of Africa, the characters in *Congo* return from their journey with tales of "cannibals and pygmies, ruined jungle civilizations, and fabulous lost treasures" (xiii). Furthermore, Crichton borrows an idea form Jules Verne's *The Village in the Treetops* by including in *Congo* an ape that can communicate not only with its own kind but also with humans.

While Crichton incorporates many traditional notions about Africa into his story, he also delivers a great deal of factual information concerning Africa to his readers. *Congo*, then, due to its didactic component, is similar to other contemporary American novels set in Africa. For example, readers are informed that Zaire (renamed Congo after a May 1997 civil war that lead to the overthrow of dictator Mobutu Sese Seko) is the "richest country in black Africa, in minerals—the world's largest producer of cobalt and industrial diamonds, the seventh largest producer of copper. In addition there are also major deposits of gold, tin, zinc, tungsten and uranium" (4). Crichton also spends several pages giving readers a condensed history of Western knowledge about Africa; he explains that although Portuguese and British explorers attempted to map the central Congo in the sixteenth and seventeenth centuries, little was known about the area until the middle of the nineteenth century (57). Crichton also informs his readers about the history of cannibalism in the Congo region: "During the Congolese civil war in the 1960s, reports of widespread cannibalism and other atrocities shocked the Western world. But in fact cannibalism had always been openly practiced in central Africa. . . . In the Congo, cannibalism was not associated with ritual or religion or war; it was a simple dietary preference" (61).

Crichton's characters have come to the Congo basin in search of a special type of diamond called "Type IIb." Type IIb diamonds are worthless as gemstones, but they can be used to develop an advanced semiconductor that will allow computer engineers to gain an advantage over competition, an advantage measured in billions of dollars (114).

The characters in *Congo* work for a company called ERTS: Earth Resources Technology Services. Team members from ERTS are sent to the Congo, an area Crichton describes as a "vast, oversized, grey-green world—an alien place, inhospitable to man" (3), and certainly the rain forest is inhospitable to the first ERTS crew sent to look for the rare diamonds. The initial ERTS team comes upon a place the natives call *kanyamagufa*, "the place of bones" (5). The area is littered with the bones of small mammals as well as with the stone ruins of an ancient city. Native legend maintains that people entering this area will have their skulls crushed by a mysterious creature. And the first team is slaughtered; the bodies—and crushed skulls—are clearly seen through the satellite hookup that sends images to corporate headquarters in Houston, Texas. In addition to the destroyed camp and the scattered bodies, the video records the face of a large male gorilla. A second ERTS team is dispatched to the Congo to obtain the diamonds and determine what destroyed the first team.

The second team is headed by Dr. Karen Ross, a tall, blonde, twenty-four-year-old genius who is "attractive though ungainly" (12). In an attempt to understand the importance of the image of the gorilla, Dr. Ross contacts a primate researcher named Peter Elliot. Elliot has taught a mountain gorilla named Amy to communicate with humans by using sign language. Amy also draws a series of finger paintings that portray a "cluster of apparently related images: inverted crescent shapes, or semicircles, which are always associated with an area of vertical green streaks" (41). Elliot publishes Amy's finger paintings, and researchers compare Amy's paintings to sketches by a seventeenth-century Portuguese explorer who claimed to have located an incredible lost city called Zinj (59). It is suspected that Amy was born somewhere near the lost city and that if she is returned to the Congo region, she might be able to lead the team to the ruins. Elliot also hopes that Amy will assist in the study of gorillas in the field (72). The second ERTS team is headed by a mercenary named Munro. Munro must get the ERTS team to the ruined city and the diamonds before the competition, a Japanese syndicate, beats them to the rare gems.

In *Congo*, Crichton touches on nearly every feature traditionally associated with African settings. While Ross, Elliot, Amy, and Munro are flying over the region, Crichton reminds his readers that Africa is a vast, empty, hostile zone: "As one sat in the air-conditioned comfort of an airplane seat, it was impossible not to recognize that this vast, monotonous forest was a giant creation of nature, utterly dwarfing in scale the greatest cities or other creations of mankind" (143).

Indeed, in *Congo*, as in many other contemporary American novels set in Africa, the natural world seems to conspire against the characters; for example, after shooting some dangerous rapids, the team is attacked by "black clouds of mosquitoes" (192) and hippos overturn one of the team's rafts. And as if a vast, hostile natural environment did not provide enough challenge to the ERTS team, the team is threatened by a civil war that breaks out in Zaire. The Zairian army is searching for rebel Kigani, a tribe of cannibals who are on the hunt (162). Surface-to-air missiles are fired at the plane carrying the ERTS team, and the team members are forced to parachute to the jungle floor (153).

However, while Crichton's employment of these standard features of African settings is notable, it is his use of science fiction traditions concerning Africa that makes *Congo* such an unusual work of contemporary American fiction. No other contemporary American author emulates so clearly the African novels of H. Rider Haggard and Edgar Rice Burroughs. In *Congo* readers encounter a new race of horrifying creatures similar to what one might expect to find in a Tarzan novel, and the city of Zinj is similar to a number of lost African cities featured in the works of Burroughs and Haggard.

In one important way, Crichton's ruined city differs from the lost civilizations found in earlier science fiction set in Africa. Haggard's and Burroughs's lost cities were always the creations of Westerners, for instance, the lost Roman city of *Tarzan and the Lost Empire* and Haggard's lost city in *King Solomon's Mines*. Crichton's Zinj, however, is the creation of black Africans. From bas-reliefs on the walls of the city, the team members determine that the inhabitants of Zinj had been "relatively tall blacks with round heads and muscular bodies" who wore "elaborately decorated, colorful long robes" (235). In the days of Haggard and Burroughs, many Westerners doubted that Africans were capable of constructing great stone cities; in Crichton's time, research—especially research at sites such as the great Zimbabwe ruins—has proven such doubts to be unfounded.

The strange creatures featured in *Congo* are no less amazing than the ruined city of Zinj. The animals are a previously undiscovered species of gorilla; these gorillas have gray fur, and, instead of being shy and fearful of humans, they attack people on sight and kill them by crushing their victims' skulls with specially designed stone paddles.

At the conclusion of *Congo*, volcanic eruptions force the ERTS team to flee from Zinj without the rare diamond. Then the team is attacked by cannibals. Finally the team escapes in a balloon after leaving Amy behind to live in peace with the mountain gorillas.

Congo makes use of many literary traditions associated with African settings: a vast and hostile landscape, dangerous wildlife, civil war, savagery, and a heavy didactic component. However, *Congo* is most notable for its use of early science fiction traditions concerning Africa. The use of these traditions in a novel published in 1980 demonstrates that traditional beliefs about Africa are very powerful and very much alive.

PART II: SAFARI, WAR, EXPLORATION, AND HISTORY

African wildlife has been a feature of fiction set in Africa since the very beginning of the English novel; for instance, Defoe sets the early part of *Robinson Crusoe* in Africa, and Crusoe has encounters with a lion and a leopard as he sails down the African coast. However, it was not until the 1850s with the publication of Ballantyne's *The Gorilla Hunters* that novelists began to make big game hunting in Africa the center of their narratives. In this century, the subject of big game hunting in Africa has appealed to American as well as English novelists. For example, America's most famous author of safari and hunting fiction, Ernest Hemingway, approaches African animals as challenges that hunters must overcome as they prove their manhood and discover their self worth. Indeed, most of the safari fiction in the American novel since 1945 is either a homage to or a reaction against such Hemingway works as "The Short Happy Life of Francis Macomber" and *Green Hills of Africa*. For Hemingway and those who emulate him, the presence of dangerous wildlife is one of the reasons that Africa is a special zone—a place free of the constraints inherent in Western, industrial culture.

Big game hunting in Africa flourished during the colonial period and remained popular until the 1930s (Murray 10); Hemingway's first African safari took place in 1933. By the 1950s, however, hunting had begun to threaten big game in Africa and big game hunting was becoming passé. When Hemingway returned to Africa for safari in 1953–54, he was more interested in observing game than in shooting it (Murray 12). The golden age of the African safari was over by World War II, and most contemporary American authors writing safari fiction either look back to Africa's colonial past or bring old hunters out of retirement because of unusual circumstances that require their special skills. Sometimes, as is the case in *Henderson the Rain King*, characters are sent not on hunting trips but on photo safaris. Safari novels, then, focus on the challenges presented by wild Africa. For the most part, these stories embrace a man versus nature theme and attempt to demonstrate that encounters with wild Africa bring out the best in Western characters.

In addition to safari novels, contemporary American novelists have written a number of works dealing with war in Africa. Certainly, historical events since World War II have provided numerous examples of war on the continent, ranging from the struggles for independence in the 1950s and 1960s to the more recent civil wars that have affected such nations as Nigeria, Chad, Ethiopia, Angola, Rwanda, and Burundi. Africa, from the early days of imperialist conquest until the recent years of Cold War conflict, has been viewed as a battleground upon which major powers could confront each other; just as the continent is seen as a diseased zone because of the many ailments one can contract in Africa, the continent is also frequently considered to be a zone where wars and civil wars flourish. It is not surprising, then, that a number of action-adventure novels written by contemporary American authors should focus on military conflicts—real and imagined—in Africa. In fact, a sort of subgenre of the action-adventure novel—novels concerning the exploits of mercenaries in Africa—has developed. For instance, both Michael Mewshaw and William Harrison have written about the exploits of mercenaries in Africa, and British authors have also written novels about the adventures of hired soldiers working in Africa. Sometimes, as is the case with the works of Robert Ruark, adventure novels set in Africa merge safari stories and narratives of war and history.

Ruark's Bloody Country: *Something of Value* and *Uhuru*

Few novelists writing after World War II have been as heavily influenced by Hemingway's African fiction as Robert Ruark, and Ruark embraces many traditional notions about Africa—especially the notion that Africa is a savage, blood-drenched place. Ruark's best known novels, *Something of Value* and *Uhuru*, follow the Hemingway tradition in that much of the action centers around the exploits of big-game hunters who confront the dangers and challenges offered by African landscapes and wildlife. However, Ruark's African novels are more than action-adventure stories about hunting. Both *Something of Value* and *Uhuru* take up a broad range of topics including the history of British colonialism in Kenya, the effects of imperialism on traditional African cultures, the Mau Mau uprising, Kenya's struggle for independence from Britain, and Kenya's transition from colony to nation. In some ways, *Something of Value* and *Uhuru* are similar to novels written about the settlement of the American West; British settlers in Kenya are challenged by harsh environments, dangerous animals, and hostile native peoples.

Below the action-adventure surface of Ruark's novels lies a didactic intent, a desire to explain Africa and African politics to American readers. As Ruark notes in the introduction to *Something of Value*, to "understand Mau Mau it is first necessary to understand Africa [and] . . . to understand Africa you must understand a basic impulsive savagery that is greater than anything we 'civilized' people have encountered in two centuries" (i). However, while Ruark clearly details instances of African savagery, he also dramatizes savage actions on the parts of the white settlers of Kenya.

Something of Value is a story about two Africas, one native and one colonial. This double vision of life on the continent is present from the beginning of the story when Ruark introduces his two main characters: Peter McKenzie, the son of a white land owner, and Kimani, the son of Karanja—the headman on the McKenzie property. Peter and Kimani begin the novel as childhood friends, but they eventually become adversaries as Kimani embraces the Mau Mau creed and the struggle for independence while Peter becomes a safari leader who forgoes the hunting of African wildlife to take up the job of hunting down the rebellious Mau Mau.

It is through Peter's eyes that readers are given information about African landscapes and animals. On one safari, for example, an American couple is introduced to the varied landscapes of East Africa: the Serengeti, the crater valley at Ngoro-Ngoro, the forested highlands, and the M.M.B.A.—the "miles and miles of bloody Africa" that stretch into Kenya's remote northern wilderness (221).

During the safari sections of the novel, Ruark adopts many of the conventional uses of African settings established by Hemingway. For instance, dangerous animals are challenges that must be overcome, and they must be overcome in an honorable, sportsman-like fashion in order for a hunter to prove his value and his courage. Americans, especially the American couple—Tom and Nancy Deane— who travel to Africa, are refreshed and renewed by the continent. Indeed, the American characters in *Something of Value* openly compare the values of colonial Kenya to those of the United States in the 1950s. Ironically, some of the comparisons that the American characters make imply that Africa, despite its remoteness and lack of industrialization, is more "civilized" than America. For example, in Africa, Nancy Deane finds a "peaceful freedom from formal fears" (346). She mingles "casually with savages in wild villages where a white woman was a complete curiosity, and she also remembered that she would not walk through Harlem or take the dogs into the park because of the muggers and perverts in New York" (346).

Their African experiences save Tom's and Nancy's marriage. Nancy thinks that the safari has changed her husband for the better. Tom Deane has had "too much money and no work to do" (346), but the safari has allowed him to demonstrate his courage and worth by facing the challenge of dangerous wildlife. Nancy feels that the safari has caused her husband to forego the playboy life in New York, a life that Nancy feels would eventually lead to a divorce that would leave her "alimonied and miserable in my minks, lunching with the girls and cursing all men while wishing to Christ I had the same man back in the same bed" (346).

Tom believes that the safari has had a positive effect on Nancy because it has enabled her to see him as a real man, a "solid man operating where his father's money and his father's reputation weren't running heavy interference for him" (349). The African experience has kept Nancy from getting "too much into that charity-ball-committee routine back in New York, with the girl lunches and the I-hate-my-husband-club they have" (349). As a result of the safari, Tom plans to buy a ranch in Kenya where he and Nancy can raise "some boy-babies and teach them to shoot and ride horses and keep them the hell away from TV and comic books and the boons of civilization" (350). Like Hemingway's characters, Ruark's characters discover that their African experiences bring out their better qualities.

In addition to describing the world of big game hunting, Ruark also informs readers about Kenyan history and politics. Much of *Something of Value* is set during World War II, and Ruark is careful to note the changes—and the contradictions— brought about by the great war and to recall the traditional ways of native Africans before the coming of the British.

For instance, in one of the more insightful sections of the novel, Karanja, Kimani's father, recalls the old days and laments the changes he has witnessed in his long life. About his youth, Karanja remembers being circumcised, killing his first Masai, getting married, mourning his father's death, and the coming of the English (76). He remembers the tribal wars between the Kikuyu and the Masai, he recalls raping Masai women and taking them as slaves (76), and he compares the old intertribal wars to the more recent European wars. Karanja notes that the white man disapproved of intertribal warfare and forbid the Kikuyu and the Masai to fight, but the English had fought two world wars and had encouraged the Kikuyu to enlist (77).

Most of all, Karanja is saddened by the way his culture has been destroyed by the coming of the whites. He observes that the young have lost respect for the elders and the old ways, preferring to move to the city where they can waste away their time drinking and gambling (61). Ruark uses Karanja's recollections to educate readers about traditional African ways of life and to highlight the differences in European ways and African ways of interpreting things. For instance, when Karanja recalls the circumcision ceremonies, he describes the procedure in a manner that is clearly didactic, detailing the differences in male and female circumcision. Female circumcision, in which the clitoris and the "two major lips" are removed, is by far the more severe of the two procedures (73).

In fact, Ruark is the first contemporary American author to describe the procedure of female mutilation, a subject that Alice Walker explores in great detail in *Possessing the Secret of Joy*. However, Ruark, unlike Walker, is content to assess the procedure from an African male point of view without commenting on the sexist nature of traditional African culture.

Karanja continues to compare African ways to Western ways when he recalls the coming of the white men and their wives. When the white men first appear, Karanja is shocked to learn that they have only one wife. Karanja believes that white women have a magical power—their tears—which enables them to weaken and control their men (78).

The comparison of African ways and Western ways is continued later in the novel when Peter offers his views about Africans to some American clients who have come to Kenya on safari: "[A]n African understands right now. He doesn't understand tomorrow, and he forgets yesterday, because he's got no sense of time" (201). Peter goes on to say that Africans don't understand such concepts as love or kindness because for African men, women are simply beasts to be bought, sold, and used. And according to Peter, African religion is based on blood, pain, and torture—both of animals and humans (202).

Ruark offers no commentary concerning Peter's remarks about Africans just as he offers no commentary to Karanja's comments about Westerners. As an American, Ruark is an outsider looking in on the workings of colonial Kenya, and while it is apparent that he sympathizes with the white settlers, he is careful to let his readers decipher the biases that lie beneath both Karanja's observations about whites and Peter's observations about Africans.While Peter is busy establishing himself as a great white hunter, his childhood friend Kimani becomes a leader in the Mau Mau revolt against the British. After a fight with Peter's uncle, Kimani joins a group of Mau Mau hiding in a remote part of the Kenya highlands. Kimani begins his career as a rebel by sacking a ranch and stealing guns from a white settler. However, because Kimani has spent many years in the proximity of whites, he must be reeducated in order to become a full-fledged Mau Mau. He learns about rebel leader Jomo Kenyatta, and he is told that there "is no such thing as a *good* white man" (267).

To ensure the security of their movement, the Mau Mau take oaths. It is in the description of the Mau Mau oath taking that Ruark most forcefully accentuates the stereotype that Africans are savage beings. According to Ruark, a typical Mau Mau oath involves cruelty and cannibalism. In a scene meant to demonstrate that the oaths were used not only to secure the secrets of the Mau Mau but also to terrorize those Africans who are reluctant to follow the Mau Mau, a rebel leader name Njogu conducts a ceremony in which a man who objects to the oath is killed; the man's son is also slaughtered and their organs are harvested for an oath-taking ceremony (326–27).

Obviously, such descriptions reinforce the Western notions that Africans are barbaric beings. However, it is not only the African characters in *Something of Value* who resort to savagery; Western characters are also quite capable of behaving in a barbaric fashion, and for both African and Western characters, war is the catalyst that triggers savage behavior. For example, as the Mau Mau threat becomes more serious, Peter gives up hunting big game and begins hunting Mau Mau, and, at one point, British settlers and Masai warriors work together to conduct a "beat" of the Kikuyu Mau Mau that is similar to a "beat" for tigers (459).

Before long, however, Peter realizes that he has sunk to a brutish level. To get the captured Mau Mau to reveal the names of their leaders, the whites apply a number of tortures. For instance, in one case, an older Mau Mau is held while a settler digs out the captive's eyes with a knife (466). Another captive is castrated (466), and a third Mau Mau's heart is cut out of his chest while he is still alive (468). Peter himself takes part in the torture, cutting out the tongue of one Mau Mau and helping to behead several others (469).

The war with the Mau Mau strains colonial society to the breaking point: settlers walk the streets of Nairobi with Sten guns slung casually over their shoulders and pistols tucked into their belts, marriages are shattered as the men spend weeks and months in the bush hunting the Mau Mau, and the heavy drinking common to the colonial culture accelerates until it reaches a nearly nonstop pace (493). Finally, Peter realizes that the colonists themselves have created the Mau Mau problem by introducing Western ways to Africans and shattering traditional African ways of life.

Something of Value ends with Kenya on the brink of achieving independence from Britain. By having Peter rescue an African child who is about to be slaughtered along with his Mau Mau parents, Ruark symbolically suggests that it might be possible for Africans and white settlers to share the land and the new nation. Peter plans to raise the child as his own and to teach him "some of the nicer things I know" (560).

While the focus of *Something of Value* is the Mau Mau uprising and the Kenyan struggle for independence, *Uhuru* is about Kenya's transition from colony to free state; indeed, *uhuru* means *freedom* in Swahili. In *Uhuru*, Ruark continues to inform readers about African life and politics while reinforcing traditional Western notions about Africa.

The main character in *Uhuru* is a hunter and safari leader named Brian Dermott. Dermott likes to take his clients to the Northern Frontier, near Lake Rudolf—now known as Lake Turkana. The Kenya of *Uhuru* is a different country than that described in *Something of Value*. The golden age of the safari is over, and special licenses are required to take game animals such as elephants. In *Uhuru*, Kenya is no longer a frontier nation of small farms where settlers can rely on hunting to make up for irregular harvests. And Ruark is one of the first to note that Africa is becoming more and more Westernized as time passes. Early in the novel, for instance, Dermott says that Nairobi "has more boulevards than Paris, and more cinemas than London. . . . And we've even got a Drive-in. This one time buffalo-wallow, this elephant tract, is a metropolis now" (65). Dermott and other white characters lament the passing of Kenya's frontier and worry about the future of Kenya's wildlife after the Africans take control of the government. Objecting to what he calls the "black logic" of Kenya's African leaders, Dermott notes that some Africans have suggested that the wildlife in Kenya should be eliminated in order to push the nation toward development: "They think that a backward country can't show progress until after all the animals are dead and the land turned to agriculture. I've actually heard politicians say . . . that America didn't become great until you killed all your bison, and that England didn't become powerful until they eliminated the wolves. . . . All this [wild Africa] must go, to make . . . room for bloody shanty towns and piddling agricultural projects" (216).

While many of the white settlers adjust to the coming of Kenyan independence by moving to England, South Africa, or Australia, the African leaders in Kenya engage in a power struggle to determine which political faction will rule when Britain relinquishes control of the country. The main rivals for power are Matthew Kamua and Stephen Ndegwa. Kamua is a trade-union leader and "already the semiofficial voice of Kenya" (81) while Ndegwa is the leader of the old Kenya Moja—one Kenya party—and is considered moderate by the whites. Ndegwa wants independence later, gradually, with the whites and Asians integrated into an African majority while Kamua wants *"his independence now, all on a platter with himself as immediate Chief Minister"* (83). There are, then, two important plot lines to *Uhuru*; white settlers must deal with the coming independence of the nation, and African leaders must compete with each other and engage in political intrigue to determine who will rule the new country. Naturally, many of the whites have a dim view of the Africans' ability to rule. At one point, Dermont asks some Americans this question: "How much progress have you seen in Haiti, which has been black and free for over a hundred and sixty years? How much progress have you noticed in Ethiopia, which has been black and free for three thousand years, for God's sake?" (273).

In *Uhuru*, Ruark also uses the political and racial situation in Kenya as a way to comment on the civil rights struggle in the United States. Just as American blacks are fighting for equality under the law, blacks in Kenya are seeking civil rights; after independence, Africans in Kenya expect that the "color of a man's skin will not make any difference in the law courts" (131). However, Kenya's African leaders have a bleak opinion of both America and American blacks. For example, at one point Ndegwa describes America in these terms:

He had watched the budding of massive riots which had not yet fully fruited, and had smelled the active fear of the white man against his own coloreds; seen the bitter hatred of the American Negro for the white American. I wonder what the hell they expect of us here, if they hate each other so in the stronghold of Democracy . . . twenty million transplanted Africans who know nothing of their own Africa all ready to rise and strike down the white man in America—America the beautiful, America the bountiful, America the generous, America the frightened, America the stupid. (466)

Uhuru repeats many of the motifs that appear in *Something of Value*, and Ruark continues to describe such common African practices as female mutilation and polygamy. *Uhuru*, then, not only comments on Kenya's transition from colony to free state but also seeks to teach and inform readers of African political and cultural affairs.

Bellow's Unsafari: *Henderson the Rain King*

Nearly everything about *Henderson the Rain King* is a reaction to and a parody of Hemingway's safari fiction. *Henderson the Rain King* opens with Eugene Henderson asking himself a question: "What made me take this trip to Africa?" (3). Henderson is fifty-five years old when he buys his ticket to Africa, and, although he is rich, he is tortured by the complications of his life and by an inner voice that constantly whispers "I want" (24). A number of factors have left Henderson confused about his life and times, but he has been most disillusioned by war. He has seen combat in World War II and has survived when nearly all the others in his outfit have been killed (20). After the war, he returns to his estate in New York, raises pigs, divorces his first wife, and considers suicide.

Henderson calls himself a sufferer, and at one point he even wonders if suffering is his profession (25). Henderson believes that a change of place may offer a cure for his malaise. He first tries Europe, spending a year in France with his new lover (and soon-to-be second wife), but the results of European trip are dismal. Only Africa—an unindustrialized place that has largely escaped the ravages of World War II—can relieve the twentieth-century madness that haunts Eugene Henderson.

In several ways, Henderson resembles Jake, the main character of Hemingway's *The Sun Also Rises*. Just as Jake, the wounded veteran of World War I, finds renewal in Spain, Henderson, the wounded veteran of World War II, finds renewal in Africa. A number of critics have noted that Henderson's adventures in Africa parody the code of manliness detailed in Hemingway's fiction. After all, Henderson and Hemingway share the same initials (Kuzna 56), and Henderson "describes himself in terms and incidents reminiscent of Ernest Hemingway, larger and more legendary than life" (Anderson 67). Kuzna believes that "Henderson has begun to chart a course away from the heroic rhetoric of the Hemingway hero" (66), and Pifer sees

Henderson the Rain King as a "parody of a quest novel in which the hero comically bumbles his way through a mythic landscape" (16). Yet, despite its parody of the Hemingway code, *Henderson the Rain King* conforms to many typical Western notions about Africa; most importantly, Africa offers Henderson a second chance at life.

The therapeutic power of Africa on Henderson is immediate. As he flies across the continent, he remarks that "Africa reached my feelings right away even in the air" (42). The climate and the landscape agree with him: "the heat was just what I craved. . . . [T]he colors themselves did me a world of good. I didn't feel the pressure in the chest, nor hear the voice within" (43). Henderson has traveled to Africa with his friend Charlie and Charlie's wife, but soon he tires of their company and decides to strike out into the more remote areas of the continent with only a guide, Romilayu.

After leaving his American companions, Henderson abandons his jeep because the area that Romilayu promises to show him is so remote that it can only be reached by foot. Soon, Henderson is lost. Being lost, however, does not trouble him because the purpose of Henderson's journey to Africa is to "leave certain things behind" (45). The things Henderson wants to leave behind are the things the of the twentieth-century Western world: mechanized war, industrialization, materialism, and estrangement from nature. What Henderson must do is strip himself of the accouterments of Western civilization so that he may come to a realization about himself; therefore, Henderson's safari is a safari of loss. As Henderson travels into the remote interior of the African continent, he loses everything: his jeep, his gun, his clothes, and, finally, his old identity when he is given a new name: Sungo.

After several days of hiking, Henderson finds himself in the middle of nowhere, and in a passage that echoes the old notion that Africa is an empty, timeless place, Henderson notes that he has finally gotten "away from everything" to a simple place where there are "no human footprints" and "no history or junk like that" (46).

Pifer observes that the "*terra incognita* Henderson discovers cannot be plotted on the map; this exotic territory eludes spatial coordinates as it defies conventional categories of time" (16). In fact, the topography through which Henderson and Romilayu travel is described in the vaguest terms; Henderson reports that "for days he [Romilayu] led me through villages, over mountain trails, and into deserts, far, far, out" (45).

Perhaps Bellow refuses to locate Henderson in any specific African place because his feelings are similar to those of Henderson who thinks geography is "one of those bossy ideas according to which, if you locate a place, there's nothing more to be said about it" (55). It is more likely, however, that Bellow is vague about the setting of his novel because of the tone and intent of his story. Vagueness about location and time are elements well-suited to both comic literature and quest stories, and Lutwack notes that quest literature often involves a journey to timeless and remote places where heroes can have visionary experiences that are either regenerative or shattering (57).

Henderson the Rain King is a highly symbolic novel that readers can interpret on several levels (King 44). Some of the best use of symbolism involves Henderson's encounters with two African tribes: the Arnewi and the Wariri. In fact, the tribes themselves symbolize two different cultural systems found in traditional Africa. The Arnewi are peaceful cattle herders, and the Wariri are warriors. Moreover, Henderson's actions toward these tribes symbolize typical Western reactions to Africans and African situations.

Henderson's encounters with the Arnewi and the Wariri come at moments of crisis for the tribes. Both the Wariri and the Arnewi are threatened by drought, and Henderson forces himself upon both tribes as they attempt to deal with problems inherent in the African environment.

While among the Arnewi, Henderson misreads every situation he encounters. Hoping to entertain some Arnewi children, Henderson lights a dry bush that "went flaming, almost invisible in the strong sunlight" (48). The Arnewi children are more frightened than entertained by Henderson's parody of Moses's biblical miracle, and they flee to the safety of their village. Henderson remarks, "I meant well" (48), but the incident only foreshadows the way in which Henderson's good intentions toward the Arnewi lead to trouble.

In fact, one of the most famous scenes in *Henderson the Rain King* is clearly meant to criticize Western good intentions and to highlight the way in which Western faith in technology has meant disaster for many Africans. Itelo, the English-speaking king of the Arnewi, explains to Henderson that the drought is killing the Arnewi cattle. But Henderson has seen a cistern full of water, and he wonders why the tribe is letting its cattle die of thirst. King Itelo explains that the Arnewi won't use the water from the cistern because frogs have suddenly and mysteriously appeared in the pond; an Arnewi taboo prevents the tribe from using water that is inhabited by animals (59). Of course, to Henderson, the Arnewi taboo seems like silly superstition. In his enthusiasm to help the Arnewi survive the drought, Henderson employs Western technology to rid the cistern of the troublesome frogs. He builds a bomb meant to kill the frogs, but the ensuing explosion destroys the stone wall that contains the water in the cistern and the Arnewi's reserve of water is lost (109). The scene involving the frogs clearly symbolizes the destruction of traditional African ways of life that has resulted from the introduction of Western technology in Africa.

The destruction of the Arnewi's water reserve marks the first of several important lessons that Henderson must learn on his African voyage to self discovery. As Pifer notes, it is not until this catastrophe that Henderson pauses to consider whether his Western technology gives him the right to tamper with the Arnewi way of life (23). Though the peaceful Arnewi still consider Henderson a friend, he leaves their village in shame, knowing that instead of alleviating their sufferings he has only contributed to their troubles.

After the fiasco with the Arnewi, Henderson and Romilayu walk on for ten more days until they encounter the Wariri. Romilayu has told Henderson that the Wariri are children of darkness (114), and Henderson believes that he will be unlikely "to do any damage . . . [to] such . . . savages" (115). Romilayu and Henderson soon find themselves facing an armed band of Wariri, and Henderson surrenders his rifle (117). The Wariri are indeed fierce; they house Henderson and Romilayu with a corpse, and they offer no food or water to Henderson and his guide. Henderson also sees a number of bodies hanging upside down from scaffolds, and he assumes, correctly, that executions are being carried out (149).

Moreover, the first impression made by Dahfu, the king of the Wariri, is not a comforting one. As he sits down to face the king, Henderson notices a large wooden bowl containing a "couple of skulls, tilted cheek to cheek" (154). Dahfu, however, turns out to be an educated and kindly man trapped by the conventions of his tribe and by his duty to his people; the skulls are only for ceremony.

Dahfu seems to lead an enviable existence—he is attended by numerous wives who fulfill his every request—but as Henderson soon learns, when the king is too old to satisfy all his wives, he will be dragged into the bush and strangled (157). Henderson has heard the roar of a lion inside the Wariri compound, and Dahfu explains that after an aging king is strangled, a lion cub is brought to the village to symbolize the reign of a new king. After a certain amount of time has passed, a priest will announce that the lion has "converted into the next king. This will be my successor" (157). The lion that Henderson hears is not the reincarnation of a dead Wariri king; she is, however, a favorite of King Dahfu who believes humans can absorb the essence of lionhood by associating with lions.

Like their neighbors the Arnewi, the Wariri are suffering from the effects of the drought. And while he is visiting the Wariri, Henderson again intervenes, complicating the situation and taking yet another step on his voyage to self discovery. Henderson breaks the drought by lifting and moving Mummah, the great stone fertility goddess of the Wariri (192). Having accomplished this feat, Henderson is given a new name, Sungo—the Rain King.

The most striking difference in Henderson's story and that of a typical Hemingway hero on safari in Africa is the role played by African wildlife, particularly the lion. In Hemingway's African fiction, big game is seen as a dangerous challenge that must be defeated to allow characters to prove their mettle, demonstrate their courage, and achieve a deeper realization of self. In the Hemingway scheme of things, nature is a hostile force, and Western characters, Macomber for example, must demonstrate their superiority over nature by slaying dangerous creatures.

In *Henderson the Rain King*, nature and African wildlife are still viewed as dangerous forces—a point demonstrated when Dahfu is killed by the lion he is assigned to capture (312)—but instead of proving his worth by slaying a wild creature, Henderson gets back in touch with nature (and, therefore, back in touch with himself) by accommodating and appreciating dangerous animals instead of slaying them.

As Anderson notes, Dahfu "is that recurring Bellowian wise man who can create the vision for Bellow's heroes that they cannot construct or call up for themselves" (71). Dahfu reshapes Henderson by forcing Henderson to expose himself to a lion named Atti. Dahfu wants Henderson to overcome his fear of the lion and develop the characteristics of a lion. About Atti, Dahfu tells Henderson, "She will have an influence upon you as she has had upon me" (225). Unfortunately, while trying to capture the lion that represents his ancestor's spirit, Dahfu is killed. Henderson is declared the new king, and to escape his eventual murder by the high priest of the Wariri tribe, he and his guide flee from the Wariri village, taking with them a lion cub that is supposed to be the vessel for the soul of Dahfu. As Henderson explains, "The king would want me to take it along. . . . Look, he's got to survive in some form" (326).

The contrast between Bellow's use of African wildlife and Hemingway's use of African wildlife is best illustrated by the conclusion to *Henderson the Rain King*. After hiking across the African wilderness for several days, Henderson and Rami-layu return to civilization. Henderson, who has been plagued by fever for most of the time he has been in Africa, is bedridden for several weeks, and, after his recovery, he returns to America with the lion cub in tow. That the African journey has reconnected Henderson with nature and put him at peace with himself is indicated by a memory Henderson recalls as he and the lion are flying across the Atlantic. As a young man who had become estranged from his father, Henderson left home and joined a Canadian carnival. Part of his job while with the carnival was to ride the roller coaster with an old, trained bear named Smolak. Henderson remembers that

Smolak and I rode on a roller coaster together before large crowds. . . . By a common bond of despair we embraced, cheek to cheek, as all support seemed to leave us and we started down the perpendicular drop. I was pressed into his long-suffering, age-worn, tragic, and discolored coat as he grunted and cried to me. At times, the animal would wet himself. But he was apparently aware I was his friend and he did not claw me. . . . And the great thing is that he didn't blame me. He had seen too much of life, and somewhere in his huge head he had worked it out that for creatures there is nothing that ever runs unmingled. (338–39)

As an adult, Henderson becomes somewhat like his old friend Smolak the bear. Before his trip to Africa, Henderson thinks of himself as a long-suffering and tragic character who has seen too much of life. His African experiences, especially those in the company of King Dahfu, have healed Henderson. The division between man and nature so apparent in the war-torn and industrialized West has been breached via Henderson's encounters with the lions of the Wariri. At the conclusion of his journey, Henderson has not solved all the dilemmas that challenge him, but he is able to face life instead of avoiding it and dreaming of death (King 50).

Both Hemingway and Bellow see Africa and African wildlife as catalysts that can spark epiphanies and changes in their characters; however, for Henderson the epiphany does not come from defeating, destroying, or controlling nature. Hender-son's experiences with the frogs in the land of the Arnewi demonstrate the futility of attempting to control nature, and his experiences with lions in the land of the Wariri demonstrate the rewards that can be found when humans regain their sense of being part of the natural order of things. *Henderson the Rain King*, then, rejects the Western idea that nature must be controlled. People must embrace the natural world just as Henderson and Smolak embraced on the frightful roller coaster rides.

Sounding an Alarm: Mewshaw's *The Toll*

Michael Mewshaw's *The Toll* differs from other contemporary American action-adventure novels set in Africa in several ways. Although the novel contains a flashback set in Nigeria, most of the action in *The Toll* unfolds in Morocco; action-adventure novels set in Africa usually take place in sub-Saharan nations, most often in East Africa. Moreover, while authors such as Ross Thomas, Robert Ruark, and John Updike employ African settings as a means of commenting on the civil rights movement and race relations in the United States, Mewshaw is alone in comparing political events in Africa to the political unrest that affected the United States in the late 1960s and early 1970s. *The Toll* is a jail-break story that uses events in Morocco as an analogy that comments on political events in America.

The Toll begins when a burnt-out, forty-year-old mercenary named Ted Kuyler meets up with a group of American young people who have expatriated to Morocco. The group of Americans is a microcosm of the American youth counterculture of the 1960s. They call themselves the Gravy Train, and, after the hippie scene in San Francisco becomes a bad trip, the commune embarks on a journey to India. The young Americans make it as far as Morocco before the group falls apart due to illness and drug abuse (33). The few remaining members of the Gravy Train, an overweight blond girl named Puff, her boyfriend Gypsy, a lame graduate student called Phil, a kid named Ants, and a pretty but unkempt young woman called Bret, team up with Polo, a former Weatherman. Polo is wanted in the United States for his part in the Chicago Days of Rage riots, and he uses the other Americans to run guns to rebels in southern Morocco. When Gypsy gets busted on a weapons charge, Polo and the others hire Kuyler to help them break their friend out of a Moroccan jail. Polo calls Gypsy a political prisoner and he wants to free the Moroccan "political prisoners" when Gypsy is liberated (10).

Kuyler says he is a soldier of misfortune because of his disappointing combat experiences. He has fought in Korea, and, after two terms in Vietnam, he quit the army. To prove his courage, be fights with the Ibo in the Nigeria–Biafra War. (American novelists who have written about this conflict always place their sympathetic characters on the Ibo side, perhaps because the Ibo were underdogs fighting for independence.) Mewshaw is one of the first to incorporate the tribal conflict in Nigeria into American fiction, and Kuyler's experience in Nigeria is particularly horrifying. After being separated from his unit, Kuyler hides in an abandoned village. When Nigerian troops occupy the village, Kuyler is forced to beat a young child to death to evade capture (25). After escaping from Nigeria shortly before the Ibo are defeated, Kuyler drifts across Morocco, looking for work and turning down several potential jobs because they are too unsavory. In fact, Kuyler has a highly developed sense of right and wrong. For instance, he decides not to work in South Africa when he discovers that he will be responsible for oppressing blacks (21). Finally, Kuyler is contacted by the members of the Gravy Train who seek his help in breaking their friend Gypsy out of a small-town jail before he is moved to the high-security prison in Casablanca.

Again and again, Mewshaw ties his characters' actions in Morocco to political events in the United States. For instance, Mewshaw compares political violence in the United States to political violence in the Third World and comments on the American counterculture's attitude toward lesser-developed nations. Recalling the attempted liberation of the Soledad Brothers from a California courtroom, an attempt that led to four deaths and left activist Angela Davis in jail for eighteen months before she was cleared of charges that she was involved in the escape attempt, Kuyler asks if the members of the Gravy Train would break Gypsy out of a prison in the United States. One of the hippies answers:

"For sure. Why not?"
"Wait a minute. Say he was at the Marin County courthouse about to be sent to San Quentin."
"Okay, I read the papers. What are you trying to do, gimme nightmares? Like I really don't believe this is the best time to remind anyone of that Jonathan Jackson horror show."
"Then you wouldn't do it?"
"All right, if Gypsy had been busted in the States, he'd be out on bail. . . . You see? And say he was convicted, he'd have umpteen appeals, a chance for early parole, and even at San Quentin he'd be better off than at Casablanca."
"What you're saying, then, is you respect the American system and wouldn't take things into your own hands. Here, in Morocco, you think you have a right to."
Phil, laboring methodically toward a conclusion, didn't laugh. "You know what it adds up to? Our plan, our whole attitude? Racism. A very subtle, condescending form of racism." (125–26)

Moreover, to point out the flaws in the American youth culture's longing to escape the United States for Third World countries such as Morocco, Mewshaw highlights the hardships faced by the citizens of Morocco. At one point, a member of the Gravy Train notes that "in a county like Morocco, going native and living organically means catching worms, hepatitis or dysentery and dying of old age at thirty-five" (137). Later, one of the other hippies in the Gravy Train remarks that "Being in Morocco has proved to me that bad as things are in the States, there's still a chance to change them. We have fantastic advantages over this country" (138).

In addition to making references to political radicalism in the United States and comparing that radicalism with violent political action in Morocco, the specter of the Vietnam War lurks behind many of the scenes in *The Toll*. Kuyler has served in Vietnam, and he notes that "even the archest patriot had to suspect that the side which was willing to sacrifice most—the side that could survive without massage parlors or smack shooting galleries—would win" (149). Eventually, *The Toll* makes the liberation of Gypsy into a metaphor for American actions in Vietnam. America destroyed Vietnam in order to save it; Gypsy is eventually destroyed by the effort that is meant to rescue him.

Just as the attempt to free the black radicals from the Marin County courtroom led to bloodshed, so does the attempt to free Gypsy from the Moroccan jail. The former Weatherman, Polo, insists on liberating all the Moroccan prisoners as well as Gypsy. This intention infuriates a Moroccan guard who has been bribed to help free the American, and in the ensuing gunfight several prisoners, the guard, and Gypsy's brother Phil are killed. Kuyler, Gyspy, and the remaining Americans flee the small town of Tazenzit in the chaos that follows the jail break. Their strategy is to escape Morocco by crossing into Algeria, a nation that, during the 1970s, was friendly to American radicals and leftists.

Once the Americans have broken Gypsy out of the small-town jail, the landscape of Morocco begins to play an important role in *The Toll*. The land and the elements seem to conspire against the Americans as they drive across a remote section of Morocco and make their way toward the border. Like many other American novelists setting works in Africa, Mewshaw describes African landscapes as empty wastelands. The first obstacle the Americans encounter on their flight to Algeria is the Anti-Atlas range: "the peaks were lost in clouds which had sunk lower until they'd massed solidly at the snow line. Devoid of sun and shadow, the land disclosed its true starkness. The mountains became a forbidding, monotonous barrier" (187). As the Americans cross the mountains in a Land Rover and a Renault, a storm gathers, fog forms, and the vehicles have a difficult time negotiating the rough road. Soon sleet begins to fall, and the road becomes a "sheet of beveled glass" (190). As they drop into a valley, the sleet changes to snow and through "the treeless waste, telephone poles were the only landmarks" (191). As the snow turns to rain, the Americans find that the road is nearly blocked by flash flooding. However, the land and the elements are not the only obstacles in the path of the Americans as they attempt to escape. While the group stops along the road to wait out the storm, Polo learns from the short-wave radio that rebels have attempted to unseat Morocco's king. Soon Polo gets his chance to fight when the Americans shoot it out with Moroccan troops near the Algerian border. Gypsy is wounded, and one by one all of the Americans except for Kuyler and Burt are killed. Their vehicles shot to pieces and the road ahead of them blocked, Kuyler, Burt, and the dying Gypsy take to the desert in a desperate attempt to hike thirty miles to Algeria. After a final confrontation with Moroccan troops, Kuyler murders a nomad for his camel and the Americans continue their trek. Again, Mewshaw descries the landscape as "empty," "sterile," and "lunar" (328–29).

Kuyler and Burt finally cross the border and reach a paved road that leads north to the Mediterranean. However, Gypsy has died along the way, and the actions Kuyler has taken to assure his and Bert's survival—particularly the murder of the Moroccan for his camel—have killed the love that Bert and Kuyler had found. *The Toll*, then, not only incorporates many conventions concerning African landscapes and nature's hostility toward humans into its plot, the novel also uses the Moroccan setting and the actions of the Americans as a way to comment on political affairs, especially the radical youth movement of the 1960s and the 1970s. *The Toll* is a warning to all who would embrace violence as a means to achieve political change;

the costs of embracing violent political action are high, and the desired results are rarely achieved.

A History of a Place: *The Covenant* by James A. Michener

Like several other contemporary American novels set in Africa—Yerby's *The Dahomean*, Chase-Riboud's *Echo of Lions*, and Harrison's *Burton and Speke*—James A. Michener's *The Covenant* is a historical novel. Michener's history of South Africa is, beyond all, well detailed. Michener begins *The Covenant* with an account of what South Africa was like in prehistoric times; he then dramatizes the entire history of the region and its people up until the time of the novel's publication. This is a lot of material, and *The Covenant* is a lengthy work—873 pages, excluding the glossary and genealogical charts. *The Covenant*, then, provides a wealth of information about Africa, and it is certainly the most straightforward, if not the most artful, of the historical novels concerning the continent.

The Covenant is arranged chronologically, and it attempts to recreate most—if not all—of the major events in South African history. While he admits that he has invented many of the characters who witness these events, Michener points out that the historical events he describes, especially the Great Trek, are "faithfully summarized" (i). Readers of *The Covenant* will quickly come to understand that the history of this region is a history of conquest in which migrating populations confront each other across a vast landscape.

According to Michener's account, the earliest inhabitants of the region, a people known as the San, stood about "four feet ten inches high" and were "yellowish brown in color" (3). For the San, the land provides food in the form of wildlife but it also presents challenges: the region is frequently plagued by drought, and the San—sometimes referred to as bushmen—often have difficulty finding water. Michener begins his tale by dramatizing the plight of one San clan and their hunt for a rhinoceros, a hunt that one of them records in a cave painting (15).

Unfortunately, Michener insists on interjecting editorial commentary into the story: "In the 1980s experts from other continents would hear of this rhinoceros and come to stand in awe at the competence of the artist who had created it" (15). Indeed, Michener stops his story in many places throughout the novel to give a commentary on the events he has described, and these interruptions do little more than weaken the pace of this immense work.

The second chapter, titled "Zimbabwe," details an incursion into the land of the San. Seeking pasturage for their herds, black Africans from the north come into contact with the small brown people, and gradually the San are pushed off the land: "There were fierce clashes between the two groups but never a pitched battle; had there been, the end result might have been more humane, because as things turned out, the little brown people were being quietly smothered" (33). The chapter also describes the construction of Zimbabwe's stone ruins. Michener correctly points out that early European explorers of the region could not make themselves believe that black Africans were capable of constructing such impressive stone buildings (61).

The following chapters deal with the South African explorations of the Portuguese, the Dutch, and the British. With each new group comes conflict with those who had previously settled the vast region. The Dutch settlers soon exterminate many of the Hottentots (108), and as the Dutch continue to explore further and further into the interior of South Africa, they are stricken by the harsh beauty and vastness of the region. Describing one exploration by the trekboers, Michener writes that "they saw wonders that no settler had ever seen before: rivers of magnitude, and vast deserts waiting to explode into flowers, and most interesting of all, continual series of small hills, each off to itself, perfectly rounded at the base" (270).

Before long, the trekboers encounter the Xhosa, a powerful tribe working its way south from central Africa: "and so the battles began, the blacks claim land which was theirs by hereditary right, the trekborer grabbing the same land because it had been promised to the children of God" (280).

The Dutch, however, find they are caught in the middle between the Xhosa to the north and the British who are occupying the region from the south, and so on "15 March 1836 the van Doorn party . . . crossed the Orange River . . . leaving the jurisdiction of England" (449). The Great Trek begins when "nearly two thousand wagons . . . move to the north" (451). The Dutch are challenged by Zulu warriors, and in a scene reminiscent of an American Western, a Boer wagon train is surrounded and the Dutch settlers fight off a Zulu attack (458).

Later, Michener details the events of the Battle of Blood River, in which 12,500 Zulu "threw themselves over a period of two hours on a cleverly entrenched foe, and without modern weapons of any kind, attempted to overwhelm a group of tough, resolute men armed with rifles, pistols and cannon" (485). In the end the trekkers slay four thousand Zulu warriors without losing a single man (486). The battle is a microcosm of the conquest of Africa; native peoples, no matter how courageous, stood little chance against Western technology.

The Covenant continues in this manner; one historical event after another—all the way up to and including the struggle against apartheid—is dramatized through the exploits of characters who are representative of the real figures. The didactic intent of Michener's detailed history of South Africa is the main strength of the novel, and, although the delivery of the information is sometimes strained, Michener has clearly done his research and the presents the data in a fair-minded way.

Who's Hunting Whom: James L. Haley's *The Lions of Tsavo*

James L. Haley's *The Lions of Tsavo* is a novelization of J. H. Patterson's classic nonfiction work, *The Man-Eaters of Tsavo*. Patterson was a British military officer who was engaged to supervise the construction of the Uganda Railway during the final years of the nineteenth century. The railway would eventually link Uganda with the port city of Mombasa, on the east coast of Africa, but construction of the line was disrupted in late December 1898 when man-eating lions began to drag Indian workers from their camps (Patterson 20). *The Lions of Tsavo* focuses on the struggle between man and nature in Africa, and the novel is also a valuable source of information about the British colonization of East Africa and the use of Indian laborers in the conquest of Kenya.

Haley begins his novel with a comment about the African landscape: "Perhaps the strangest thing about the wilderness was its sameness. It was not 'scenery.' White Europeans, who were used to the pastoral countryside of a casual holiday, were not prepared for the deep fastness of a realm so primitive that it knew man before he was man, and accorded him no importance" (1).

In *The Lions of Tsavo*, nature is hostile, not indifferent, to humans; wild Africa seems to conspire to halt the progress of Europeans as they attempt to conquer the continent. The dangers presented by the wildlife of Africa are apparent from the early pages of the story. Patterson and two companions set up a tent alongside the tracks after a day's ride on the train. In the middle of the night, one of Patterson's companions is dragged from the tent by a man-eater (6). Moreover, lions are not the only wild creatures that the railway builders must battle. Elephants searching for water in the arid land that surrounds the Tsavo river valley dig up and turn over bridge works (10), and Patterson and another British officer, Dalgairns, must hunt down and kill the elephant responsible for the destruction (18).

The landscape of the East African wilderness also has traumatic effects on the British and their families. For example, Margaret Dalgairns is at first very unhappy with her husband's African assignment, and her unhappiness is sparked, at least in part, by the African landscape. When asked why she hates Kenya, Margaret replies: "You can't ever see the sun go down. We can look across the valley to the east and see it come up, but the whole time we've lived here I've yet to see a proper sunset. The days just aren't symmetrical, somehow, without that" (29). However, Margaret, like so many other characters in contemporary American fiction set in Africa, eventually comes to love Africa, and her life is transformed by Africa. At the conclusion of the novel, she has forgotten the hardships that the continent presents and takes great pleasure in schooling African children (259).

Like many other contemporary American authors setting their works in Africa, Haley sees the continent in traditional terms; therefore, Haley frequently uses the words *empty* and *primitive* to describe Africa. Moreover, in addition to fighting the climate and the hostile wildlife, the builders of the railroad are also faced with numerous diseases; both the British and the Indian workers are threatened by dysentery, malaria, black water fever, and bilharzia.

Beyond the description of the hunt and the promotion of the old notions that Africa is an empty and primitive zone hostile to humankind, *The Lions of Tsavo* offers a number of important lessons about Africans and the Indians the British have brought to Africa. For example, readers are told about the slave trade that flourished in East Africa before being halted by the British: "The Masai would go out and catch all the Kikuyu, or whomever they could . . . and conduct them down to the coast" (171), and about the customs of the Masai: "They will greet you with much spitting on your hands and your faces. You must accept this and do it also with them. Do not show offense at their spit" (189). Haley also provides details about the punishment Masai girls suffer if they become pregnant before they are circumcised: "They saw on the ground before them the body of a girl—naked, pinned to the ground by stakes through her hands and thighs. Her belly had been ripped open and most of her organs eaten; the hyena tracks . . . were still fresh" (192).

Haley's story also makes it clear that the British are afraid of their Indian workers. When Patterson and the other British officers hear a scream from the Indian camp, they assume that the lions have struck again, but the British are reluctant to investigate because, as Dalgairns explains, "A European? Go in the uproaring collie camp, after dark? Certainly not; it would be folly" (24).

The Indian workers become so afraid of the lions that they consider the lions to be spirits or devils, not ordinary animals. The British soon acknowledge the fact that they must hunt down and kill the lions before the workers strike and refuse to help with the construction of the railroad. Eventually, a professional hunter named Pieter Verwoerd, a "Boer from South Africa" who has "experience with man-eaters" (94) takes up the task of dealing with the lions that plague the Tsavo railway.

Verwoerd attempts to ambush the lions by staking out goats for bait and waiting for the lions to appear while he is protected inside a railway car with boarded up windows. However, when the "coolies had boarded up the windows, they had not made the loopholes [for the rifle barrel] wide at all, and while the air inside was hot and stagnant . . . Verwoerd could press his face against a crack and tell that the air outside had cooled" (111). Eventually, tired of waiting for the lions to appear, Verwoerd steps outside the car for air. When he goes back inside, he forgets to latch the door, and he dozes off to sleep. He awakes to find a lion biting off his face (112). When Patterson and Dalgairns discover Verwoerd's remains the next morning, all they find are a "number of long bones" and his head; "the tongue and fleshy parts of the face had been bitten away" (116).

Eventually, Patterson is successful in his quest and the lions are killed, but for much of the novel, it is the lions that are on safari and the hunters become the hunted. All of African nature seems to be hostile to the construction of the Tsavo railway, but it is the man-eaters that best symbolize natural Africa's resistance to Western imperialism and its advanced technology, technology destined to forever change an Africa that the West had considered timeless for many centuries.

Africa According to William Harrison

William Harrison has set four novels in Africa: *Africana, Savannah Blue, Burton and Speke,* and *Three Hunters. Africana* is a war story that employs African settings to promote the theme that violence and terror are at the heart of what passes for "civilization." *Savannah Blue* is a murder mystery that draws attention to the ways in which Western materialism and industrialization have destroyed much of Africa. *Burton and Speke* is a fictionalized account of the mid-nineteenth-century race to discover the source of the Nile, and *Three Hunters* is a safari novel that contrasts past and present-day Kenya while alerting readers to the horrors of the refugee camps that have sprung up across Africa in recent years. To some degree, all of Harrison's African novels touch on the notion that the modern world has become dominated by corporations and bureaucracies that have stripped away the worth of the individual, a value that can only be fully understood when people exist in natural or wild environments and directly face the challenges offered by these environments.

Africana is, in some ways, a fable that comments on the violence that characterizes the twentieth century. Harrison begins *Africana* with language that establishes the fable-like tone of the novel: "There was once a soldier named Leo who was also a philosopher. He had a small private army of mercenaries in Africa, was in love with a woman named Val, and had a friend named Harry of whom he was afraid. They went to Africa because that was a well-known place for savages. There they met many people as well as various ghosts and shadows" (15).

Furthermore, Harrison's description of Africa in the early pages of the novel also helps to establish the tone of *Africana*. The story begins with a passage that provides a condensed description of the entire continent and reinforces the notion that Africa is a mysterious, unsettling zone that is hostile to humankind. Harrison informs his readers that the harmattan, a dry wind that blows down from the Sahara, covers the jungles of central Africa with a "fine dust" (15). Natural Africa is depicted as a hostile element against which people must continually struggle: "A few farms have been hacked out of this middle jungle that goes around the continent like a thick belt"; farmers must "beat back the undergrowth" to plant crops, and, after a while, the forest grows back and "orchids creep in like delicate killers" (16). As Leo, one of the main characters in the novel, observes, a person's relationship to the jungle "becomes episodic, like war; the creature of the field survives only one embattled day at a time" (16). One can easily lose one's bearings in such a setting where "nature overgrow[s] all strategies and directions and claims everything while the *harmattan* obliterates definition" (17).

From this beginning, Harrison proceeds to weave a story that describes the horror and violence that have affected much of Africa since World War II, a story that implies that violence, even random violence, is the most characteristic feature of "civilization." The African settings are essential to the theme of *Africana* because by playing on the commonly held notion that Africa is a savage, brutal, and uncivilized region, Harrison is able to expose the violent underbelly of Western culture. For Harrison, the irony is that the West sees Africa as savage yet the West is at least as violent and savage—if not more so—than any African culture.

In addition to this thematic statement about the nature of "civilization," *Africana* contains a wealth of information about the African continent; therefore, like numerous other contemporary American novels with African settings, *Africana* has a substantial didactic component. Much of the information about Africa is released in the form of notes from Val's journal. Val, the most important female character in *Africana*, is a Londoner who longs for a life of adventure. She goes to Africa as a journalist, hooks up with Leo, then decides she prefers Harry. Harrison drops paragraphs from Val's journal into the novel on a number of occasions, and each comment contains some unusual fact about Africa. For example, from Val readers learn that tourists driving across the Serengeti are chasing the cheetah and causing the big cats to die of heart attacks (36). In fact, Harrison incorporates a wealth of information about African wildlife into his novels. The creature that for Harrison best symbolizes the nature of Africa is the leopard, an animal that appears as both a character and a symbol in *Africana* and *Three Hunters*. Unlike lions, leopards have not become accustomed to the presence of humans.

While Val writes, Harry, Leo, and the Elite Rifles fight in the Congo, where they secure a fortune, and in Biafra, where they battle for the Ibo and their doomed dream of independent statehood. Leo delivers much of the thematic content of *Africana*. As a reward for his service in Africa during World War II, the Crown grants Leo a tract of land in Kenya. He sells his land and establishes a private police force that helps white settlers combat the Mau Mau rebels who threatened Kenya in the 1950s.

Describing Leo's opponents, Harrison writes: "These were black men who practiced all the taboos and wild fancies of a mysterious jungle protocol; . . . these were a people to whom the white man had sent missionaries and clothes. Now the outside world had sent its other manifestation, Leo" (24). And, later, Harrison comments on Leo's war against the Mau Mau in these terms: "Welcome to real savagery: play this on your drums village to village" (25). Leo, then, is meant to symbolize an important component of Western civilization; he can even be considered the true incarnation of Western values.

Leo is given to drinking Carlsberg beer and delivering speeches to his troops. These speeches contain the essence of Leo's philosophy. For instance, in one speech, Leo tells his men: "*Civilization has rules for war, chivalrous ways of harming people. . . . The rules are always broken and in terrible ways. . . . [S]o let there never be any rules, nothing too bloody or horrible*" (18).

Later, Leo tells his friend Harry that it "takes courage to see the world as it really is, the veils ripped away. . . . Nations are built on guns, not constitutions—only honest men can admit that. . . . Only the strong will admit that and survive" (107). Foreshadowing his final action in the novel, Leo says, "*The domestic life is a bacteria covering the earth! It breeds shops and apartments and idle, fat people. It's a killing disease . . . it kills off freedom and vitality!*" (108).

Harry is Leo's comrade in arms during two of Africa's most serious civil wars: the conflict between the Congo and its largest and most wealthy province, Kaatanga, a conflict that lasted from 1965 through 1967, and the fight between Nigeria and its province, Biafra, which lasted from 1967 to 1970 and in which a million people died. Harry has distinguished himself in combat in Korea, and he is recruited by the American CIA. He requests assignment in Africa because "You go there to take your gut temperature" (46). Harry is a savvy warrior who is torn between the exhilaration he finds in combat and his desire for a normal, domestic life with Val.

After barely escaping death in Biafra at the hands of Nigeria's federal troops, Harry and Val retire to Texas and Leo flees to Kenya. In his retirement, Leo dissolves into drunken madness. His last action—a murderous shooting spree on the beach at Mombassa—is a sort of acting out of the comments that Kurtz, in *The Heart of Darkness,* scrawls across the final pages of his report: "Exterminate all the brutes" (87). Leo has brought his version of Western civilization—violence and death—to the continent.

While *Africana* focuses on the civil wars that plagued Africa in the 1960s, *Savannah Blue* laments the changes—particularly urban blight and the destruction of traditional African cultures—that the twentieth century has brought to Africa. *Savannah Blue* is a murder mystery that takes the form of a safari in which American businessmen, instead of African wildlife, are stalked and killed.

The settings of *Savannah Blue* include most of Africa's major cities as well as Washington, DC. The novel opens in Lagos, Nigeria, when Harrison's hero—Quentin Clare—arrives by plane and takes a taxi across the city. As he rides through the town, Quentin stares out the window of the cab and sees a group of children playing on a putrid trash pile a block long and fifteen feet high (9). Musing on the urban nightmares that are African cities, Quentin thinks of "Cairo, Tangier, and all the other places awash with human flesh like this. . . . The cities of his continent were sewers. He was at war with the men who manufactured such litter, and he thought of himself not so much as a killer, but as a soldier, an army of one" (10).

Quentin is a white African whose parents had settled in Kenya. His father and mother loved Africa, the "continent's legacies: wild nature, the primitive undertow" (85), and it is Quentin's desire to take revenge on those who have destroyed these legacies. Quentin has adopted his father's politics. According to Quentin's father, the Western world intended "to take away culture, adventure, personal freedom, the arts, true science, nature, and any other wild spirit; it meant to instill efficiency, production, conformity, comfort, and the consumer mentality" (163).

It is the Westernization of Africa that most troubles Quentin. He has seen the slow change come to Kenya, especially to Nairobi: "Colonel Sanders' Kentucky Fried Chicken. American items in the supermarkets. Blue jeans in the shop window. A thumping music from the storefront loudspeakers. *Playboy* on the newsstands" (167). Quentin believes that these changes can never "be turned back with a few . . . soft cultural amenities, with piano lessons or Russian novels or a few intelligent pieces of architecture; it had to be fought and destroyed, if possible, because its hideous, plastic, loudspeaker values were too pervasive" (168).

In some ways, Quentin echoes the philosophy espoused by Leo in *Africana*. For example, Quentin sees urbanization as a disease just as Leo sees civilization as a disease. For Quentin, cities such as Cairo and Lagos are "catastrophes . . . the world's sores. In the desert beyond, men stood out like monoliths, tall and important" (64), but in the urban slums of Africa, individuals have little merit and humanity has been degraded.

However, in the final analysis, Quentin's campaign is carried out not for black Africans, because although their "suffering and hardships are real and pathetic enough . . . they were also easily bought off by any coin" (194). Quentin's fight is for "raw, wild nature itself" (194). Readers may see Quentin's outrage concerning the destruction of African wildlife as justified because African wildlife may completely vanish by the early decades of the twenty-first century. According to Calder, "The forests and savannas of Africa have sustained wildlife for countless centuries, but there may be room for nothing but people within decades" (H4). By giving this motive to Quentin's quest for revenge, Harrison accomplishes the nearly impossible task of making readers sympathize with a cold-blooded killer.

In *Savannah Blue* Harrison uses one of Africa's great animals as a symbol for the entire continent. The animal is a legendary old elephant called Juju; Juju is said to carry a hundred bullets in his body, bullets left by "mindless men from far away [who] had come to destroy nature itself. But the magnificent Juju . . . would not die. . . . Then it was gone. Dead, perhaps, although no one really knew" (103–4). Harrison highlights the symbolic quality of the elephant by writing that Juju is "Africa itself carrying the spiteful, thoughtless iron of the modern world inside its body" (104).

The method of murder that Quentin chooses perfectly fits his purpose of taking revenge against those who have destroyed wild Africa; Quentin poisons his victims with a form of cobra venom. Even though Quentin refines the venom so that it kills in a matter of seconds instead of minutes, the cobra's poison is a natural element that links Quentin's revenge with the wildlife of Africa.

Soon Treasury Department agents in Washington, DC, become aware of the fact that someone in Africa is killing American businessmen. A team is formed and sent to Africa in an attempt to determine who is responsible for the attacks. The team is headed by Charlie Hazo, a professor who is associated with an intelligence-gathering organization called Africa International. After Quentin succeeds in assassinating businessmen in Durban, Kinshasa, Monrovia, Algiers, and Lagos, Hazo's team attempts to lure the killer into striking one of the agents who is posing as a businessman.

Quentin finally turns to hunting the members of the team that has been sent to hunt him, and the final scenes of the novel unfold not in Africa but in Washington where Quentin is shot after attempting to assassinate a government official. Quentin's last thoughts as he bleeds to death are of Africa: "He wanted to see Africa again. . . . [H]e didn't want to die in this sad, metallic country on the wrong side of the world" (283).

As in *Africana*, Harrison uses African settings in *Savannah Blue* to make a thematic statement about the nature of Western materialism and the way in which modern times have destroyed anything, animal or human, that retains individuality, freedom, or a wild spirit. The use of Africa as a setting appeals to Harrison because Africa, although it is rapidly being destroyed by twentieth-century technology and industrialization, is the last home of the great wonders of nature, the last place where humans are not "barnyard creatures" but "upright figures on an open landscape" (168).

Harrison's third African novel, *Burton and Speke*, is his most didactic because its story dramatizes the actual exploits of Richard Francis Burton and John Haning Speke—the famous explorers who searched for the source of Nile. The Africa of *Burton and Speke* is just beginning to be explored fully by Europeans. Previous attempts to find the source of the Nile had failed because, from its mouth near Cairo, the river wanders through more than three thousand miles of desert, making it impossible for mid-nineteenth-century explorers to discover its source by simply following the great river inland.

When the novel opens, Burton has already established himself as a hero by disguising himself as an Afghan pilgrim who joins a caravan to Mecca; thus Burton becomes the first European to visit the forbidden city. Burton is a linguist who has mastered Arabic and numerous other languages, and his ability to communicate with the many inhabitants of the regions he explores is very useful. Speke has been on duty with the British army in India for ten years before joining Burton in Africa, and when asked by Burton why he wants to go to Africa, Speke replies, "I want to go to Africa . . . to die" (11). Speke comes close to getting his wish a number of times.

Using Burton as a spokesman, Harrison releases numerous bits of information about Africa and African cultures. For example, readers are informed that "Africans are not truly fighters. . . . Perhaps because they walked a continent of superior beasts—the great cats, the invincible rhinos and elephants, their confidence was low. But the word for war in Africa was *barouf*, the Arab word for gunpowder, or actually, the sound of powder as it harmlessly exploded. War was common in most tribes and peoples of the continent, but death in battle was rare" (27).

However, the Somali who attack Burton and Speke on their second attempt to move into the interior seem quite effective in battle, killing many of Burton's men and seriously wounding both Burton and Speke (43). Burton and Speke return to England to recover from their wounds, and eventually Burton convinces the Royal Geographical Society to fund another attempt to locate the highland lakes that are rumored to be the source of the Nile.

While the vastness of the African continent and the threat of hostile Africans are significant obstacles for the explorers, the greatest challenges that Burton and Speke confront come from diseases and wildlife. For instance, both Burton and Speke suffer from fevers most of the time they are in the interior. Burton is stricken with a swelling of the legs that makes it nearly impossible for him to walk (161), Speke temporarily loses his vision because of an eye ailment (162), and cholera is a constant threat in the villages along the coast when they return form their journey (194).

Dangers also come from African insects. At one point the explorers' camp is overrun by a column of bulldog ants: "Speke was bitten on the leg; it felt like a long, hot needle entering the flesh, and he heard himself cry out" (111). One night Speke lights a candle in his tent, and "[h]undreds of black beetles began crawling toward the light." He awakes to find a beetle "eating its way deep into his ear. He could hear its legs and jaws working, but couldn't get it out" (170). Speke removes the beetle with his pen knife, an experience that leaves him deaf in that ear.

Big game also poses threats to the explorers. For example, at one point, Speke is charged by a buffalo:

He had always pictured himself in this fix except, in his imagination, a lion, not a buffalo, would charge; he would have one bullet and one chance. Perhaps, with a lion he would wait until that final leap, catching it with this shot at the last second. But the lion would be a soft, easier target; now . . . as he began to squeeze the trigger, he could hear each separate beat of the hooves and see only that wall of horn. This shot, he felt, would fail. Death drew a tight string around his heart. . . . [However the shot] somehow deflected off the horn and severed the bull's spine. It lay dead at their feet. (279–80)

The explorers find one great lake (Tanganyika) but are unable to determine that a river flows out of it to the north. While Burton is recovering from the mysterious illness that caused his legs to swell, Speke and a small group of men go on to explore yet another lake, one that Speke names Victoria Nyanza (Lake Victoria). Speke believes that this lake is the source of the Nile, but, lacking hard evidence, Burton remains unconvinced and a rift develops between the two adventurers.

Speke returns to Africa on yet another search to substantiate that Lake Victoria is the source of the Nile; however, the results of this second exploration are similar to those of the first. Although history will prove him correct, Speke's second expedition fails to establish for certain that the lake is the birthplace of the Nile.

Burton again travels to Africa late in the novel when he is sent as a representative of the British government in an attempt to persuade King Gelele of Dahomony to end the slave trade in West Africa. In contrast to the East Africans that Burton has dealt with, Gelele seems a savage tyrant. Burton argues that the British will "stop all of the slave trade in coastal waters" (383) but Gelele is unimpressed. When Burton protests against the Gelele's frequent indulgence in human sacrifice, Gelele reminds Burton that "Criminals are put to death in your land. . . . As for the others, this is a religious matter. . . . You will not worry about our religion" (383).

In *Burton and Speke* Harrison captures the immensity of the African continent by detailing the struggles of the British explorers as they spend months and years making their way into the heart of East Africa. Readers of the novel gain a great deal of information not only about the exploits of the famous explorers but also about the African continent itself.

Harrison's most recent African novel, *Three Hunters*, is part safari story, part family drama, part history, and part commentary on East Africa's growing refugee problem. Harrison incorporates several familiar features of African settings into this tale of a man-eating leopard that preys on refugees who inhabit the desolate shore of a crocodile-infested lake.

The novel begins when Trey Nichols, a beautiful American physician who has come to Kenya to work with refugees, meets Lucien Cavenaugh, the youngest son of a retired big game hunter named Chili. Lucien's older brother is a rogue named

Coke, and when Coke and Lucien aren't hunting game they are busy pursuing each other's women, a habit that has caused serious ill feeling between the brothers. Indeed, the entire Cavenaugh clan is divided; Coke has inherited his father's traits concerning drink (whiskey and beer are important foods), women (all are fair game), and the hunt (danger is the ultimate high). Lucien takes after his mother, Audrey; he is fond of music, books, and business, but he has learned hunting and the safari trade from Chili and has proven his courage against charging lions and other dangerous African creatures.

Dr. Trey has "inherited" the refugee camp because her Kenyan supervisors have abandoned the project. When he first arrives, Lucien finds that the camp is "desert squalor along the mud flats at the lake. . . . The refugees huddled under their canopies and lean-to huts, searching for whatever shade they could find, lying there listless and helpless" (20). To run the camp efficiently, Lucien sorts the refugees into groups: "Ethiopian families who had fled the drought, a few rebels from the ongoing wars over in Uganda, a dozen Somalis, some long-time lake inhabitants including the reluctant fishermen" who fear the crocodiles that seem to be the only creatures that thrive in the region (21). Lucien is making excellent progress both with the camp and Dr. Trey until the appearance of a leopard that begins taking refugees from the camp during the nights. The appearance of the man-eater requires that Lucien contact Chili so that they may conduct a safari and hunt down the dangerous leopard. Unfortunately, at least from Lucien's point of view, Coke flies Chili into the camp.

The appearance of Coke troubles Lucien because Lucien knows that Coke will attempt to steal Trey away. However, Lucien is glad to have experienced hunters help him in his pursuit of the leopard because the leopard has hidden in some hills just north of the lake. Even Chili believes that the hunt will be extremely dangerous because of the topography of the area (90). As Lucien explains, there are only three of the hunters, and with three men "the leopard can move between us and flank us. Hell, *he'll* be hunting *us*" (111). This added danger suits Chili who "wanted danger and little else. . . . Life was sweetened only by jeopardy. Only by risk was anything confirmed or understood, and if possible you risked everything: fortune, family, and the blood that ached in your veins" (111). It is his love of hunting dangerous wildlife that has kept Chili in Africa for many years; once he thought of returning to his home state—Arkansas, but the "big four in Arkansas were only bear, razorback hog, deer, and coon—hardly worth the effort" (61).

Harrison artfully intersperses chapters that deal with Kenya's past between chapters set at the lake. Readers learn about the Cavenaugh family history and about life in colonial Kenya. Kenya's role in World War II is also recalled. For instance, Harrison details Chili's exploits as a soldier during the war. In the last months of the conflict, Chili was given the job of hunting lions that had become accustomed to eating the flesh of Italian soldiers who had been wounded or killed in battle (93).

Indeed, a number of scenes in *Three Hunters* describe the conflicts between man and nature. One particularly interesting encounter between humans and African wildlife occurs when the "croc man" appears at the lake. The croc man is a loner who emerges from the desert annually to kill as many crocodiles as he can. He is almost a superman in appearance: "the raw physical presence of the visitor was a measure of any man at the north end of the lake. Shiny black pectorals, biceps, sinew of neck, set of jaw: he made Coke look puny and made the poor refugees resemble cadavers" (130). The croc man is armed only with a dagger, a pistol, and a coil of rope.

Because of the crocs, his appearance is cause of celebration for the refugees:

[A]ll year long the crocs ruled the lake and the shore. . . . During Trey's first weeks at the clinic a croc had seized the arm of a young girl as she bent in the shallows to wash away the sting of a bee. Her parents began a tug of war with the croc, losing ground, inching into deeper water, the mangled arm between them and the brute, until a second croc arrived, got the mother's and father's legs in one bite, and the whole family disappeared into the waves. (131)

Coke is fascinated by the croc man, and he joins the croc man in this hunt, shooting the crocs with a pistol as they approach. Coke and the croc man, because of their courage in facing hostile African wildlife, are examples of what Harrison calls "upright figures in an open landscape" (*Savannah* 168).

In all of his novels set in Africa, Harrison is careful to portray Africans in a fair manner. Some of the African characters in Harrison's fiction, for instance, a tribal leader in *Three Hunters* who wants to sell Lucien a young girl so she can be used as bait for the leopard, are savages who conform to Western stereotypes. But in each of Harrison's African novels there are also African characters who are noble, brave, and wise. In *Burton and Speke*, that character is Sidi Bombay who guided numerous expeditions across the continent and became the "only man in the nineteenth century to cross Africa from both south to north and east to west" (420). In *Three Hunters*, readers not only meet the fearless croc man, they also encounter Abba, a wise old guide who has an extra pair of ears; he has dried the ears of his dead cousin and attached them to his own ears like rings. The extra set of ears allows Abba to hear voices from the underground. Abba was attracted to the lake "because of much voices here" (137). It is Abba who explains to Trey and the hunters that "all the voices from the lake are sad" and that in "this place the leopard and all the people are very much lost and confused" (137).

The hunt for the leopard provides the Cavenaughs with an opportunity to patch up the feuds that have divided the family for years, and this use of hunting and the challenges provided by African wildlife to bring out the strengths in characters and cause them to reach a fuller understanding of themselves harkens back to the early examples of safari literature, especially such stories as Hemingway's "The Short Happy Life of Francis Macomber" and *Green Hills of Africa*.

At the conclusion of *Three Hunters*, it is the leopard that brings the family together and heals the discontent that has smoldered between the Cavenaughs, especially between Coke and Lucien. While the hunters are stalking the leopard in the boulder-strewn hills north of the lake, the leopard stalks the three men. Before anyone can raise his rifle, the beast pounces on Coke, breaking his collarbone and taking off a large section of his shoulder. Neither Chili nor Lucien dares to fire at the leopard for fear of hitting Coke, so Lucien draws his knife and wounds the big cat, distracting him long enough for Chili to get off a good shot.

Dr. Trey patches up Coke's wound so that he can take off in the plane, but she fears he may bleed to death. As Coke gets weaker, Lucien pilots the plane, and the four of them—Trey, Chili, Coke, and Lucien—fly away from the lake, the refugee camp, and the dead leopard. In Nairobi, Dr. Trey and the local surgeon manage to save Coke's arm.

Neither the use of African wildlife and landscapes as challenges for characters nor an interest in dramatizing African history is unique to Harrison. However, no other American author is so successful in linking African landscapes and creatures to the notion that humankind suffers when what is wild, both in people and in places, is lost. For Harrison, Africa—at least the Africa of the recent past—offers an example of the alternative to the false "civilization" of the West that has resulted in a homogenized corporate culture and the devaluation of what it means to be a free individual instead of a "barnyard animal."

To summarize, most genre novels with African settings rise above the standards expected of genre fiction and delve into substantial themes associated with serious literature. For instance, the work of William Harrison questions the very existence of Western "civilization" and implies that the West and its materialistic values have destroyed the natural world and have diminished the worth of human beings. In *The Wild Boys*, William Burroughs uses African settings to comment upon the divisions that exist between the wealthy and the poor and to predict what might happen to the developed West if the problems of overpopulation and poverty in the Third World are not addressed. Moreover, most genre novels with African settings contain strong didactic elements; these novels, even such "entertainments" as *Congo* and *The Covenant*, incorporate a wealth of factual data about Africa, Africans, and African history into their stories. Behind the didactic elements and the thematic concerns of many of these genre novels set in Africa, however, is a reinforcement of traditional Western notions about Africa. In the works of Ruark, for example, Africans are often portrayed as savage beings, and in Bellow's *Henderson the Rain King*, Africa is seen as a timeless, empty space existing outside the realm of history.

In contrast to these genre novels, postmodern novels set in Africa sometimes question, rather than reinforce, Western stereotypes about Africa. In such works as Maria Thomas's *Antonia Saw the Oryx First* and Richard Dooling's *White Man's Grave*, for example, African ways of seeing reality are contrasted with Western ways of seeing reality, and these postmodern novels imply that the West may learn something important from these alternative visions of the world.

Chapter 6

Africa: Postmodern, Postcolonial, and "Other" Wise

Works of postmodern fiction are often set in zones that are "discontinuous and inconsistent," zones that juxtapose "worlds of incompatible structure" with the intent of undermining established norms or ways of perception (McHale 44). Because Africa is often viewed as being in binary opposition to the West and because African methods of perceiving the world are frequently seen as being different from Western methods of perception, a number of contemporary American novelists use African settings to indicate that the Western way of thinking is not necessarily the only way in which reality can be understood.

Moreover, Westerners have traditionally considered Africa an empty space, and McHale observes that "if the map is blank, the corresponding area of the real world too must be a kind of empty space offering minimal resistance to the realization of adventurous fantasies" (54). Therefore, postmodernist texts may not "reflect objective African realities, but they do faithfully reflect our culture's ontological landscape, which allots a certain space to an unreal zone called Africa" (McHale 55). Because Westerners tend to think of Africa as "unreal," alternative visions of reality thrive in postmodern fiction set in Africa. Furthermore, in addition to this interest in undermining established norms, postmodern fiction is also concerned with the status of the "other" (Linn 63), and several contemporary American novels, beginning with Paul Bowles's *The Sheltering Sky*, examine the role of Westerners as "others" in Africa.

Indeed, the status of outsiders such as Westerners and Asians is a major concern of novels set in postcolonial Africa. Novelists such as Paul Theroux, Maria Thomas, and Richard Dooling examine the status of outsiders in postcolonial Africa and detail the political and social situations in newly independent African states. While critics argue that some of these novels, particularly the work of Maria Thomas, challenge the "Africanist" conventions—the notions that Africa lags behind the West and that the West is in binary opposition to Africa—found in much Western literature set in Africa (Gruesser 128), Theroux and others reinforce the traditional Western concepts about Africa and Africans. Theroux's African fiction indicates that Africa is indeed different from the West, that postcolonial Africa does lag behind the West in terms of economic and political development, and that Westerners and Asians living in postcolonial Africa are frequently subjected to racism and violence.

PART I: PAUL BOWLES

Lost and Found in North Africa: *The Sheltering Sky, let it come down,* and *The Spider's House*

Paul Bowles is the first American novelist working after World War II to feature African settings in his narratives, and few Americans are as qualified as Bowles to write about the role of Americans as "others" in Africa. As Patteson notes, Bowles's "self-chosen status as an outsider . . . stamps his art with an indelible mark, and his works often involve journeys out—away from the apparently safe and domestic, toward the dangerous and the alien" (ix–x). In three of Bowles's novels, *The Sheltering Sky, let it come down,* and *The Spider's House,* these dangerous and alien locales are in North Africa. While these novels embrace numerous Western conventions about Africa and Africans, Bowles challenges the uses of African settings employed by Hemingway in the 1920s and 1930s. In all of Bowles's African novels, however, the settings—both cultural and natural—are agents that influence the outcome of the narratives. As Oates observes, readers may even be disoriented by a writer such as Bowles "whose focus of attention is not upon human beings but upon primitive forces—land or cityscapes—that express themselves through human beings" (Introduction xv).

The Sheltering Sky, Bowles's first novel, is the story of three Americans—Port Moresby, his wife Kit, and their friend Tunner—who travel "into the Sahara, farther and farther away from what they had known as reality" (Halpern viii), and deep into a land that is both hostile and deadly. Few American novels set in Africa make as extensive use of setting as a narrative tool as does *The Sheltering Sky,* and, for the most part, the notions Bowles associates with African landscapes in this book are familiar ones. In *The Sheltering Sky,* Africa is a timeless, empty place, a harsh, disease-ridden zone populated by natives who are often hostile. It is a place where Americans can easily lose their identities, their minds, and their lives.

The Americans in *The Sheltering Sky* have come to Africa for the usual reasons, reasons popularized by Hemingway in his African fiction; they are seeking an authentic experience, and they are hoping that Africa can revitalize them. At one point, for example, Port tells Kit that "We've never managed, either one of us, to get all the way into life. We're hanging on to the outside for all we're worth, convinced we're going to fall off at the next bump" (101). Their journey to Africa is an attempt to "get all the way into life."

For the Americans in *The Sheltering Sky*, Africa also represents a world that is unspoiled by World War II, a conflict that has ended only a few years before Port, Kit, and Tunner journey to the Sahara. Readers are informed that the "war was one facet of the mechanized age [that Port] wanted to forget" and that Port's intention is to keep "as far as possible from the places which had been touched by the war" (14). Indeed, upon their arrival on the coast of North Africa, the Americans discuss the effects of the war. Looking about the coastal city, Kit remarks that the "war has certainly left its mark here" (15). Port agrees, saying that "There were troops passing through for a year or more" (15). Kit goes on to note that the world has been homogenized by the war: "The people of each country get more like the people of every other country. They have no character, no beauty, no ideals, no culture—nothing, nothing" (16). Port replies that Africa will be different: "Everything's getting gray, and it'll be grayer. But some places'll withstand the malady longer than you think. You'll see, in the Saraha [*sic*]" (16). In terms of a concern with the effects of the war, Bowles's Africa is something like Hemingway's Spain in *The Sun Also Rises*. Spain, because it had been largely untouched by industrialization and by World War I, was Hemingway's last good country (Stanton 15); for Port, Africa is the last good continent.

One reason that Port is certain that Africa will be different from much of the war-torn world is that Africa, in Port's view, is a timeless place. For instance, after bribing an official into giving him and Kit seats on a bus, Port remarks that the original ticket holders won't mind being bumped from their places because "What's a week to them? Time doesn't exist for them" (177). Kit also comes to share this notion about Africa's timeless quality; as they pass groups of riders who are draped in "indigo veils that hid their faces," Kit thinks that it is rather "wonderful" to see "such people in the Atomic Age" (185).

In addition to seeking an escape from a world ravaged by war, the Americans in *The Sheltering Sky* have journeyed to Africa is search of revitalization, and, in the case of Kit and Port, they have come to the continent with the hope that a trip to Africa will somehow strengthen their marriage (Patteson 39). However, unlike characters such as Hemingway's Macomber—who discovers that the challenges offered by Africa bring out the best in him—or Harry, the main character of "The Snows of Kilimanjaro," who finds that African settings help him come to important assessments about his life, Port and Kit obtain only madness or death as a result of their African adventure.

As the Americans travel deeper and deeper into the interior of Africa, the environment becomes more and more hostile. For instance, after traveling to Boussif, the Americans book passage on a bus to Aïn Krorfa, a town in the interior. They take the night car to "avoid the heat, which is oppressive" (104), but even before they reach the town they are attacked by flies. The bus driver warns them that in the town the flies are like "black snow, over everything" (112). Later in the novel, the desert begins to affect the moods of the characters. When Port is ill, for example, a sandstorm blows up, covering everything with fine dust, and Kit notes that the natural environment is mirrored by the lack of human sympathy in the residents of the region; she becomes aware "for the first time of how cruelly lacking in that sentiment [sympathy] was the human landscape here" (212).

Later, when she is deep in the Sahara with the Arabs who have made her a sex slave, Kit notes that the entire natural world seems hostile: "The sand had been left far behind, and so had the great dead stony plains. Now there was a gray, insect-like vegetation everywhere, a tortured scrub of hard shells and stiff hairy spines that covered the earth like an excrescence of hatred. The ashen landscape as they moved through it was flat as a floor. Day by day the plants grew higher, and the thorns that sprouted from them stronger and more cruel" (275–76).

Novels set in Africa frequently feature disease as a motif, and disease plays a central role in *The Sheltering Sky*. For instance, upon reaching the town of El Ga'a after an arduous bus ride, Port becomes ill and Kit discovers that there is no lodging to be found in the city because of a meningitis epidemic (192). Port, however, contracts typhoid, not meningitis, and he spends his last days dying of fever in a cell-like room in a French fort.

For Kit and Port, Africa is not a land that generates self discovery; it is a place that strips them of their identities. This loss of identity comes just as the Americans are penetrating the interior of the continent. When Port's passport is stolen, he reports the loss to a French official and explains that "ever since I discovered that my passport was gone, I've felt only half alive. But it's a very depressing thing in a place like this to have no proof of who you are, you know" (159–60). Port, however, will have little use for his passport since death requires no identification papers.

Kit also seeks a renewal in Africa, specifically a renewal of her relationship with Port, but all the continent offers her is loss of identity and madness. Even before she reaches the interior of the Sahara, Kit is distraught because she has betrayed Port's trust by sleeping with Tunner, and her long days spent caring for Port have further affected her mind. When Port dies, she flees from Tunner and leaves the protection of the French fort where she and Port have taken refuge. She joins a caravan whose destination she does not know because the leaders of the caravan do not speak English or French and Kit knows no Arabic. Before long, the Arabs in charge of the caravan have made Kit their sex slave, raping her repeatedly each night as the caravan crawls across the vast desert. Eventually, the younger of the Arabs, a man named Belqassim, takes Kit for his own. Kit's loss of identity is symbolized by the loss of her Western clothing, her name, and eventually, all of her possessions except for her passport. Specifically, Belqassim forces her to discard her Western clothes and take an Arab name: Ali (277).

For several months she is confined to a small room in Belqassim's house and treated as a sex slave. Finally, Kit breaks free and runs into the streets of an unnamed African city in the Sudan. She is again taken in by an Arab male and again used for sex. When she is at last rescued by the authorities, Kit has gone completely mad. She does not remember her name (309), and she laughs deliriously and soils herself on the flight from Sudan to the North African coast. Finally, Kit vanishes into the native quarter of a coastal city rather than face Tunner and her old way of life. For Kit and Port, the great hope that an African journey would bring renewal and insight is a false hope; their journey to Africa brings only madness and death.

In *The Sheltering Sky*, the harshness of the Sahara is a factor that affects the mental conditions of the characters. In *let it come down*, the rain that falls on the North African coast mirrors the mental state of an American named Nelson Dyar, but in *let it come down*, cultural aspects—rather than natural aspects—of the North African setting push Dyar toward madness and isolation.

Dyar is like many characters in contemporary American fiction set in Africa in that he has traveled to the continent in search of a fresh start. A heart murmur kept him from serving in the war, and he spends his days as a bank teller in New York City where he feels that his "life was a dead weight" (7). When he gets an offer from an old friend, Jack Wilcox, to work as a travel agent in Tangier, Dyar sails for North Africa with a few hundred dollars and hopes that his African experience will provide him with a new sense of life and deliver him from the feeling of "despair that had weighed on him for so long" (9). Dyar believes he has taken a great step toward achieving self realization by leaving New York and sailing to Morocco: "All the way across on the ship to Gibraltar, he had told himself that it was the healthy thing to have done, that when he arrived he would be like another person, full of life" (9).

In some ways, *let it come down* is a novel of intrigue because most of the action takes place in Tangier when the city is still part of Morocco's International Zone and because the plot involves stealing and smuggling currency (Patteson 47). The International Zone is an exotic place populated by a strange collection of characters; for instance, while he is in the Zone, Dyar has encounters with a prostitute named Hadija, an alcoholic American lesbian named Eunice Goode, a wealthy socialite named Daisy de Valverde, and an attractive Russian agent named Mme. Jouvenon. And Jack Wilcox, Dyar's employer, is more interested in smuggling currency than in arranging tourist itineraries.

As the days pass, Dyar becomes more and more concerned about his dwindling funds. Wilcox has arranged for Dyar to transport a large amount of smuggled money through the Zone, and Dyar decides to flee to Spanish Morocco with Wilcox's cash. However, despite the plot's reliance on smuggling and intrigue, *let it come down* is more a novel about an existential search for meaning than an adventure tale. Dyar is an existential character who feels his "life is a dead weight" (7); unfortunately, only by committing a senseless murder is Dyar is able to obtain a feeling of being alive (Patteson 16).

Assisting Dyar in his escape from Wilcox and the International Zone is a Moroccan named Thami. Thami smuggles Dyar into Spanish Morocco and hides him in an abandoned house that is perched high upon a hillside like a "fort" (256). Dyar has vaguely formed plans of escape; he thinks he might first go to French Morocco and then "hop on a train and just keep going down into Africa, to the end of the line" (192). As Dyar attempts to exchange the stolen currency for francs, he becomes more and more suspicious of Thami. The catalyst of Dyar's paranoia is a drug commonly used in Morocco: hashish. Indeed, Dyar's use of hashish and kif "increasingly propel him on a course of action that leads to his complete isolation" (Patteson 122).

Dyar is first introduced to hashish by Daisy de Valverde, who gives him some of the drug in a piece of candy. Daisy tells him that the Arabs "eat it all the time" but that Americans and Europeans would consider the use of the drug as an act of depravity (216). After his first experience with the drug at Daisy's house, Dyar constantly smokes kif and eats hashish until the end of the novel. Dyar himself admits that the drug is "treacherous stuff" (290), yet he seems driven to smoke kif, and he consumes a large amount of candied hashish with Thami.

In fact, the hashish he eats causes Dyar to hallucinate, and the room that he and Thami share turns into a "magic room" that is transformed into a "red grotto, a theater, a vast stable with a balcony that hung in the shadows. Up there was a city of little rooms, a city inside a pocket of darkness" (299). After Thami passes out from the effects of the hashish, Dyar's hallucinations intensify until he loses all conception of reality. His language and thoughts degenerate into a "mass of words" such as "Many Mabel damn. Molly Daddy lamb. Lolly dibble up-man. Dolly little Dan" (301). As he attempts to hammer the door of the cabin shut with a nail, the wind seems to rush through his head: "[H]is head . . . was a single seashell of grottoes; its infinitely smooth pink walls delicate, paper-thin, caught the light of the embers as he moved along the galleries. 'Melly diddle din,' he said, quite loud, putting the point of the nail as far into Thami's ear as he could. He raised his right arm and hit the head of the nail with all his might" (302). When he recovers his senses, Dyar finds the "ear in the head beside him. The little steel disc with the irregular grooves in it. He had known it would be there" (303).

Dyar has traveled to Africa in an attempt to fill the void that is his life, and the use of kif and hashish, features of North African culture, spark in him a paranoid vision that causes him to kill Thami. Dyar, whose life in America is marked by its emptiness, discovers in Africa that he is the ultimate outsider, a man who at last fills the void within himself and establishes a "precise relationship with the rest of men. Even if it had to be one of open hostility" (311). Like other contemporary American novels set in Africa, *let it come down* is the story of an American who travels to Africa in search of a fresh start in life; however, Dyar's African journey is a nightmare voyage of isolation.

Bowles's third African novel, *The Spider's House*, is more complex in terms of narrative structure and point of view than either *The Sheltering Sky* or *let it come down*; however, because *The Spider's House* is highly didactic and because the Americans in the novel are influenced in a positive way by their African experiences, *The Spider's House* is more conventional in its uses of African settings than either of Bowles's earlier African works. *The Spider's House* informs readers about the threat that modernization presents to traditional Islamic culture while detailing the struggle for Moroccan independence. Furthermore, because much of the novel is presented from the view point of Amar, a fifteen-year-old Moroccan boy, Bowles is able to compare the Islamic way of life with the Western way of life in order to dramatize the changes that modernization has brought to Africa. Moreover, the Americans in *The Spider's House*, a writer named John Stenham and a tourist named Polly Burroughs, are "others" not only because they are Americans in Africa but also because they are not French, and, therefore, have no stake in maintaining colonial rule of Morocco. Stenham and Burroughs provide Amar with a link to the modern world, a link that symbolizes the transitions that Morocco and other African nations will experience as they become modernized (Patteson 34).

The majority of the action in *The Spider's House* takes place in the medieval Moroccan city of Fez. Fez is an appropriate setting for a novel concerned with the changes that Morocco experiences as it moves into the postcolonial era because Fez is actually two cities, one old and one new. Amar and Stenham live within the old city; the French live mostly in the new city that has been built outside of Fez's walls. Like the entire nation of Morocco, then, Fez is divided between the old ways that have prevailed for centuries and the new ways that the French have introduced. Indeed, Stenham recognizes the symbolic value of old Fez in a passage that highlights the novel's major thematic concern—the destruction of traditional culture that colonialism and modernization have brought about: "The city was, in a rough sense, a symbol. . . . It represented everything in the world that was subject to change or, more precisely, to extinction" (205).

Indeed, even the old city has changed in the years in which Stenham has lived in Fez. For instance, at one point, Stenham leads Burroughs though some of Fez's slums. As the Americans walk past dwellings "made with packing cases, thorn bushes and oil cans, tied together with rope and strips of rags," they see naked children playing "on the refuse-strewn waste land between the huts, where the ground glittered with tin and broken glass" (244). Stenham explains that the slums are a recent addition to Fez: "None of this existed a few years ago" (244). After seeing the "intense squalor" in which many Moroccans live, Burroughs tells Stenham, "I wish you hadn't taken me through there. It somehow spoils the rest of the place for me." Stenham replies that the slums inside the city walls are "about one twentieth of what there is outside the walls" (245).

In fact, Stenham has a romantic attachment to traditional Moroccan culture and he is "an apologist . . . for the old Moroccan way of life" (Patteson 34). But although Stenham has lived among Islamics for years, he doesn't pretend to understand them. Early in the novel he notes that "unaccountable behavior on the part of Moslems amused him, and he always forgave it, because, as he said, no non-Moslem knows enough about the Moslem mind to dare find fault with it. . . . We haven't an inkling of the things that motivate them" (6).

Stenham feels that Western ways will destroy traditional Morocco and that Westerners come in two types: missionaries and modernists. Polly Burroughs is a missionary type; she sees the Moroccans as "backward onlookers standing on the sideline of the parade of progress; they may be exhorted to join, if necessary pulled by force, into the march. . . . The modernizer offered nothing at all, save a place in the ranks" (252). At first, Stenham and Burroughs seem to have little in common, but, by the conclusion of the novel, they have become lovers and allies; the two outsiders are united by the challenges presented by North African culture and by their sympathy for the Moroccans who are brutally oppressed by the French.

Anticipating violence and unrest, the French force Stenham and Burroughs to leave the old city of Fez, and it is only when the Americans flee the city and travel to the mountains that they encounter a pure form of Moroccan culture that is uncorrupted by modernization. For example, the rebels have ordered the Moroccans in Fez not to observe the feast of Aïd, a religious ceremony that requires each family to sacrifice a sheep. As Amar notes, "Never before had such a strange thing happened" (118). And Amar's father explains that the Istiqlal, the Moroccan freedom fighters, have threatened to kill anyone who makes a sacrifice (121). According to Amar's father, "In five years no one will remember it [the feast of Aïd]. This is the end of Islam" (121).

However, in the mountains, the feast is still observed. The mountain people are quite different from the Moroccans who live in Fez's slums. Upon first encountering the country folk, for instance, Polly Burroughs finds their cleanliness "astonishing. . . . It was not only their bodies and clothing that seemed clean. . . . It was as much the expressions of their faces, the aura of their collective spirit; they made her think of the purity of mountain streams, untouched regions" (311).

The journey to the mountains links Amar to Stenham and Burroughs, and one of the reasons that *The Spider's House* is an exceptional novel is that Amar is one of the few fully developed African characters to appear in contemporary American fiction set in Africa. Amar enables Bowles to deliver numerous details about Moroccan culture and about the African reaction to Western ways, and Amar's friendship with the Americans is a symbolic link that connects traditional Morocco to the ways of the modern world. As Patteson explains, Amar is "apart from his own father, the novel's most loyal Moslem. Amar is genuinely shocked by his encounters with Moslems who drink alcohol" or in some other way violate Islamic law, yet Amar is moving toward modernism without fully realizing it (34). Amar is a symbol of the changing times in Morocco; he longs for the security of his father's religion, yet he also desires European goods. The revolution that breaks out in Fez forces Amar to align himself with Stenham and Burroughs, and Amar's attitude toward Westerners is changed by his exposure to the Americans.

For example, at the beginning of the novel, Amar sees Christians, Jews, and Westerners as enemies, as savage barbarians who "were still murdering Moslems every day [in Jerusalem] and putting their flesh in tins to be shipped abroad and sold as food" (33). And throughout the novel, Amar is shocked by Western women, especially Polly Burroughs. Indeed, while Amar becomes friends with the Americans, he never fully comes to an understanding of Western ways. Moreover, the status of women in the Western world is one of the most important ways in which Morocco differs from the modern world. For Moroccans, Allah clearly intended for men to rule over women (268). This cultural gap concerning the role of women is dramatized by Amar when he wonders how Stenham can stand to make conversation with Polly Burroughs. Amar thinks that women are, by Allah's design, inferior to men in all ways (280).

The contrast of Western ways and African ways is continued when Bowles hints at a concern that will be the subject of his long story "Too Far From Home," the notion that Westerners and Africans have different methods of perceiving and shaping the world. Amar believes he has magical powers "that no one else possessed" (19). Specifically, Amar thinks he has special healing powers; he believes he can cure the ill with a touch and a prayer (19). The interest in alternative ways of perceiving and dealing with the world, especially ways of healing that are different from Western ways, are subjects touched on by Bowles and explored in more detail by later American authors such as Maria Thomas and Richard Dooling.

Bowles also informs his readers that Moroccans reason in ways that are different from Western ways of thinking. At one point Stenham explains to Burroughs that things are fated by Allah to unfold as they do: "[Y]ou must always remember it's a culture of 'and the' rather than one of 'because,' like ours" (187). In fact, Stenham does not believe that Moroccans are rational in the Western sense of the word: "If they were rational beings . . . the country would have no interest" (210).

By the conclusion of the novel when Polly Burroughs has given Amar a large sum of money—money and material wealth are the most apparent trappings of Western life and modernization in Amar's eyes—Amar has moved away from the traditions of the past and toward the world that Stenham and Burrough represent. In fact, *The Spider's House* ends on a symbolic note: Amar, the primitive Moroccan, chases after the car that transports Stenham and Burroughs away from the ancient city of Fez. Amar, like Morocco on the eve of independence from France, is stranded between two worlds—the ancient Islamic world of Fez and the modern world of the West with its liberated women, advanced technology, and material wealth.

PART II: PAUL THEROUX

On the Outside Looking In: *Fong and the Indians, Girls at Play*, and *Jungle Lovers*

While Paul Bowles examines the roles of Americans as "others" and outsiders in colonial North Africa, Paul Theroux devotes three novels, *Fong and the Indians*, *Girls at Play*, and *Jungle Lovers* to the adventures of Westerners and Asians who are "others" in postcolonial Africa. Specifically, *Fong and the Indians* deals with the experiences of Asians in East Africa, *Girls at Play* describes the situations encountered by white women in postcolonial Kenya, and *Jungle Lovers* dramatizes the exploits of an American insurance agent and a French-Canadian insurgent in the central African republic of Malawi.

To some degree, these novels are didactic in that they inform readers about the ways in which African nations have changed since independence, and they describe African attitudes about "others" in postcolonial Africa. Furthermore, each of these novels comments upon American notions, both political and cultural, concerning postcolonial Africa. Gruesser maintains that Theroux updates "African discourse to suit postcolonial conditions" and relies "heavily on major African conventions" such as the notions that Africa and the West are in binary opposition, that Africa is a blank or empty space, and that Africa lags behind the West in terms of political and economic development (46). Gruesser finds this reliance on traditional notions about Africa disturbing. However, Threoux lived in Africa for five years (Gruesser 71), and his ideas about Africa are grounded in his experiences on the continent.

Fong and the Indians is set in East Africa—which Theroux explains is a region of Africa, not a specific nation—where Sam Fong, a Chinese immigrant, runs a grocery store. Theroux begins *Fong and the Indians* with an author's note that explains the situation in which Asians living in East Africa find themselves: "There are roughly 400,000 'Asians' . . . who consider East Africa their home. The majority of Africans feel differently; they often say it is time for the Asians to leave, and sometimes they deport them" (1).

Fong is the ultimate outsider. Having sworn never to trust a black man or a white man because of the way he is treated by them (8), Fong turns to the Indian community for support and advice. However, while the Africans have little love for him because he is from the East, the other Asians in East Africa—the Indians—don't consider Fong one of them either. The Africans call Fong an immigrant, but he has lived in the nation longer than the black prime minister. As Fong puts it, "to be one Chinaman in a country of seven million Africans is not easy: you stand out; the East cannot save you" (4).

Fong is carpenter, but he is forced to quit his position as foreman in the carpentry shop of the Ministry of Works when the nation achieves independence. At the time of independence, the Englishman who supervises the works instructs Fong to find a "native, African chap" to be trained as foreman (5). A suitable candidate is found, sent to England for training, and returns to replace Fong as shop foreman even though the African has learned little about carpentry during his training period.

Pushed out of his position by an affirmative action policy, Fong buys a grocery shop from a fast-talking Indian named Fakhru who forces Fong to buy all his goods from him (9), including a vast load of canned milk that has been stolen from the "Milk for Moroccan Mothers Crusade" (29). Much of the novel's plot depends on this milk and how Fong will dispose of it. Fakhru convinces Fong that the milk is a good buy because at any time the train from Nairobi might fail to arrive and white women will buy the milk to feed their children (43). Eventually, Fong loses all his capital to Fakhru, and as his financial situation worsens, he frequently beats his wife Soo, and the family is forced to eat grasshoppers go survive (20). Moreover, every time an African dressed in a suit and tie comes into the store, Fong fears that he will announce that the new owner is an African (20).

Both Fong and Fakhru realize that they have a precarious status in Africa; they could be deported at any moment, and they are always prepared for disaster (45). Indeed, Fong and the other Asians are constantly victimized by Africans. For example, Fong is forced to give fifty shillings to an African representing the Young

Pioneers; the African tells Fong that if he does not give him the money, the store windows will be broken and Fong's wife will be "handled" (58).

In *Fong and the Indians*, Africa has a negative effect on a number of Asians. For instance, Z.F.R. Mehboob comes to "Africa a quiet man . . . given to prayer and impulsive acts of good" (82). However, Africa forever changes Mehboob: "He was a Moslem South Indian; but the kinship between Dravidian and Negro was too close for Mehboob to bear and literally overnight he became Persian" (82). The feeling of "otherness" is so great for most of the Asians shopkeepers that they rarely leave their shops (83), yet in order to make a living, Mehboob drives up-country once a month to sell wholesale goods. On each trip, Mehboob fears that he is watched by naked savages and he has heard terrible rumors of Asians being tortured by Africans (83).

One day two Americans—Bert and Mel—enter Fong's store. Bert is white and Mel is black. The Americans are the source of much of the humor and satire in *Fong and the Indians*, and Fong immediately notes that there is something unusual about these men. For one thing, they seem to be extremely healthy (27). The Americans are arrogant government agents who are incredibly ignorant about Africa and Africans. The black American, Mel, introduces himself to Fong by saying, "Ah'm an Amirican Negro and I wanna tell you, friend, the Amiricans's really cleanin up their own backyard. Why, back in the States the white min pick up the trash" (34). Fong is at a loss; he understands little English, and thinks that whites talk too much and have "disgusting habits" (35).

Since Fong knows little English, Fakhru acts as a translator for the American agents. At first Fakhru cannot understand why the two Americans are so anxious to do business with Fong, but the agents explain that their mission is to counter a possible Chinese takeover of the country (77). The Americans believe they are engaged in a power struggle with China for the future of newly independent African nations, and this notion is consistent with the idea, present in Western fiction since the days of the Brontës, that Africa is a battleground for the world powers. Fakhru, never one to miss a chance to make a profit, thinks that because the Americans know nothing of Africa he can make a fortune by dealing with them (79).

As the political affairs of the nation worsen, the prime minister has the members of his cabinet arrested, and the Asians become more concerned about their status. The Asians assume the Africans are savage, and these beliefs are reinforced by the rumors that sweep through the Asian community. For instance, the shopkeepers have heard that the prime minister has eaten the hearts of some of his opponents and sexually tortured others (93). The Asians brace themselves for the disaster that they have long been expecting, and disaster strikes when terrorist gangs set up roadblocks, trash Asian shops, and rape white and Asian women (94–95).

The Africans also hear rumors about the Asians. It is said that the Asians are part of a conspiracy to take over the country and outbreed all the Africans. These rumors lead to even more violence against Asians, and during the worst of the riots, "Sam Fong nailed his children into a packing crate and he and his wife rolled themselves into reed mats where they stayed for most of the day, like pastries" (95). Finally, a state of emergency is declared, soldiers patrol the streets, and Fong and his family are forced by the Young Pioneers to listen to a speech by the prime minister who declares that "Asians . . . had better walk on tiptoes from now on" (102).

After this warning, Fong boards up his shop, lives on canned food, and hears gunfire in the night (103). It is at this point in the novel that Fong most feels like an "other" in Africa. He has spent years on the continent, yet all he has is an empty grocery store and a country full of enemies (105). Fakhru's situation is little better; he realizes that he could be deported at any moment and find himself broke and homeless in Pakistan (108).

As the political situation deteriorates, several Asians are deported, and Theroux makes it clear that there is little regard for justice or civil rights in postcolonial East Africa. For example, one of the first Asians to be deported is V. R. Gupta, who "spoke four African languages and knew most of the tribal customs" (125). Throughout the colonial period, Gupta had fought for independence, and he often proclaimed that because he was born in Africa, he was an African (125). Gupta is deported for advocating free elections (128).

Nor are the Asians the only "others" in East Africa; Mel, the black American agent, also finds that he is an outsider. At one point Mel had looked forward to working in Africa, he had even thought of Africa as home (109), but he quickly comes to understand that he has little in common with Africans. When he had first arrived in Africa, he had believed that Africans were his people, but after a year on the continent, he has changed his mind. Mel gets especially upset when his colleagues tell him about "your [typical] African" (111). Mel can't help but think his colleagues are talking about him, that each "statement indicated plainly that Mel (and family) were no different from those people down there on the street . . . Africans whom he had grown to dislike so much" (111–12).

The Americans mistakenly think that Fong is a Chinese agent "responsible for this here emergency thing" (160). Fakhru tells the Americans that they are mistaken, but Mel insists that the blacks wouldn't do such things "Cause I'm black and I know" (162). According to Mel, the Chinese always make it appear that Africans are unable to govern themselves. Mel says, "[I]t ain't the Africans screwing up this country. It's the Commies. I tell you, Fong's our man" (163). The Americans spread about a lot of money in an attempt to buy Fong's friendship. By making Fong wealthy, the agents hope to use him as a propaganda tool in the fight against Communism (160). However, every dollar the Americans give Fong quickly ends up in Fakhru's bank account.

Meanwhile, an actual Chinese agent named Chen appears at Fong's grocery, calls Fong a "running dog," and leaves the collected works of Mao (in English) at Fong's store. Mel, seeing the books later, thinks that they confirm his suspicions about Fong (168).

The conclusion of *Fong and the Indians* is a hilarious satire of American foreign policy and attitudes about Africans and Asians. Fong is invited to an embassy party by Mel and Bert, but, when he wonders off, the Americans mistake Chen for Fong; apparently all Chinese look alike to Americans. Chen speaks English much better than Fong, but Bert and Mel figure that Fong has just been pretending not to know English. After the party, Chen—now assumed by all the Americans to be Fong—is invited to tour the United Sates. In America, Chen visits the cities, meets with some American Indians who call him Chief Fong, and becomes a propaganda spokesman for the United States. Whether Chen is working as a double agent or has succumbed to American materialism is unclear.

Back in East Africa, Fong sinks deeper and deeper into poverty; finally he becomes a true African by giving up Chinese food and taking up an African diet (197). Finally Fong comes to terms with his status as an outsider in Africa; he no longer fears Africa, and, in fact, he becomes "African" because he has no other community—certainly not that of Fakhru and the Indians—to turn to. Although he will never be fully accepted by the Africans, Fong knows that Africa is his home. Fakhru and the other Asians, however, continue to experience the hatred of their African neighbors (195).

Postcolonial African politics and attitudes are sharply criticized in *Fong and the Indians*, a fact that troubles critics such as Gruesser. However, Theroux is even-handed in his criticism; he not only attacks Africans for their racist treatment of Asians and Westerners, he criticizes America's inane foreign policy in Africa as well as American attitudes about Asians and Africans.

While Fong and the Asians do not find life as "others" in Africa easy, they fare far better than do the outsiders—a group of single white women—who are the main characters of *Girls at Play*. The setting of the novel is a girls' school in the highlands of Kenya in the years just after Kenyan independence. The white women in *Girls at Play* have traveled to Africa for the usual reasons; they want adventure and romance. Miss Poole, the headmistress of the school, is the daughter of a settler; she can't bear life in England. Miss Heather Monkhouse, the English teacher, is a refugee from a London shop, and B. J. (Bettyjean) Lebowitz is a nineteen-year-old Peace Corps worker from southern California. Heather and B. J. will die in Africa, and Miss Poole will be deported; the message is that postcolonial Kenya is a dangerous place for "others" who are at the mercy of those who rule the new nation. *Girls at Play* clearly reinforces the old notion that Africa is a hostile and dangerous zone; this is a notion that Gruesser challenges as being "Africanist," yet Theroux is simply informing his readers about his view of postcolonial Africa. As demonstrated not only by *Girls at Play* but also by his third African novel, *Jungle Lovers*, Theroux believes that outsiders cannot help Africans, and Africans may well hurt or destroy those "others" who come to the continent.

In *Girls at Play*, the school itself is both a prison and a refuge for the women who staff it. The campus is enclosed by a "high leafy wall of bulging green. . . . On all sides . . . were green juicy barriers; an African cage" (1). Heather thinks of the school as a prison camp fenced with trees instead of barbed wire (40). Outside this cage lurks danger, and sometimes this danger invades the sanctuary of the campus. For instance, Miss Poole lives in fear of African intruders, and she spends most of her time shut up in her room. Poole believes some are still seeking revenge against whites even though the Africans have had independence for seven years (6).

Poole has not always feared Africans; she sometimes fondly recalls life on her father's farm in the years before independence. Poole voices the settler philosophy; farming communities were "safe and green" and "came alive when the morning bell sounded, the Africans scampering like hounds" (31–32). This simile is an appropriate one for the relationship that existed between the white settlers and the native peoples in the colonial days. For Poole African history is a story of one brutal conquest after another until the arrival of the British settlers. Only the British, it seems, are strong enough to put order to the chaos that is Africa (120). Needless to say, Kenya's new rulers have no fondness for Poole or the settler philosophy; she is an "other" not only because she is an eccentric white woman in a black country but also because she is one of the former oppressors of the people in whose nation she now resides.

Miss Poole's adversary at the school is Heather Monkhouse, whom Poole refers to as Heather Mongoose. Heather has fled England to escape the dullness of life as a shopkeeper; she goes to Africa "to get away from it all: the filthy crowded subways, the sooty church steeples, the wilted working-class faces everywhere" (13), and although she has no training, she accepts a position as an English teacher in Kenya. During her voyage to the continent, her fellow travelers warn her of East African brutality. As the old African hands put it, "she had never been to Africa before and had not the slightest idea of what it was like to live in a country populated with savages" (16). By the time the ship lands in Kenya, Heather begins to "imagine Africa as a huge black carcass, inert in the ocean, with evil at its center and all Africa's vastness radiating mishap off its shores in dark smelly eddies" (18). But once Heather actually reaches Africa, she discovers that she likes it: "Nairobi was the most exciting city she had ever been in," and she finds that she is considered "young, upper middle-class, desirable; men were good to her" (23). Africans are "all around her, but she never saw them; she found she did not even have to hate them: they kept their distance" (24). Indeed, all goes well for Heather until a sex scandal forces her to leave Nairobi and transfer to the remote girls' school in the highlands.

Another outsider in the story is the American girl B. J. Lebowitz. B. J. is the ultimate "other" in the novel; she has no connection to colonial Kenya because she is an American, and the British women at the school look at her as an outsider because she is a "Yank" and a Jew. B. J. has come to Africa because she thinks Africa will be as great and mysterious as it is portrayed to be in the media. Her experiences in Kenya, however, soon convince her that the popular image of Africa is a myth. Indeed, B. J. feels cheated by actual Africa. Africa, she discovers, is not the exciting, romantic, adventurous place of books and films. It is instead the "dullest place B. J. had ever been, the biggest zero on the globe" (110–11).

B. J. gets a close look at real Africa when she accompanies her African suitor, Wangi, to his home village, and her experiences in the village reinforce her belief that Africa is empty, nothing, a "zero." Wangi, a former Mau Mau, is head of the electricity board even though he has no training or education, and B. J. dates him not out of any feelings of affection but because "of a sense of obligation to the Peace

Corps" (115). Wangi's village is little more than a smattering of thatch huts in the wilderness. Instead of "drums, the dancers with the lion mane headdresses, [and] the fantastic-tailed birds" there is only dirt, smoke, and silence (138). After a few hours in the village, B. J. could "feel the filth clinging to her hands like gloves" (139). Her trip to the village makes her identify with the early European explorers who "could not have reported the silence" or the decay and, therefore, had invented a literature that mythologized Africa as a place of "savage warriors, slim back girls, lustful rumble of drums, fearsome yelling, and . . . wet trees and lovely birds" (139).

Ultimately, it is B. J.'s continued association with Wangi—her encounter with a "real" African—that leads to disaster. After a night of heavy drinking, B. J. tells Wangi that she intends to return to the United States. Wangi rapes the young American, and the next day she apparently commits suicide. Wangi's crime is covered up by his relative Wilbur, who is the District Education Officer. Wilbur makes a deal with Heather to hide Wangi's crime; then he fires Miss Poole and makes Heather headmistress of the school. Heather is just about to call the police and testify against Wangi when Rose, Miss Poole's loyal African servant, kills Heather to revenge Miss Poole's dismissal.

Girls at Play, then, is similar to *The Sheltering Sky* and *let it come down* by Bowles in that the characters in these novels come to Africa expecting adventure and romance, but they find only death and disaster.

Theroux's third African novel, *Jungle Lovers*, continues to explore the role of "others" and outsiders in postcolonial Africa, and the story indicates that neither of the West's most important ideological exports, capitalism or Marxism, offers viable solutions to Africa's problems (Gruesser 81). These Western ideologies are represented by an American insurance salesman named Calvin Mullet and a French-Canadian insurgent named Marais. Both of these characters travel to Africa with the hope of helping Africans; both of these characters realize, by the conclusion of the novel, the futility of their endeavors (Gruesser 81). Like *Fong and the Indians* and *Girls at Play*, *Jungle Lovers* indicates that in postcolonial African nations the response to outsiders is often harsh and racist.

Jungle Lovers is set in the central African nation of Malawi. Theroux served in the Peace Corps in Malawi, and he was deported from the country in 1965 after being falsely accused of plotting to kill Prime Minister Hastings Banda, the dictator of that nation (Gruesser 70). Theroux's disgust for Banda—whom he calls Hastings Osbong in the novel—is evident throughout *Jungle Lovers*. Osbong requires that his official photograph grace every room in Malawi. The photo shows Osbong wearing his school tie and a fur hat trimmed with rat tails (18–19). The legend under the picture reads, *"They call me a Dictator! If I am, then I am a Dictator for the People, by the People, and of the People"* (19). However, while Osbong's photograph is everywhere, Osbong himself is "seldom seen except through the windows of his Rolls" (19). Furthermore, Calvin comes to realize that Malawi is not really a nation (104). Malawi has a president, a flag, a national anthem, and a seat in the United Nations, but Malawi "wasn't a country. . . . [I]t was a situation, a patch of jungle in central Africa" (104–5).

However, at the beginning of the novel, when Calvin is dispatched to Malawi to open an office for Homemakers' Mutual Insurance Company, he thinks highly of the country: "He loved being in a place where you could spit where you pleased and piss by the door" (16). Moreover, Calvin has a real sympathy for Africans; in fact, Calvin is quite sensitive and open-minded for an American. He travels to Malawi with his American wife, but he is offended by her racism, and he boycotts food and products from South Africa because of that nation's racist policies. Before long, Calvin's wife files for divorce, and she returns to the United States after winning all of Calvin's "goods and chattels, so called, and half of his salary" (3).

Calvin suffers from a curious American ailment; he wants to help everyone. He wants to better the lives of Africans by encouraging them to buy insurance and save for their future, and he travels the backcountry in search of customers. However, Africans are slow to take to Calvin's product, and the African reaction to insurance is a criticism of American materialism. One potential customer suggests that Calvin look at life the African way: "Drink. Be happy. No worry" (8). And as Calvin eventually discovers, Africans have little use for insurance.

When one of Calvin's customers is beheaded by Marais's rebels, Calvin concludes that the "sort of insurance that Africans needed, Homemakers' Mutual did not sell. . . . Extra money wouldn't help anyone. . . . A person who appeared the least bit prosperous was nationalized and burgled; if he refused he got his skull cracked by the Youth Wingers. Insurance: there was no future in it" (135).

A few months after his divorce, Calvin marries Mira, the sister of a customer who has been killed by the rebels. Calvin quits selling insurance and begins drinking beer all day long; indeed, he appears to have adopted an African philosophy about life: "Drink. Be happy. No worry" (8). Calvin begins to eat African foods such as fried ants—he finds them quite tasty—and he has an African-like attitude when he discovers that Mira is expecting. He is glad the Mira will have a baby because the "childless were paupers—children were insurance in its purest form" (199). Calvin believes that the "Africans were right in valuing children. . . . Barrenness was the only poverty" (200). In fact, Calvin begins to think of Malawi as home, and he begins writing *The Uninsured*, a book about the plight of the Africans he has met. "*Would you insure me?*" asks the African narrator of Calvin's story: "*I have been beaten, robbed and nearly killed a thousand times. I live at the worst end of a bad world*" (85).

Eventually, Calvin's book is stolen by the rebels and printed as a manifesto that inspires the people of Malawi to revolt. Indeed, one of the novel's postmodern features is that Calvin's text within a text becomes a determining factor in the plot of *Jungle Lovers*. Ironically, the rebellion that is inspired by Calvin's book causes Calvin to reconsider his feelings about Africa; as the rebels make more progress, the mood of the Africans begins to change and racism toward whites becomes apparent. Africans force Calvin off the road and rough him up at the bars he frequents. Clavin is abused because he is white, the "violence was the African's reply, the savagery his denial that he was a savage" (239).

Before long, Africans begin to threaten Calvin and Mira, telling them that they will "keel new boat," which Mira translates as "kill you both." On other occasions, Africans call Calvin a "white sheet," a "bloody sheet, a useless sheet, a stewpeed sheet. The Africans were sinisterly equipped to abuse; their English was no good, but their mood was dark" (239–40). Eventually, Osbong's thugs nationalize Calvin's insurance agency, and after the birth of his son, Calvin realizes that there is no place in Malawi for a white man with a child of mixed heritage. Calvin is unable to help the Africans by insuring them, and the Africans refuse to allow him to live peacefully in Malawi.

Like Calvin, Marais has come to Africa with good intentions; he wants to help the citizens of Malawi liberate themselves from Osbong, and he wants to use the nation of Malawi as a staging area in the ongoing war against the white-controlled nations of Rhodesia and South Africa. Marais arms a group of fifty rebels and begins a trek through Malawi, moving from north to south. At first, Marais is idealistic, even romantic, about his quest. All the men in Marais's army are considered equal and the mission to overthrow Osbong is a noble one (12). However, after the rebels have some success, they become crazed by power. Some take to looting; others to rape (14). In fact, after Marais and his men capture a major city, his troops rebel against him and hold him prisoner while they loot the town.

Marais concludes that the struggle to liberate Malawi is hopeless because the rebels are as bad as Osbong and his thugs. He realizes that it "was a mistake to try to start a popular revolt here. No one cares. The biggest error was arming fifty men. I made them dangerous" (214). Marais thinks that Malawi is "still a tribal village. . . . When we leave, as we must, it will go back to being a village, slightly scarred with the memory of deaths. It was always cows and children. Osbong knew that" (214).

Marais dies in an attempt to end the revolution that his and Calvin's *The Uninsured* have imported to Malawi. In *Jungle Lovers*, as in *Fong and the Indians* and *Girls at Play*, Theroux leaves little doubt that postcolonial Africa is a hostile zone for outsiders and "others."

According to Gruesser, Theroux's three novels about Africa chronicle the West's initial attitude of hope for postcolonial Africa, an attitude that quickly turned to disillusionment that reinforced "Africanist thinking," the idea that Africa is less progressive than the West and in binary opposition to the West (89). Certainly, five years in Africa helped to shape Theroux's opinions about the continent. After all, in 1968 when Theroux was an instructor at Makere University in Uganda, he and his wife were attacked by students protesting the racist policies of Rhodesia (Gruesser 71). Theroux, then, has firsthand experience with the ways in which "others" are treated in postcolonial Africa. While Gruesser implies that any rein-forcement of traditional Western notions about Africa are erroneous and racist, Theroux's own experiences in Africa and the three novels he has written about Africa suggest that the "Africanist" notions that Gruesser criticizes actually de-scribe conditions in postcolonial Africa.

PART III: THOMAS PYNCHON AND WALTER ABISH

V. and *Gravity's Rainbow*: Pynchon's African Connection

Critics agree that one important theme shared by *V.* and *Gravity's Rainbow* is a concern with the nature of history and the relationship of past events to the present (Weisenburger 141). In both *V.* and *Gravity's Rainbow*, Pynchon uses African settings to comment on the nature of history and to explain why things have gone so terribly wrong in the twentieth century. The African scenes in both of these novels indicate that the decline of Western civilization—a decline evidenced by two world wars and the Holocaust—is linked to colonialism.

The main use of African settings in *V.* occurs in a chapter titled "Mondaugen's Story," a chapter that details Mondaugen's adventures in Southwest Africa in 1922. Inside this story is an account of the struggle between Africans and Germans in 1904, a struggle that led to the extermination of a number of African tribes. Mondaugen's job in Southwest Africa is to monitor "atmospheric radio disturbances; sferics for short" (213). Mondaugen uses amplifiers to alert him when a sferic occurs, and the noise created by these amplified radio disturbances frightens the native people and causes them to revolt against the settlers—mainly Germans who remained in Southwest Africa after control of the colony was shifted to the British at the conclusion of World War I. Mondaugen is told to collect his gear and "tell them at Foppl's what you've heard here. Hole up in that fortress of his" (215).

The news of the uprising causes those at Foppl's farm to engage in a siege party that lasts for two months. During this party, Mondaugen learns of the atrocities committed in 1904 by the Germans who controlled the colony. In stark contrast to the traditional uses of African settings in contemporary American fiction, Pynchon's tale of the 1904 struggle between the Germans and the Africans indicates that the Westerners—not Africans—are savage beings. Pynchon describes the German actions of 1904 in these terms: "In August 1904 . . . German forces were ordered to exterminate systematically every Hereo man, woman, and child they could find. . . . Out of the estimated 80,000 Hereos living in the territory in 1904, an official German census taken seven years later set the Hereo population at only 15,130. . . . Similarly the Hottentots were reduced in the same period by about 10,000, the Berg-Damaras by 17,000. . . . This is only 1 percent of six million, but still pretty good" (227). Pynchon's allusion to six million deaths clearly links the slaughter of the Africans with the slaughter of the Jews in World War II, and Newman believes that Pynchon views the "horrors enacted by the Germans in Southwest Africa . . . as a logical extension of the capitulation to the void which V. personifies and to which twentieth-century life has succumbed" (48–49).

Weisenburger notes that many of the descriptions of the atrocities committed against Africans in 1904 are derived from a book titled *South African Cinderella: A Trek through EX German South West Africa* (151). The author of this volume, an Englishman named Rex Hardinnnge, "describes many of the variations on field

execution Pynchon tells of in *V.*—hangings, disembowelings, and the slow stran-
gulation of victims by stringing them up between the (yes) v-shaped branch of a
tree" (Weisenburger 151–52). Indeed, the descriptions of the German atrocities in
Southwest Africa will sound familiar to those acquainted with the tortures devised
by Nazis in Hitler's Germany. For instance, Pynchon writes about "natives already
exterminated—sleeping and lame burned en masse in their pontoks, babies tossed
in the air and caught on bayonets, girls approached with organ at ready, their eyes
filming over in anticipated pleasure or possibly only an anticipated five more
minutes of life, only to be shot through the head first and then ravished" (245).
Moreover, the Germans apparently first use concentration camps in Southwest
Africa: "The barren islets off Luderrizbucht were natural concentration camps. . . .
Their [the Africans'] bodies, so terribly thin and sick . . . lay drawn together to pool
what marginal warmth was left to them" (249).

As the German colonist Foppl explains, General von Trotha, the man who
ordered the killing of the natives, is a hero to the Germans because he "taught us
not to fear. It's impossible to describe the sudden release; the comfort, the luxury;
when you knew you could safely forget all the rote-lessons you'd had to learn about
the value and dignity of human life" (234). *V.* indicates that Germany's colonial
experience in Africa has dehumanized the colonists and infected them with a terrible
evil that is carried home where it lies dormant until it explodes within Germany—
the heart of European darkness—and results in the horrible events of the Holocaust.

Gravity's Rainbow continues Pynchon's examination of the "lessons of history
and the consequence of ignoring those lessons" (Newman 96), and, like *V.*, *Gravity's
Rainbow* highlights this concern with history by asking readers to consider events
that occurred in German-controlled Southwest Africa. Pynchon again returns to the
notion that the German experience in Africa prepared the way for the Holocaust in
Europe. For instance, as one of the Africans in *Gravity's Rainbow* explains: "Forty
years ago, in Suydwest, we were nearly exterminated. There was no reason. Can
you understand. *No reason.* We couldn't even find comfort in the Will of God
Theory. These were Germans with names and service records, men in blue uniforms
who killed clumsily and not without guilt. . . . It went on for twenty years. Their
orders came down from a human being, a scrupulous butcher named von Trotha"
(362). The Germans in Southwest Africa are much like their World War II counter-
parts; they are simply following orders, simply doing their duty, when they
exterminate a race of people considered inferior to themselves.

Pointedly tying the German colonial experience in Southwest Africa to the
events of World War II, Pynchon writes that

[C]olonies are the outhouses of the European soul, where a fellow can let his pants down
and relax. . . . Where he can fall on his prey roaring as loud as he feels like, guzzle her blood
with open joy. . . . Where he can just wallow and rut and let himself go. . . . Christian Europe
had always been death . . . and repression. Out and down in the colonies, life can be indulged,
life and sensuality in all its forms, with no harm done to the Metropolis, nothing to soil those
cathedrals, white marble statues, and noble thoughts. . . . No word ever gets back. The

silences down here are vast enough to absorb all behavior, no matter how dirty, how animal it gets. (*Gravity's* 317)

However, both *V.* and *Gravity's Rainbow* indicate that the word did finally get back, and the actions of the Germans in Southwest Africa infected an entire nation and caused its citizens to forget the "rote-lessons" of civilization and engage in one of history's most brutal events—the extermination of more than six million people. In both *V.* and in *Gravity's Rainbow*, Pynchon suggests that the seeds of Western destruction lie in the colonial experience; the events in German-controlled Southwest Africa are just the beginning of a long fever that has destroyed twentieth-century Western civilization.

Alphabetical Africa: Africa by the Letter

One of the most experimental of the contemporary American novels set in Africa is Walter Abish's *Alphabetical Africa*. *Alphabetical Africa* contains many of the features readers have come to expect from postmodern fiction: a challenge to conventional narrative forms, an interest in metafiction, and a use of parody. *Alphabetical Africa* describes the exploits of jewel thieves who are chasing their partner across Africa, but the characters—Allen, Alex, and Alva—are thinly developed and the story line is comic, even silly.

The challenge to narrative convention is the most important postmodern feature of Abish's novel. The story is constructed of fifty-two chapters. The first twenty-six chapters follow the order of the alphabet; for instance, chapter one uses only words beginning with the letter *A*, chapter two uses words beginning with *A* and *B*, and so on until chapter twenty-six, which employs words that begin with all of the letters. In the second twenty-six chapters, Abish reverses the process and works his way back through the alphabet from *Z* until the final chapter, like the first, contains only words that begin with *A*. As McHale explains, *Alphabetical Africa* is a text "in which even the details of space, time, description, narration, plot, and character are subject to the determination of letters" (158). *Alphabetical Africa*, then, is more about the nature of narration and language than about Africa; Abish's Africa is a metaphor for the work of art, an "alibi for investigating a possible world of fiction" (Martin 231).

Yet even in this highly experimental work, Abish makes use of many traditions associated with African settings. Because *Alphabetical Africa* is a work of postmodernism, however, these conventions are parodied rather than seriously applied to the story. For instance, Abish parodies the notion that Africa is constantly plagued by war by beginning *Alphabetical Africa* with a passage dealing with war: "an awesome African army assembled and arduously advanced against an African anthill, assiduously annihilating ant after ant" (1). While the parody is apparent, the message is serious. Schirato points out that the ants are metaphorical, noting that "ants are not normally annihilated [but] a race of people or the inhabitants of a country, city, or village might be" especially if "like Africans to Western eyes, they are seen as inferior 'others' " (134). Moreover, the Americans seem to be at war with Africa in Abish's novel; the "American airforce bombs Ashanti beaches," and later American bombs fall on imaginary beaches in Chad—a landlocked nation.

Abish also parodies the Western notion that Africans are brutal savages capable of all types of atrocities. For instance, early in the novel an "African army captain attends a Bach concert at an army camp. As always bugler cautiously blows Bach, beautiful Bach, as an army captain, citing duty, calmly cuts down drummer, chopping at arms, at body, also cutting down bugler, clean convenient cuts, and dismembering a dozen conductors, all crawling among ants, all dreading clean convenient cuts" (8).

Furthermore, Abish employs parody to comment on the familiar Western idea that Africans are childlike beings incapable of culture: "Congolese cannot create a culture, can barely cook cucumbers, curds, and cauliflowers," and arriving in Chad, "Alex and Allen coldly consider childlike Chad attitudes, and calculate, can Chadians afford American cosmetics" (6). African weather is another topic that interests Abish: "You must avoid having nothing to say and nothing to do in this heat, the French Consul said to Alfred. It can cause irreparable damage to your nervous system" (74), and African wildlife can be deadly in Ablish's parody: "A day after their arrival they lost their faithful African guide to a man-eating snake" (83).

Abish also plays with the notion that Africa has no history: "all history in Africa is hearsay, and, consequently, although Africa indubitably exists, history cannot correct certain highly erroneous assumptions" (21). Indeed, history is a thematic concern in *Alphabetical Africa* just as it is in Abish's later works, *How German Is It* and *Eclipse Fever*. As Martin notes, by "choosing to write about Africa, the archetypal territory of colonial exploitation, [Abish] is also choosing to write about history" (232). What does *Alphabetical Africa* say about the Western role in Africa's history? As Schirato points out, in *Alphabetical Africa*, "Western intervention in Africa is rationalized . . . in terms of Africa's apparent lack of discernible shape, order and not least of all, authority" (135). By expanding and shrinking Africa along alphabetical lines, Abish is reminding his readers that the West has traditionally seen the African continent as a formless zone that needs to be shaped and ordered before it can be consumed by Western powers.

Alphabetical Africa successfully accomplishes the goal of much postmodern fiction: an upsetting of established norms and methods of perception. Abish hopes that his use of parody and unconventional narrative technique will cause readers to realize the shortcomings inherent in many of the traditional Western notions concerning Africa.

PART IV: MARIA THOMAS AND RICHARD DOOLING

Two Worlds Side By Side: *Antonia Saw the Oryx First*

Maria Thomas's *Antonia Saw the Oryx First* is a postmodern work that examines the status of whites as "others" in postcolonial Africa and asks readers to consider the possibility that there are African methods of healing that challenge the conventions of Western science. The novel also comments on conditions in postcolonial Africa and on the way Western infrastructures and technology have deteriorated since African nations achieved independence. Maria Thomas lived in Africa for twelve years, she spoke several African languages, and she met a tragic death in Ethiopia in a 1989 plane crash that also took the life of Congressman Mickey Leland of Houston (Gruesser 122). Although Thomas finds numerous faults with conditions in postcolonial Tanzania, she is sympathetic toward African cultures and African problems. The concern with alternative ways of knowing the world and of healing the sick makes *Antonia Saw the Oryx First* a postmodern novel in terms of theme, but the book is traditional in structure and narrative technique.

Antonia Saw the Oryx First is set mostly in Dar es Salaam, the capital of Tanzania. The main character of the novel is Antonia Redmond, a doctor who works in the city's hospital. Antonia was born in Tanzania of American parents, but after independence, the government nationalizes her father's property (14). By the time of the main action of the novel, Antonia's father has died, and her mother has returned to the United States where she hopes to "reclaim America" but is "daunted by the place, the speeding freeways, the confusion of machines" (41).

Although Antonia considers herself an African, the socialist government of Tanzania allows her to remain in the nation only because she is a physician whose skills are sorely needed. In fact, Antonia is one of the most assimilated to Africa of all the Western characters featured in contemporary American novels set in Africa. This high degree of assimilation is evident from the very first line of the book: "Like an African, the white doctor came to work on foot" (1). However, Antonia's assimilation is not voluntary. She walks to work not because she chooses to but because she has been waiting over a year for her car to be repaired. Her assimilation is brought about by conditions inherent to Africa, not from a desire to live as a majority of Africans live.

Antonia's supervisor at the hospital is an African named Paul Luenga. Paul and Antonia meet while in college in Boston; they are drawn together because they are both Africans attempting to deal with the climate and culture of North America. Their difference in race is transcended by their affinity to place; they both miss Africa, and, after graduation from medical school, Antonia returns to Dar es Salaam to work and live with Paul even though he has a wife in his home village. However, Paul and Antonia break off their affair, and the cause of the breakup is political. Paul sees everything in political terms, even "their sex life. She worried about getting on top for fear he'd see some parallel to the colonial situation in it" (48). Antonia, however, doesn't care to discuss what might have been if Africa had not been ruined by Europeans.

Although Antonia socializes mainly with Westerners whose governments have assigned them to duty in Dar es Salaam, she has friendships with many Africans. In the case of Esther Moro, the major African character in the novel, this friendship transcends not only race but also class and education. Esther—one of the few fully developed African characters in contemporary American fiction set in Africa—is a vehicle for delivering comments that show how Africans view the West and how Africans are affected by Western culture. Most importantly, Esther seems to have a mysterious ability to heal the ill, a power that she associates with Christianity. And according to Alex Haley's *Roots, moro*, Esther's last name, is an African term for a religious leader or teacher (104).

The things that draw Esther and Antonia together are disease and healing, and few settings are so well suited to an examination of methods of healing as is Africa. After all, one of the major conventions about Africa in Western literature is that Africa is a disease-ridden zone. In fact, Esther's entire adult life is shaped by a concern with disease and healing, and this concern is one of the most important ways that Thomas highlights the notion that Africa and the West are "two worlds . . . side by side" (20). Esther's father, Musumbi, is an assistant to a German doctor, and he has learned many things about Western science. Musumbi tells Esther that there "are two truths . . . theirs and ours. They know only one, their own" (171). Although Musumbi believes in Western medicine, he is a sort or African folk doctor who can heal by using native plants and medicines (30). However, Musumbi remains opposed to the *mganga*, the witch doctors whose cures—they often force people to drink dog urine—are questionable (31).

When her father dies, Esther is sold as a child bride to Josephat, an elderly man who has several wives and who sexually torments the young Esther but refrains from sleeping with her because she has not yet begun menstruation and has not yet been circumcised. Esther hates Josephat and his tribe, and she fears genital mutilation because she knows it has caused the death of many young women. When she has her first period, Esther flees Josephat's village to avoid mutilation; it is at this point that Esther begins her encounters with the Western world.

Once she arrives in Dar es Salaam, Esther takes a job doing washing for a French family. She soon realizes that Westerners have lives that are much different from the lives most Africans lead. Since she is a Christian, Esther speculates that somehow Westerners are "favored by God" because of their health and material wealth (96). Indeed, Western ways seem as mysterious to Esther as African ways seem to many Westerners, and this view of how Africans react to Western culture is one of the most intriguing features of *Antonia Saw the Oryx First*. For instance, Esther thinks that it is strange that the Europeans paint their toes and sunbathe (96), and she finds the music that the French play on their phonograph odd (97). Esther's next job in Dar es Salaam is cooking for a family of Indians, and she finds that the Indians are just as strange as the Europeans. Indeed, Esther is not at ease with outsiders who have come to live in her country, and she has a suspicion that "being Hindi, or French, or even German was a kind of demon possession itself, a madness" (107).

Eventually, Esther becomes a prostitute, and even in this profession she learns that Westerners are different from Africans. For example, Esther's friend Hadija tells her that Americans are simply little boys who, when the sex is finished, want to be sure the girl is happy (101). It is Esther's contact with a Greek sailor that brings her to Antonia's attention. After a night of heavy drinking, the sailor uses a broken bottle to cut at Esther's genitals in a sloppy version of the circumcision that Esther had hoped to avoid (29).

Antonia saves Esther's life, but Esther returns to the hospital with pain caused by scar tissue. However, Esther believes that the pain is caused by frogs in her stomach, and, after hearing Esther's explanation for the pain, Antonia "envies the *mganga* their clever blend of psychology and herbs and magic. A *mganga* would have treated Esther for what she thought was wrong, frogs in the stomach" (56). Esther's curiosity about medicine leads Antonia to befriend the girl, and soon Esther tells Antonia about her healing abilities.

Among the people whom Esther has healed is an Indian girl who suffers from fever. Esther lays hands on the girl and throws "away the fever" (108). Another time Esther heals a girl who has a terrible skin condition. Esther bathes the girl and cleans away the foul pastes that the *mganga* have used to treat her. The girl soon recovers (92). Yet another of Esther's cures involves a boy who is stricken with polio. Inspired by Antonia's descriptions of hydrotherapy, Esther takes the boy swimming in the sea until his leg muscles are strengthened and he can walk. Esther tells Antonia that "I told them this is therapy like you said so that they don't think I am a witch" (155). While some of Esther's cures can be explained in terms of Western science—for instance, the girl with the skin condition improves not because of Esther's touch but because Esther bathed the girl, and the boy with polio walks again not because of magic but because of physical therapy—others are unexplainable.

Antonia is naturally puzzled by the cures that Esther performs, and she thinks of some possible explanations for these events. Could the cures be explained by the powers of suggestion or by spontaneous remission? Antonia concludes that Esther's healing is "only another absurd situation like all of Africa" (184). In any event, Antonia realizes that Esther truly believes she has special powers and that many people think that Esther has cured them (185). Furthermore, Antonia notes that Esther thinks about disease in terms different from those used by Western physicians. Esther speaks of "drawing off" disease and "rebalancing" the body while Westerners conceive of disease in war-like terms (149). However Antonia clearly doubts Esther's power because nothing she has seen in her years as a physician indicates the validity of alternative methods of healing (270).

Eventually Esther leaves the city and travels into the country in the company of a refugee from South Africa. The man's name is Nkosi, and he is a rebel soldier in the army of guerrillas who intend to liberate South Africa from white rule. Nkosi claims to have seen Esther heal (285), and he believes that Esther's powers come from a special talent she was given at birth.

After reading a newspaper account of Esther's healing ceremonies, Antonia travels into the bush in search of Esther because Antonia knows that, due to the political situation in Tanzania, she may never have another opportunity to talk with her friend. When Antonia does find Esther, she is reminded that there are many conditions that neither Western medicine nor Esther's power can remedy. Specifically, neither Esther nor Antonia can save Nkosi, who suffers from a terminal liver condition.

Despite her doubts, Antonia apparently is willing to believe in Esther's powers if she sees proof. At the conclusion of the novel, Antonia has a vision of Nkosi recovered from his terminal condition: "She thought of the miracle—Lazarus" (290). However, when she runs to see Nkosi, she is told that he has died. About her vision Antonia thinks, "Perhaps hallucination tells you more about yourself than about the world" (290).

Antonia finally concludes that both Western and African healing rely on "myths and blindness" (252), that, obviously, the state of human knowledge, be it Western or African, is limited. Moreover, through various observations about Western medical techniques as seen through Africa perspectives, Thomas demonstrates how such techniques can seem very strange to non-Westerners, as strange as African ways sometimes seem to those from the West. For example, the Africans find it very odd that organ transplants are common in the West, and when Antonia visits a hospital in the lake country, a nurse asks if it is true that American women can get a penis "stitched on" or that American men can have operations that will give them breasts (208). Obviously, such Western practices might appear strange, even magical, to Africans.

The discussion of Western and African ways of healing is just one aspect of a major theme in the book: that there are numerous realities and that, as postmodernists insist, reality is subjective. For instance, to explain the seasons in the northern hemisphere to her servant Charles, Antonia says the days in the north get shorter in the winter and longer in the summer. Charles wonders how people can sleep under such circumstances, and Antonia explains that, in other countries, people are used to the sun rising at slightly different times each day. For Charles, however, this is puzzling because at the equator "the sun rose at the same time every day" (242).

The Africa of *Antonia Saw the Oryx First* is also postmodern in its mixing of cultures, especially the mixing of American pop culture with African culture. Esther's prostitute friends are infatuated with Western goods and styles. The African character who most embraces Western pop culture is Esther's friend Hadija. Hadija believes that she can only be happy by being modern. For her, happiness means wearing Western fashions and frequenting nightclubs (113). And it is not only the prostitutes who embrace Western styles; the Bantus like neckties, wrist watches, and shoes (10). Antonia has her own thoughts about the way Western culture has invaded Africa. She knows that Western influence has been destructive, but she realizes that history cannot be undone (18).

While Western pop culture thrives in postcolonial Africa, Western technology fails and falls short of it promise. Indeed, Thomas uses the introduction of Western technology to Africa as a metaphor for the effects of colonialism on the continent. The most powerful of these metaphors concerning colonialism and technology comes when Antonia travels to the lake country in search of Esther. The Germans had long ago introduced a species of perch into the lake: "Perch of frightening proportions, brought from abroad by a foreign scheme, were eating all the other species in the lake" (209). The giant perch that consume the indigenous species are like Western values and technology that have consumed traditional African ways.

The signs of decay and technological collapse are everywhere in Tanzania, but Antonia is most upset by the failure of the postcolonial government to maintain standards at the hospital. The hospital has gone to ruin after the departure of the British. Indeed, Antonia knows that some Westerners think that Africa was better off in colonial days (159). Paul Luenga sees such decline from an African point of view; he thinks the decay is actually progress: "A seed must rot before it germinates. . . . Only when you completely ruin us will you understand how much of it is your fault and then you might leave us alone" (159).

The hospital is only one of many colonial institutions that have gone to ruin under the postcolonial government. Antonia lives in a government housing project that only allows her two gallons of water a day, and, when the gas supply is disrupted, Antonia starts cooking on a kerosene-powered stove. She worries that soon she will be reduced to using charcoal and eventually, when there are no more trees, she will not be able to cook her food (252). Because Antonia is African and because she loves her homeland, she takes no happiness in these developments, and she thinks disdainfully of those who find joy in Africa's troubles (248).

However, even those who have come to Africa to help sometimes have doubts about Africa's postcolonial status. For instance, Antonia's lover is an American official named Ted Armstrong who had worked with the Peace Corps in Nigeria before coming to Tanzania (121). Armstrong has been disillusioned by Western ways of attempting to help Africans. According to Armstrong, Westerners have relied too much on technology to solve Africa's problems. For example, he tells Antonia that millions of dollars have been wasted building dams that can never hold back lakes because in arid regions rivers often change their paths (125). Yet despite his lack of confidence in Western projects that are designed to help Africans, Armstrong feels that the West will eventually be forced to take a greater role in African affairs. He predicts another colonial period, one that Africans will willingly accept in the face of starvation (226).

Finally, most of the Westerners, including Antonia, are forced by the oppressive postcolonial government to leave Tanzania, and the conditions at the airport cleverly demonstrate not only the extent of the decline of Western technology in postcolonial Africa but also the loss of a sense of place that characterizes the postmodern world. The automatic flight board at the airport no longer works, and "arrivals and departures were scrawled in chalk on a wall that had been painted black. Poorly erased, the wall had a dusty, surreal look—Lonoroma, Bomanfurt—layers of place names as though the world had been suddenly altered, shaken together and respelled to harrow tourists" (244).

Antonia is an African by birth and her attachment to Africa is deep. As she prepares to leave Tanzania, she thinks that leaving behind "landscapes, seascapes, and skies like these" is harder than leaving behind people because more than a background to her life, the "graying, glowing billowing sky seasoned with the winds of Asia" is "her context" (224). However, despite her attachment to Africa, Antonia is an "other," an outsider who is no longer welcome in her home country because she is white. And although the people of her country are in great need of her medical skills, Antonia knows she will be deported along with the Indians and other outsiders who attempt to make postcolonial Tanzania their home.

Gruesser maintains that "Antonia realizes that her career and Western medicine in general are based on an Africanist mentality. According to Thomas, the intention of both is not to reach out and soothe Africans in pain but rather to stop the infection of Africa from spreading to the West" (127). This is a serious misreading of an important novel, and, curiously, Gruesser cites no passage to support his claim. However, Antonia is open to the possibility that African ways of healing may be real, and she certainly realizes that Western medicine is limited and does not hold all the answers to the problems of Africa or the world. Gruesser also claims that despite "all the progress she has made toward reducing the alienation she feels in Africa, Antonia gives up short of true communion with the continent and its people" (129). Again, Gruesser offers no passage from the novel to support this assertion, and, in fact, Antonia's relationships with Africans, Paul Luenga, Esther, and the nurses at the lake-district hospital, for example, are lengthy and rich. Antonia does not want to leave Africa and would be content to stay in Tanzania and serve her nation and her people. However, because she is white, she is forced to leave the country by the distrustful, racist postcolonial government that rules the nation.

Bewitched in Sierra Leone: *White Man's Grave*

Like *Antonia Saw the Oryx First*, Richard Dooling's *White Man's Grave* is postmodern in its thematic concerns but traditional in structure and narrative technique. *White Man's Grave* promotes the idea that the West African method of explaining the physical world, a method that relies on magic and belief in spirits that influence everyday affairs, is "real" because it works as well for Africans as science does for Westerners. The novel is heavily didactic; it provides a wealth of information about the history of Sierra Leone and about conditions in that West African nation. Moreover, *White Man's Grave*, like many other contemporary American novels set in Africa, uses the comparison of Africa and the United States as a method of critiquing contemporary American society. To some degree, Dooling's strategy, like Thomas's in *Antonia Saw the Oryx First*, is to describe Western ways in a manner that makes them seem as "unreasonable" as African ways sometimes seem to Westerners.

White Man's Grave begins when Randall Killigan, a senior partner in the largest law firm in Indianapolis, receives a mysterious package from Sierra Leone where his son works as a Peace Corps volunteer (1). Randall Killigan is the novel's symbol of American capitalism and aggression. He thrives on stress and conquest and takes pleasure in destroying the careers of opposing attorneys (15).

The package from Africa is a "black bundle of tightly wrapped rags the size of a small football, with a two-inch hollow red tube made out of some kind of porous stone or mineral sticking out of the apex" (7). The day he receives the package,

Randall learns that his son Michael is missing in the bush country of Sierra Leone. Later that evening, Randall has a vision in which he believes he sees a giant bat in his bedroom (70).

Randall discusses his vision with a physician, Dr. Bean, telling Bean that the bat "was hideous, like something out of Africa" (77). Dr. Bean thinks that Randall is a stressed-out attorney and that the law consists mainly of magic spells and incantations (74). This analogy concerning law and magic is only the first of many in which Dooling compares Western institutions and beliefs with African institutions and beliefs.

Randall's son Michael has rejected the American way of life and rebelled against his father by enlisting in the Peace Corps. After he is sent to Sierra Leone, Michael writes numerous letters to his best friend, Boone Westfall, and the two plan to travel around the world when Michael finishes his fourth year in West Africa. Michael's letters reflect his change in attitude as he spends more time in Sierra Leone. At first the letters are "celebrations of African village life," but later, Michael's love of Africa turns into a hatred of America (31).

Boone, like Michael, is the product of a liberal arts education that has left him unprepared to earn a living in the United States. After working a year for his father's insurance company, where he learns that high school graduates are hired to spot fraudulent claims and that his job, as a college graduate, is to find ways to refuse legitimate claims, Boone decides to save his money and see the world (25). He is tired of "life in the Land of TV" (23). Boone is waiting in Paris to meet Michael when he learns that Michael is missing from his village in Sierra Leone.

The accounts of Michael's disappearance are alarming; U.S. officials maintain that after an attack on his village, Michael dissapeared. They suspect rebels are holding him captive (21). The official report also maintains that locals in Sierra Leone believe that Michael has assumed the shape of a "bush devil," and that he roams the bush seeking revenge against those who destroyed him (22). When Boone learns of his friend's disappearance, he gathers some information about Sierra Leone and flies to Freetown, the nation's capital.

In *White Man's Grave*, information about Sierra Leone is released from three sources: the guidebooks on Sierra Leone that Boone obtains in Paris, a disillusioned Peace Corps volunteer named Sam Lewis, and an American anthropologist named Sisay who has made Sierra Leone his home for more than twenty years. From the guidebooks, Boone learns that Sierra Leone got its name from Portuguese sailors who, in 1462, thought they heard lions roaring in the hills (48). He also discovers that the British colony of Sierra Leone was founded in 1787 as a country for liberated slaves. The British ruled Sierra Leone until 1961, when the nation achieved independence (49). The guidebooks also explain that it rains six months a year in Sierra Leone, that the per capita gross national product is 240 U.S. dollars, and that 166 of every 1,000 infants in Sierra Leone die before their first birthday (46). Beyond a description of the history, weather, and economy of the nation, Boone also learns from his guidebooks that garbage is piled to the rooftops in

Freetown, that West Africans have a hatred of whites, and that, aside from diamonds, "disease was Sierra Leone's biggest export" (42).

Boone's research also provides clues as to the contents of the mysterious package that Michael's father has received. The strange package contains a *ndilei* medicine. A person becomes a witch via association with the medicine, and once "under the medicine's power, he is committed to the life of cannibalism which witches lead" (44). The *ndilei* is perfectly suited to Randall Killigan because he makes his living by "cannibalizing" bankrupt corporations and "destroying" enemy attorneys. In fact, the conclusion of the novel implies that Randall's very being has been shaped by his merciless attitude, an attitude that serves him well in court but also bewitches him into thinking that he is living a worthy life.

After his arrival in Freetown, Peace Corps officials warn Boone against traveling into the interior to search for Michael. Boone is told that his stateside inoculations against yellow fever, cholera, and typhoid will do him little good because there are more than 250 other tropical diseases that he might contract if he ventures inland (53). However, Boone is befriended by Sam Lewis, a Peace Corps worker who knows Michael and promises to help Boone locate his lost friend.

Lewis is one of the more intriguing characters in the novel; he is, in fact, a foil for Michael who has gone native and been initiated into the Poro cult—a secret men's society whose initiation rites include ritual scarification. Lewis tells Boone that Sierra Leone "runs on bribes . . . graft, thievery, witchcraft, and juju" (57). Lewis also maintains that, because it is election time in Sierra Leone, the politicians will resort to ritual cannibalism to make powerful medicines (216).

Lewis tells Boone that Michael is friends with an American anthropologist named Aruna Sisay who has gone native, taken three wives, and refuses to speak anything except Mende (61). Lewis maintains that Sisay is in Sierra Leone in search of personal gain, despite the fact that Sisay claims to despise materialism. As Lewis explains it, Sisay is happy in Sierra Leone because he is "running half the country. . . . He's up there. He's connected" (213). Lewis thinks Sierra Leone appeals to men like Sisay because they can rent farms for only a few dollars, and they can buy as many wives as they like: "[Y]ou can get the cream of the crop—big teats, no diseases, a young tight one with good training—for under a hundred. . . . This ain't suburban Indiana, pal. Women are chattel, got it?" (214).

Boone travels to Sisay's village in hopes of learning Michael's whereabouts. Sisay explains that he came to Sierra Leone to study the Mende, but someday he hopes to return to the United States so he can study the "savage, violent, unspeakable greedy people who live there" (99). Dooling uses Sisay to release additional information about life in Sierra Leone. For instance, Sisay informs Boone that in West Africa the right hand is used for eating and the left hand is for cleaning oneself after using the latrine. It is, therefore, very bad form to eat with the left hand or to even touch someone with the left hand (97). Sisay also warns Boone about the dangers of "bush devils," telling him not to travel into the bush at night for any reason (107).

In one of the more important thematic moments of the novel, Sisay explains the validity of witchcraft to Africans by comparing witchcraft's effects to the effects of Western science. According to Sisay, Westerners always want to know if African magic is "true" because they think that science is "true." Westerners, however, only think science is "true" because it works; science heats their homes and powers their cars, yet few can actually explain how the wonders of science are accomplished. African witchcraft is also "true," at least in Sisay's view, because it too "works" by protecting crops and destroying a person's enemies (104). Westerners simply don't understand how magic and witchcraft work in West Africa.

Sisay also informs Boone that Michael may not be missing; he may be hiding because he has become involved in a political dispute. Because Michael speaks Mende, he has become "too African" (105). According to Sisay, Michael has made a number of enemies because he is honest; he will not allow Western aid to be diverted to corrupt officials (106). Moreover, Michael has also fallen in love with a Mende woman named Jenisa who is one of the wives of an important section chief (116).

From Jenisa, readers learn about the status of women in Sierra Leone and about the Sande Society—the women's secret society whose initiation rites include genital mutilation (114). Indeed, *White Man's Grave* frequently compares the status of women in West Africa to the status of women in the United States. For instance, after he makes the mistake of helping the village women process their rice crop, Boone learns that all jobs are gender specific in Sierra Leone. Sisay tells Boone that the villagers think he is mentally ill because hulling rice is woman's work (150).

Continuing his strategy of indicating that Western ways are just as "savage" and "unreasonable" as African ways, Dooling gives readers an African view of women's rights in the West. Some of the feminist Peace Corps volunteers set up workshops in which they attempt to convince the Mende women that they are the victims of a male conspiracy to oppress them. The volunteers denounce polygamy and genital mutilation and urge the Mende to resist these oppressive policies. Some of the Mende women are even listening to these arguments until they learn about abortion rights in the United States. At one workshop, a Mende women explains that in America "they let medicine men cut healthy peekins [babies] out of their mothers' bellies, then they throw the peekins into latrines. How's that for savagery?" (147). When the Mende women hear this description of abortion in the United States, the volunteers' feminist movement dies.

Dooling also compares Western religion to West African beliefs, indicating that there is not so much difference in the two as some might suspect. For example, Dooling compares African witchcraft to the religious beliefs held by Randall's wife, Marjorie. Marjorie believes so strongly in prayer that she hires nuns to design special prayers just for her (188). Dooling implies that Marjorie's actions are similar to those of West Africans who hire witches to assist them in their communication with the spirit world. The comparison of Africa and Western religions is continued when Randall attends church for the first time in many years and has to decide if he should accept the Eucharist. The Eucharist strikes Randall as a "primitive, savage ritual" in which a priest changes wine and bread into the blood and body of Christ. Randall then thinks of his son who is lost in Africa and is who is probably being chased by "cannibals" (238).

In an attempt to understand the mysterious package he has received and to prepare himself for his journey to Sierra Leone, Randall consults a U.S. government official who gives him background information on Sierra Leone and West Africa. The official is named Warren Holmes, and his comments provide yet another example that the belief systems of the West and Africa are not as different as they might appear to be. Specifically, Holmes compares Western science to African witchcraft and religion by saying that Africans do not understand the laws of physics. Africans believe in an invisible world of spirits and think the spirits share the earth with them and influence the every day lives of the living (133). Dooling's point is that Westerners also live among invisible "spirits"; however, Westerners call these invisible elements *science*. Holmes says that Africans are "so ignorant they don't realize that everything is actually made up of molecules, consisting of electrons, muons, and neutrions in orbit around atomic nuclei, together with protons, neutrons, pi mesons, mesons, baryons, kaons, and hadrons . . . no one's ever 'seen' these elementary particles . . . [but they] conform to perfectly rational laws of physics. Does that sound like witchcraft?" (133–34). The tone of this passage clearly indicates that Dooling expects his readers to answer *yes* to the question posed by Holmes. However, Dooling's comparisons fare better when he examines African religions and Western religions. His comparisons are less convincing when he attempts to equate African magic with Western science.

After Boone witnesses a ceremony in which a witchman apparently cuts out his own tongue and then replaces it without causing himself any harm (298), Boone is kidnapped by rebels and taken to Michael. Boone and Michael are able to escape the rebels because the rebels think Boone is a witch, and they are afraid to kill him because his witch spirit might haunt them (347). Witchcraft "works" in Sierra Leone because Boone's status as a witch allows him to escape his captors.

In the meantime, Randall Killigan flies to Africa in search of his son. However, upon his arrival in Freetown, Randall realizes that "he had crossed a forbidden threshold into another dimension . . . where his life was suddenly as cheap as those of the beggars and urchins swarming around him" (368–69). While in Freetown, Randall sees a five-hundred-year-old cotton tree that is a local landmark. He thinks that people have decorated the tree with "spectacular capes that hang from every limb" (373). The capes turn out to be fruit bats like the one Randall imagined seeing in his bedroom shortly after receiving the mysterious package from Sierra Leone. When he sees how people live in Freetown, Randall decides to forego searching the bush for his son, and he returns to the United States.

Eventually, Michael, Jenisa, and Boone are able to escape Sierra Leone, and Randall returns to his law office to discover that one of the opposing lawyers whose career he has ruined has died of a stress-related heart attack. However, Randall's brief African experience has apparently changed him; as he walks through his law office he realizes that for years he has worked with nearly two hundred people without bothering to learn any of their first names. But it is not until he has traveled to Freetown that he thinks there is anything unusual about this. The concluding lines of the novel continue the comparison of law and witchcraft, indicating that Randall is like a witch who had "convinced himself that he was only using bad medicine to protect himself . . . but before long . . . discovers that he has a witch spirit, and the witch spirit has gradually . . . taken over" (386). Randall Killigan suddenly realizes that his career as an attorney, a career in which he takes much joy in the destruction of competition, has in fact infected him with a spirit similar to that of the evil magic practiced by the witchmen of Sierra Leone. Randall's realization, a realization brought about by his African experience, implies that evil is a force that is within all people and that this evil force is powerful enough to take over a person's being.

In summary, because African methods of understanding and coping with the world are often quite different from Western methods of perceiving reality, some contemporary American novelists have employed African settings as ways to promote the postmodern notion that all reality is subjective. Furthermore, because Westerners have traditionally viewed Africa as an uncharted zone where anything is possible, readers are able to suspend their disbelief about such mysterious events as Esther Moro's healing powers in *Antonia Saw the Oryx First* and the powers of the witchmen in *White Man's Grave*.

While Dooling and Thomas are content to use traditional narrative techniques in their thematically postmodern novels, other contemporary American authors, especially Walter Abish and Thomas Pynchon, have incorporated African settings in novels that are postmodern in form as well as theme. Moreover, Paul Theroux has carried on the tradition begun by Paul Bowles by examining the status of "others" in contemporary Africa. Most of these postmodern and postcolonial novels with African settings contain significant didactic passages that inform readers about conditions in postcolonial Africa.

As the works of Abish, Pynchon, Thomas, and Dooling demonstrate, some of the most significant challenges to stereotypes about Africa in contemporary American fiction come from authors who write postmodern novels set in Africa. Yet, in his postcolonial African novels, Theroux reinforces the notion that Africa is a hostile zone for outsiders who dare to travel there. Postmodern and postcolonial novels with African settings are, therefore, like the larger body of contemporary American fiction featuring African settings; these novels both challenge and reinforce the traditional Western conceptions of Africa and its peoples.

Chapter 7

Conclusions:
Africa—A Continent of Words

The early examples of English novels with African settings establish a tradition that associates specific thematic concerns with Africa. These thematic concerns—slavery and the slave trade, the conflict between humans and the natural world of Africa, and the notion that Africa is the home of lost cities and civilizations—continue to interest contemporary American authors who feature African settings in their works. Africa has traditionally been seen as an empty, mysterious, disease-ridden, and fearsome place that is in binary opposition to the West; and, in both British and American fiction, African environments are often described as harsh, challenging, and deadly, and Africans are frequently portrayed as primitive, savage, and hostile. Images of Africa and Africans in contemporary American fiction are usually either extensions of or reactions to notions about Africa popularized by earlier English and American authors.

For many contemporary American novelists, the appeal of Africa as a literary setting is its "otherness," its difference from the United States. Because Africa is frequently considered to be in opposition with the West, authors often employ African settings in their novels as ways to measure and assess Western culture by comparing Western and American ways of living with life in Africa. American novelists writing since World War II also look to African settings as a way of commenting upon themes such as courage, death, religion, and war as well as the relationship between an individual and his or her society. Africa, then, is a place where characters in American novels go to discover the truth about themselves and their culture by comparing their values with African values and by testing themselves against the challenges provided by African landscapes, animals, and peoples. Ironically, even those novels that challenge Western assumptions about the nature of reality by comparing Western "reality" to African "reality" are grounded in the idea that Africa is a strange, mysterious zone where anything is possible.

Perhaps the most striking feature of contemporary American novels set in Africa is their didactic quality. This didactic quality permeates all types of fiction set in Africa. For example, novels set in imaginary African nations release didactic information about Africa to enlighten readers about the conditions that exist in various regions of Africa and to explain to readers that many of Africa's problems are the legacy of colonialism. Like actual African nations, the invented African nations in contemporary American novels are divided by political, tribal, and religious conflicts that are the result of different peoples being grouped together under a single flag. Novels set in invented African nations also remind readers that imperialism, in the guise of Cold War conflicts in which the superpowers use Africa as a battleground, is still a powerful force in contemporary Africa.

There is an especially strong didactic component in the African novels by contemporary African-American authors. However, the lessons presented about Africa in works by black Americans are quite different from those in novels by white authors. While white authors often portray Africa as a changeless, timeless place without a history, African-American novelists who set works in Africa usually write historical accounts that challenge stereotypes about Africans and Africa. Specifically, African-American novelists seek to remind readers that Africa is the home of many great cultures and the scene of one of the greatest crimes against humanity in all of history: the slave trade to the Americas. Moreover, Alice Walker uses African settings in three of her novels not only to "correct" stereotypical notions about Africa but also to promote her feminist concerns. In writing about these concerns, Walker constructs a "history" of the world that explains the origins of patriarchal societies and the beginnings of such common African practices as polygamy and the genital mutilation of women. In fact, Walker's best known African novel, *Possessing the Secret of Joy*, details the horrors of genital mutilation and urges readers around the world to help bring a halt to this custom.

Even genre novels set in Africa—novels of adventure, war, safari, history, and science fiction—are heavily didactic. Crichton's *Congo*, for example, releases a wealth of factual information about Africa while relying on the old notion that Africa is a strange and mysterious place of lost cities and fantastic creatures. Several of these works, for instance Harrison's *Burton and Speke*, are actually nonfiction novels that detail the adventures of historical figures. Many of the genre novels set in Africa are also warnings, warnings about the price of violent political actions or warnings that Western ways are destroying much of what is valuable in the world. Genre novels with African settings, therefore, often rise above the standards expected of genre fiction and delve into substantial themes associated with serious literature.

Works of postmodernism set in Africa, novels such as Thomas's *Antonia Saw the Oryx First* and Dooling's *White Man's Grave*, are also heavily didactic. In fact, Dooling incorporates passages from actual guidebooks about Sierra Leone into his story, and Thomas provides her readers with a wealth of information about conditions in postcolonial Africa. Moreover, novels such as Theroux's *Fong and the Indians* and *Jungle Lovers* provide readers with details about the conditions Asians and whites face in repressive postcolonial nations. The didactic nature of contemporary American novels set in Africa demonstrates that American authors setting their works in Africa have learned that Africa is a history—a lesson waiting to be conveyed—as much as it is a physical place to be explored.

However, the physical qualities of African landscapes do play an important role in contemporary American novels that feature African settings. For instance, in Paul Bowles's *The Sheltering Sky*, the Sahara desert becomes a "character" that helps to determine the outcome of the story. In a similar way, Michael Mewshaw uses the harsh topography of Morocco as a plot-shaping device in his novel *The Toll*, and in *Roots* Alex Haley describes the weather of West Africa as a force that determines the nature of village life. And of course, African animals, especially the lions in *The Lions of Tsavo* by James Haley and the leopards that appear in William Harrison's *Africana* and *Three Hunters* are also "characters" that affect the outcomes of these novels; these animals and others like them often serve as symbols for the entire continent of Africa.

While many contemporary American novels with African settings reinforce traditional notions about Africa, a number of these novels challenge Western stereotypes about Africa and Africans. Nowhere is this challenge more clear than in novels by black Americans. African-American novelists frequently set their works in Africa in order to "rewrite" the history of Africa so that African accomplishments are acknowledged. The stereotypical notion that Africa is a savage, barbaric continent is also challenged by a number of white novelists who are intent on promoting the idea that the West, not Africa, is the heart of darkness. For example, Michael Mewshaw's *Land Without Shadow* implies that the West, in the form of governments and multinational corporations, is more than willing to allow Africans to starve if that will ensure a profit, and William Harrison uses *Africana* and *Savannah Blue* to deliver a scathing criticism of Western culture, a criticism that suggests that the West has destroyed all that is valuable and free as the world surrenders to the homogenization of the marketplace. And one of the many lessons about history incorporated into Pynchon's *V.* and *Gravity's Rainbow* is that the horrors of colonialism in German-controlled Southwest Africa led to the nightmare of Nazi Germany.

American writers have not limited their use of African settings to novels, and future studies would do well to consider the use of African settings in contemporary American short fiction. For example, Paul Bowles has written a number of short stories set in Africa, and his collections—*The Delicate Prey* and *A Hundred Camels in the Courtyard*—should be of special interest to critics. Bowles's most recent African story, "Too Far From Home," is also worthy of critical examination because it reflects the interest in Africa as a suitable setting for postmodern fiction. Additionally, Maria Thomas has published two collections of stories set in Africa, *Come to Africa and Save Your Marriage and Other Stories* and *African Vistas*. Although Thomas's career was cut short by her death in a plane crash in Africa, she is a superb author whose works are certain to become more appreciated as time passes, and her short fiction is surely worthy of study. Another contemporary American author who has set short stories in Africa is Martha Gellhorn; her collection *The Weather in Africa* is an outstanding work that certainly deserves further critical investigation.

Of course, British authors writing since World War II have also frequently set their works in Africa, and an examination of the uses of African settings in contemporary British fiction would be useful. While there has been some critical discussion of the African works of such well-known British authors as Graham Greene, critics should also consider works by black British authors such as Caryl Phillips, whose *Crossing the River* develops a story similar to Sarah J. Hale's *Liberia*.

Furthermore, critics would do well to study African settings in novels by African writers to see how these authors employ African settings in their works. As indicated in Chapter 1, African authors such as Chinua Achebe and Cyprian Ekwensi make extensive use of the natural aspects of African settings in their works. White African authors such as Doris Lessing and Nadine Gordimer have also included aspects of natural Africa in their works, but little has been written about the role of African settings in novels and short stories by Africans.

This study is limited to a discussion of African settings in contemporary American novels written between 1949 and 1994, but recent American involvement in African nations such as Somalia and the political unrest in Zaire (recently renamed Congo), Liberia, Sudan, and Kenya, will provide American authors with material that can be shaped into fiction. Will works written in the early decades of the twenty-first century continue to reinforce traditional notions about Africa, or will the old notions associated with Africa pass away to be replaced by new traditions? Will Africa continue to be a suitable setting for science fiction novels if the continent becomes so familiar to readers that they no longer expect Africa to harbor strange creatures and lost civilizations? Or will some new and terrible African disease—perhaps something similar to the AIDS virus—spark the interest of those who want to write about the future? And since wild Africa continues to vanish—perhaps forever—will future novels set in Africa deal with the fight to save Africa's remaining wildlife? Moreover, as postcolonial African nations mature and struggle for democracy, will forthcoming novels continue the tradition of delivering political assessments concerning Africa? The answers to these questions are likely to determine the role of African settings in American novels written in coming decades.

Africa has been a rich literary territory for American authors writing since World War II; these writers have created a continent of words, a literary Africa that both preserves and challenges Western traditions about Africa, and this continent of words will surely grow as American authors continue to explore Africa as a setting for their novels.

Bibliography

Abish, Walter. *Alphabetical Africa*. New York: New Directions, 1974.

———. *How German Is It*. New York: New Directions, 1980.

———. *Eclipse Fever*. New York: Knopf, 1993.

Achebe, Chinua. *Things Fall Apart*. 1959. New York: Fawcett, 1969.

———. *Hopes and Impediments: Selected Essays*. Garden City, NJ: Doubleday, 1989.

Anderson, David D. "Hemingway and Henderson on the High Savannas: Or, Two Midwestern Moderns and the Myth of Africa." *Saul Bellow Journal* 8.2 (1989): 59–75.

Andrews, William. L. "The First Century of Afro-American Autobiography: Theory and Explication." *Studies in Black American Literature: Black American Prose Theory*. Ed. Joe Weixlmann and Chester J. Fontenot. Greenwood, FL: Penkevill, 1984. 4–42.

Appiah, Kwame Anthony. *In My Father's House: Africa in the Philosophy of Culture*. New York: Oxford UP, 1992.

Archer, Armstrong. "A Brief View of the Author's Descent from an African King on One Side, and from the Celebrated Indian Chief Powhattan on the Other." *Steal Away: Stories of the Runaway Slaves*. Ed. Abraham Chapman. New York: Praeger, 1971. 39–45.

Atkinson, C. William. "At the Inner Station: Conrad, Greene, and Naipaul on the Congo." Diss. Emory U, 1992.

Azim, Firdous. *The Colonial Rise of the Novel*. London: Routledge, 1993.

Ballantyne. R. M. *The Gorilla Hunters*. London: Collins, n.d.

Barthold, Bonnie J. *Black Time: Fiction of Africa, the Caribbean, and the United States*. New Haven: Yale UP, 1981.

Bartholomew, John. Preface. *The Times Atlas of the World: Southern Europe and Africa*. Boston: Houghton, 1956. xi.

Behn, Aphra. *Oroonoko: or, The Royal Slave*. 1688. New York: Norton, 1973.

Bellow, Saul. *Henderson the Rain King*. New York: Viking, 1959.

Berghahn, Marion. *Images of Africa in Black American Literature*. Totowa, NJ: Rowman, 1977.

Bontemps, Arna, ed. *Great Slave Narratives*. Boston: Beacon, 1969.

Bowles, Paul. *The Sheltering Sky*. New York: New Directions, 1949.

———. *let it come down*. New York: Random, 1952.

———. *The Spider's House*. New York: Random, 1955.

———. *A Hundred Camels in the Courtyard*. San Francisco: City Lights, 1962.

———. *The Delicate Prey*. 1950. Hopewell, NJ: Ecco, 1972.

———. "Too Far From Home." *Too Far From Home*. Ed. Daniel Halpern. Hopewell, NJ: Ecco, 1993. 295–327.

Bristow, Joseph. Introduction. *The Story of an African Farm*. By Olive Schreiner. Oxford: Oxford UP, 1992.

Brontë, Charlotte. *The Twelve Adventurers*. London: Hodder, [1925].

Buckman, Alyson R. "The Body as a Site of Colonization: Alice Walker's *Possessing the Secret of Joy*." *Journal of American Culture*. 18.2 (1995): 89–93.

Burroughs, Edgar Rice. *Tarzan of the Apes*. 1912. New York: Ballantine, 1963.

———. *The Eternal Savage*. 1914. New York: Ballantine, 1992.

———. *Tarzan and the Ant Men*. 1924. New York: Ballantine, 1963.

———. *Tarzan and the Lost Empire*. 1928. New York: Ballantine, 1963.

———. *Tarzan and the Lion Man*. 1934. New York: Ballantine, 1964.

Burroughs, William S. *The Wild Boys*. New York: Grove, 1969.

Burton, Richard. *Two Trips to Gorilla Land and the Cataracts of the Congo*. 2 Vols. London: Sampson Low, 1876. New York: Johnson Reprint, 1967.

Byerman, Keith. "Walker's Blues." *Alice Walker*. Ed. Harold Bloom. New York: Chelsea, 1988. 59–66.

Calder, Josh. "Vanishing Points." *Fort Worth Star-Telegram* 29 Dec. 1996, city final ed.: H1+.

Caputo, Philip. *Horn of Africa*. 1980. New York: Harper, 1991.

Cary, Joyce. *Aissa Saved*. 1932. New York: Harper, n.d.

———. "*Aissa Saved*: A prefatory essay by the author specially written for the Carfax edition." *Aissia Saved*. By Joyce Cary. New York: Harper, n.d. 213–19.

———. *An American Visitor*. 1933. New York: Harper, n.d.

———. *An African Witch*. 1936. London: Michael Joseph, 1951.

———. *Mister Johnson*. 1939. New York: Harper, 1951.

Chapman, Abraham, ed. *Steal Away: Stories of the Runaway Slaves*. New York: Praeger, 1971.

Chase-Riboud, Barbara. *Echo of Lions*. New York: Morrow, 1989.

Chukwu, Augustine. "The Dreamer as Leader: Ellelloû in John Updike's *The Coup*." *Literary Half-Yearly* 23.1 (1982): 61–69.

Conrad, Joseph. *Heart of Darkness*. 1902. London: Penguin, 1983.

Courlander, Harold. "Kunta Kinte's Struggle to be African." *Phylon: A Review of Race and Culture* 47 (1986): 294–302.

Crichton, Michael. *Congo*. New York: Knopf, 1980.

Defoe, Daniel. *Robinson Crusoe*. 1719. New York: Bantam, 1988.

———. *Madagascar; or, Robert Drury's Journal, During Fifteen Years' Captivity on That Island*. 1729. New York: Negro UP, 1969.

Dickens, Charles. *Bleak House*. 1853. New York: Signet, 1964.

Dinesen, Isak [Karen Blixen]. *Out of Africa*. 1937. New York: Vintage, 1970.

Dooling, Richard. *White Man's Grave*. New York: Farrar, 1994.

Doyle, Paul A. "Evelyn Waugh." *Dictionary of Literary Biography* 15. 1983.

Early, Gerald. "Understanding Afrocentrism: Why Blacks Dream of a World Without Whites." *Civilization* Jul./Aug. 1955: 31–39.

Eiland, Howard. "Updike's Womanly Man." *Centennial Review* 26 (1982): 312–23.

Ekwensi, Cyprian. *Burning Grass.* 1962. London: Heinemann, 1968.

Equiano, Olaudah. "The Life of Olaudah Equiano or Gustavus Vassa: the African." *Great Slave Narratives.* Ed. Arna Bontemps. Boston: Beacon, 1969. 4–192.

Etherington, Norman. *Rider Haggard.* Boston: Twayne, 1984.

Fishkin, Shelley Fisher. "The Multiculturalism of 'Traditional' Culture." *Chronicle of Higher Education* 10 Mar. 1995: A48.

Forester, C. S. *The African Queen.* 1935. New York: Random, 1940.

———. Foreword. *The African Queen.* By C. S. Forester. New York: Random, 1940. ii.

Gallagher, Winifred. *The Power of Place: How Our Surroundings Shape Our Thoughts, Emotions, and Actions.* New York: Poseidon, 1993.

Gellhorn, Martha. *The Weather in Africa.* New York: Dodd, 1978.

Gikandi, Simon. *Reading Chinua Achebe: Language and Ideology in Fiction.* Portsmouth, NH: Heineman, 1991.

Gohdes, Clarence. "American Novels of Muckraking, Propaganda, and Social Protest." Introduction. *Liberia; or, Mr. Peyton's Experiments.* By Sarah J. Hale. 1853. Upper Saddle River, NJ: Gregg, 1968. n.p.

Goonetilleke, D.C.R.A. *Developing Countries in British Fiction.* Totowa, NJ: Rowman, 1977.

Greene, Graham. *A Burnt-Out Case.* London: Heinemann, 1961.

Gruesser, John Cullen. *White on Black: Contemporary Literature about Africa.* Champaign, IL: U of Illinois P, 1992.

Haggard, H. Rider. *King Solomon's Mines.* 1886. London: Cassell, 1965.

———. *She. Five Adventure Novels of H. Rider Haggard.* New York: Dover, 1951. 1–238.

———. *Allan Quatermain.* 1887. *Five Adventure Novels of H. Rider Haggard.* New York: Dover, 1951. 417–636.

Hale, Sarah J. *Liberia; or, Mr. Peyton's Experiments.* 1853. Upper Saddle River, NJ: Gregg, 1968.

Haley, Alex. *Roots.* Garden City, NJ: Doubleday, 1976.

Haley, James L. *The Lions of Tsavo.* New York: Bantam, 1989.

Halpern, Daniel. Preface. *Too Far From Home.* Ed. Daniel Halpern. Hopewell, NJ: Ecco, 1993. vii–xii.

Harris, Eddy L. *Native Stranger.* New York: Vintage, 1993.

Harris, Joseph E. *Africans and Their History.* New York: Mentor, 1987.

Harrison, William. *Africana.* New York: Morrow, 1977.

———. *Savannah Blue.* New York: Merek, 1981.

———. *Burton and Speke.* New York: St. Martin's, 1982.

———. *Three Hunters.* New York: Random, 1989.

Hemingway, Ernest. *The Sun Also Rises.* New York: Scribner, 1926.

———. "The Snows of Kilimanjaro." *The Snows of Kilimanjaro and Other Stories.* 1927. New York: Scribner/Macmillian, 1986. 3–28.

———. "The Short Happy Life of Francis Macomber." *The Snows of Kilimanjaro and Other Stories.* 1927. New York: Scribner/Macmillian, 1986. 121–51.

———. *Green Hills of Africa.* New York: Scribner's, 1935.

Holtsmark, Erling B. *Tarzan and Tradition: Classical Myth in Popular Literature.* Westport, CT: Greenwood, 1981.

Howard, Lillie P. "Benediction: A Few Words about *The Temple of My Familiar*, Variously Experienced, and *Possessing the Secret of Joy*." *Alice Walker and Zora Neale Hurston: The Common Bond*. Ed. Lillie P. Howard. Westport, CT: Greenwood, 1993. 139–46.

Johnson, Charles. *Middle Passage*. New York: Atheneum, 1990.

Johnson, Samuel. *The History of Rasselas, Prince of Abissinia*. 1759. Oxford: Clarendon, 1937.

Katz, Tamar. " 'Show Me How to Do Like You': Didacticism and Epistolary Form in *The Color Purple*." *Alice Walker*. Ed. Harold Bloom. New York: Chelsea, 1989. 185–93.

King, Kathleen. "Bellow the Allegory King: Animal Imagery in *Henderson the Rain King*." *Saul Bellow Journal* 7.1 (1988): 44–50.

Kuzna, Faye I. "Mental Travel in *Henderson the Rain King*." *Saul Bellow Journal* 9.2 (1990): 54–57.

Lathrop, Kathleen. *"The Coup*: John Updike's Modernist Masterpiece." *Modern Fiction Studies* 31 (1985): 249–62.

Linn, Ray. *A Teacher's Introduction to Postmodernism*. Urbana, IL: NCTE, 1996.

Livingston, David. *Missionary Travels and Researches in South Africa*. New York: Harper, 1858.

Lutwack, Leonard. *The Role of Place in Literature*. Syracuse, NY: Syracuse UP, 1984.

Markle, Joyce. *"The Coup*: Illusions and Insubstantial Impressions." *Critical Essays on John Updike*. Ed. William R. Macnaughton. Boston: Hall, 1982. 281–301.

Marshall, Paule. *Praisesong for the Widow*. New York: Plume, 1983.

Martin, Richard. "Walter Abish's Perfect Unfamiliarity, Familiar Imperfection." *Journal of American Studies* 17 (1983): 229–41.

McHale, Brian. *Postmodernist Fiction*. New York: Methuen, 1987.

Mewshaw, Michael. *The Toll*. New York: Random, 1973.

——— . *Land Without Shadow*. Garden City, NJ: Doubleday, 1979.

Michener, James A. *The Covenant*. New York: Random, 1980.

Milbury-Steen, Sarah L. *European and African Stereotypes in Twentieth-Century Fiction*. New York: New York UP, 1982.

Morrison, Toni. *Song of Solomon*. 1977. New York: Plume, 1987.

Murray, John A. *Wild Africa: Three Centuries of Nature Writing From Africa*. New York: Oxford UP, 1993.

Newman, Robert. *Understanding Thomas Pynchon*. Columbia: U of South Carolina P, 1986.

Ngugi wa Thiong'o. *Weep Not Child*. 1964. London: Heinemann, 1984.

Norris, Frank. *The Octopus*. 1901. New York: Signet, 1964.

Oates, Joyce Carol. *"The Coup* by John Updike." *Critical Essays on John Updike*. Ed. William R. Macnaughton. Boston: Hall, 1982. 80–86.

——— . Introduction. *Too Far From Home*. Ed. Daniel Halpern. Hopewell, NJ: Ecco, 1993. xiii–xviii.

Oliver, Pasfield. Introduction. *Madagascar: or, Robert Drury's Journal, During Fifteen Years' Captivity on That Island*. By Daniel Defoe. New York: Negro UP, 1969.

Patterson, J. H. *The Man-Eaters of Tsavo and Other East African Adventures*. 1907. London: Macmilian, 1949.

Patteson, Richard F. *A World Outside: The Fiction of Paul Bowles*. Austin: U of Texas P, 1987.

Phillips, Caryl. *Crossing the River*. New York: Knopf, 1994.

Pifer, Ellen. "Beyond History and Geography." *Saul Bellow Journal* 7.2 (1989): 16–34.

Pinsker, Sanford. "Magic Realism, Historical Truth, and the Quest for a Liberating Identity: Reflections on Alex Haley's *Roots* and Toni Morrison's *Song of Solomon.*" *Studies in Black American Literature: Black American Prose Theory.* Ed. Joe Weixlmann and Chester J. Fontenot. Greenwood, FL: Penkevill, 1984. 183–97.

Pratt, Mary Louise. *Imperial Eyes: Travel Writing and Transculturation.* London: Routledge, 1992.

Pynchon, Thomas. *V.* Philadelphia: Lippincott, 1963.

———. *Gravity's Rainbow.* New York: Viking, 1973.

Ratchford, Fannie Elizabeth. *The Brontës' Web of Childhood.* New York: Russell, 1964.

Ruark, Robert. *Something of Value.* Garden City, NJ: Doubleday, 1955.

———. *Uhuru.* New York: McGraw, 1962.

Sanders, Lawrence. *The Tangent Objective.* New York: Putnam's, 1976.

———. *The Tangent Factor.* New York: Putnam's, 1978.

Schama, Simon. *Landscape and Memory.* New York: Knopf, 1995.

Schirato, Anthony. "Comic Politics and Politics of the Comic: Walter Abish's *Alphabetical Africa.*" *Critique* 32.2 (1992): 133–44.

Schreiner, Olive. *The Story of an African Farm.* 1883. Oxford: Oxford UP, 1992.

Schueller, Malini. "Containing the Third World: John Updike's *The Coup.*" *Modern Fiction Studies* 37 (1991): 113–28.

Secord, Arthur W. *Robert Drury's Journal and Other Studies.* Urbana: U of Illinois P, 1961.

Stanley, Hanley Morton. *In Darkest Africa.* 1890. 2 Vols. New York: Scribner's, 1891.

Stanton, Edward. *Hemingway and Spain: A Pursuit.* Seattle: U of Washington P, 1989.

Swift, Jonathan. "On Poetry." *The Poems of Jonathan Swift.* Ed. Pat Rogerrs. New Haven: Yale UP, 1984. 522–36.

Theroux, Paul. *Fong and the Indians.* Boston: Houghton, 1968.

———. *Girls at Play.* Boston: Houghton, 1969.

———. *Jungle Lovers.* 1971. New York: Ivy, 1990.

Thomas, Maria. *Antonia Saw the Oryx First.* New York: Soho, 1987.

———. *Come to Africa and Save Your Marriage and Other Stories.* New York: Soho, 1987.

———. *African Vistas.* New York: Soho, 1991.

Thomas, Ross. *The Seersucker Whipsaw.* 1967. New York: Mysterious, 1992.

"Togolese woman given U.S. asylum for fear of mutilation." *Fort Worth Star-Telegram* 14 Jun. 1997, city final: A6.

Tuan, Yi-Fu. *Space and Place: The Perspective of Experience.* Minneapolis: U of Minnesota P, 1977.

———. *Landscapes of Fear.* Minneapolis: U of Minnesota P, 1979.

Updike, John. *The Coup.* New York: Knopf, 1978.

Verne, Jules. *The Village in the Treetops.* 1901. Trans. I. O. Evans. New York: Ace, 1964.

Walker, Alice. *The Color Purple.* New York: Harcourt, 1982.

———. *The Temple of My Familiar.* New York: Pocket, 1989.

———. *Possessing the Secret of Joy.* New York: Harcourt, 1992.

Waugh, Evelyn. *Black Mischief.* 1932. Boston: Little, 1946.

———. *Scoop.* London: Chapman, 1938.

Weisenburger, Steven. "The End of History? Thomas Pynchon and the Uses of the Past." *Critical Essays on Thomas Pynchon.* Ed. Richard Pearce. Boston: Hall, 1981. 140–56.

Wiedner, Donald L. *A History of Africa South of the Sahara.* New York: Vintage, 1962.

Winchell, Donna Haisty. *Alice Walker.* New York: Twayne, 1992.

Wren, P. C. *Beau Geste*. 1924. New York: Stokes, 1925.

Yerby, Frank. *The Dahomean*. New York: Dial, 1971.

"Zimbabwean leader rips U.S. lawmakers." *Fort Worth Star-Telegram* 19 Aug. 1995, city final ed.: A4.

Index

About the Author

DAVE KUHNE is a Writing Specialist at the William L. Adams Writing Center and Instructor of English at Texas Christian University. His articles and short stories have appeared in such publications as *CCTE Studies*, *Lamar Journal of the Humanities*, and *New Texas 91*.

ISBN 0-313-31040-8

HARDCOVER BAR CODE